AWS Certified ML Specialty Guide

Navigating the AWS Certified Machine Learning
- Specialty exam from novice to expert

Arun Arunachalam

bpb

www.bpbonline.com

First Edition 2026

Copyright © BPB Publications, India

ISBN: 978-93-65896-428

To View Complete
BPB Publications Catalogue
Scan the QR Code:

Dedicated to

My beloved dog Lucky, whose gentle presence turned our house into a home and reminded us that love is the most powerful force of all

About the Author

Arun Arunachalam, a senior solution architecture leader and a generative ambassador at Amazon Web Services, is notably recognized for his expertise in machine learning and generative AI. With over two decades of experience in digital transformation and innovation across various sectors, Arun has a strong foundation in cloud computing and AI technologies. He has multiple AWS certifications that include the coveted AWS Certified Machine Learning - Specialty certification. He has extensive experience in applying ML techniques like classification, regression, and clustering using AWS tools such as SageMaker, Lambda, and Glue. This expertise is further exemplified in his book *AWS Certified ML Specialty Guide,* where he provides a comprehensive roadmap for mastering ML on AWS. His work emphasizes the transformational impact of ML and AI, demonstrating his commitment to driving innovation and educating in these fields.

About the Reviewers

❖ **Deepak Pandey** is an AI/ML and data science engineer passionate about building intelligent, scalable AI solutions. A B.Tech graduate in electronics and communication engineering from NIT Jamshedpur, Deepak works extensively with cloud-native technologies like AWS, GCP, PySpark, Docker, and Kubernetes. His core expertise lies in machine learning, deep learning, NLP, generative AI, and large language models.

He has contributed to impactful projects in cybersecurity, document intelligence, reputation intelligence, financial insights chatbot and privacy-focused data engineering. His work includes fine-tuning LLMs, RAG, developing modular inference pipelines with LangChain and agentic AI, and implementing scalable ETL workflows on cloud platforms. Deepak is passionate about automation and designing clean, reusable AI architectures.

He is an AWS Machine Learning – Specialty certified engineer and winner of the 2023 Global Data Science Challenge, where he helped develop an AI solution for clinical diagnostics using deep learning. He is also a published researcher—his paper *Encryption and Authentication of Data Using the IPSEC Protocol"* was featured in the Proceedings of the Fourth International Conference on Microelectronics, Computing & Communication Systems.

Beyond tech, he is an avid reader with deep interests in international relations and global politics, blending analytical thinking with a global perspective.

❖ **Hatim Kagalwala** is an applied scientist specializing in machine learning, generative AI, causal inference, and credit risk modeling. Currently working at Amazon, he designs and implements large-scale machine learning systems and has led projects generating significant business impact through innovative AI solutions. Previously, Hatim worked at American Express, where he focused on developing advanced models to detect and prevent credit and fraud risks. He holds a master's degree in financial engineering from New York University. Passionate about research and writing, Hatim regularly contributes to technical publications and conferences. He enjoys translating complex algorithms into practical, real-world applications. In his free time, Hatim loves reading, playing board games, and spending time outdoors with his golden retriever.

❖ **Ramesh Mohana Murugan** is a seasoned technology expert and senior IEEE member with more than 17 years of experience in the IT industry. He has collaborated with top-tier companies such as Meta Platforms, AWS, Amazon, and major financial institutions, spearheading innovation and excellence in data engineering/analytics and machine learning. Throughout his career, Ramesh has designed and implemented state-of-the-art data solutions that drive key products like Instagram Feed Recommendations, Meta Shops Ads, AWS Worldwide Revenue, and Alexa Shopping, processing billions of data points and reaching a global user base to accelerate business growth.

Additionally, Ramesh is an active reader and reviewer of technical content in his field. He has contributed to the advancement of technology by reviewing journals and books, including Time Series Analysis with Spark, LLM Fine Tuning, and SQL Crash Course: Mastering the Essentials of SQL Programming, among others.

Acknowledgement

I am deeply grateful to my family for their unwavering support throughout this journey. To my wife Lakshmi, my daughter Shakthi, and my son Karthick, thank you for your patience and encouragement. A special mention to our beloved dog Lucky, who kept me company during countless writing sessions and is truly an integral part of our lives.

I extend my gratitude to everyone who continues to teach me daily, my friends, colleagues, and the wonderful students I work with. your insights and questions constantly inspire my learning.

My heartfelt appreciation goes to BPB Publications for their expert guidance and collaboration in bringing this book to fruition. This lengthy journey of revisions was made possible through the valuable contributions of reviewers, technical experts, and editors.

Finally, thank you to all readers who have shown interest in this book. Your support and encouragement have been invaluable in making this work a reality.

Preface

The machine learning revolution is transforming industries across the globe, much like the advent of electricity once did. As organizations increasingly rely on data-driven insights and intelligent automation, the demand for skilled machine learning professionals who can harness the power of cloud computing has never been greater. Amazon Web Services has emerged as the leading platform for building, deploying, and managing machine learning solutions at scale.

This book is designed to be your comprehensive guide to mastering machine learning on AWS and successfully passing the AWS Certified Machine Learning - Specialty exam. It bridges the gap between fundamental cloud computing knowledge and advanced machine learning expertise, taking you on a journey from understanding basic concepts to building production-ready ML solutions.

Throughout this guide, you will gain hands-on experience with essential AWS services, including Amazon SageMaker, AWS Glue, Amazon Kinesis, AWS Lambda, and many others. The book is structured around the four key domains of the AWS ML Specialty certification, that is,data engineering, exploratory data analysis, modeling, and machine learning implementation and operations. Each chapter builds upon previous concepts while providing practical, real-world examples that you can apply immediately.

This book is intended for aspiring machine learning specialists, data scientists, data engineers, cloud architects, and professionals seeking to validate their expertise in AWS machine learning technologies. Whether you are beginning your machine learning journey or looking to formalize your existing knowledge, this guide will equip you with the skills and confidence needed to excel in the rapidly evolving field of cloud-based machine learning.

With this book, you will not only prepare for certification success but also develop the practical skills necessary to drive innovation and make a meaningful impact in your organization through the power of AWS machine learning.

Chapter 1: Creating Data Repositories for Machine Learning- This chapter establishes the foundation for any ML project by exploring how to identify diverse data sources and select appropriate storage solutions on AWS. The chapter covers databases, Amazon S3, Amazon EFS, and Amazon EBS, providing best practices for data repository design and integration strategies that ensure your data infrastructure can support robust machine learning workflows from simple batch processing to complex real-time analytics.

Chapter 2: Implementing Data Ingestion Solutions- This chapter discusses the critical process of moving data into your ML pipeline, covering both batch and streaming data ingestion patterns. You wi'll learn to leverage Amazon Kinesis, Amazon EMR, AWS Glue, and other AWS services to orchestrate and automate data pipelines, including scheduling and managing complex data ingestion jobs for various data types and volumes across different organizational needs.

Chapter 3: Transforming Data into Insights – This chapter focuses on converting raw data into formats suitable for machine learning analysis. The chapter explores ETL processes using AWS Glue and Amazon EMR, handling ML-specific data transformations with MapReduce, Apache Hadoop, Spark, and Hive, while providing optimization techniques to prepare data for various ML algorithms and ensuring scalable transformation workflows.

Chapter 4: Data Sanitization and Preparation- This chapter addresses the crucial task of ensuring data quality and readiness for modeling. You will learn to identify and handle missing or corrupt data, implement data cleaning and preprocessing techniques, and apply normalization and scaling methods. The chapter emphasizes data augmentation strategies and quality assessment practices essential for successful ML outcomes while maintaining data integrity throughout the preparation process.

Chapter 5: Feature Engineering- This chapter explores the art and science of extracting meaningful features from diverse data sources including text, speech, and images. The chapter covers feature identification techniques, dimensionality reduction methods, and feature transformation approaches, with practical examples demonstrating how to enhance your datasets for optimal ML model performance using AWS tools like SageMaker Feature Store and processing capabilities.

Chapter 6: Data Analysis and Visualization- This chapter teaches you to create insightful visualizations and interpret key statistics that inform ML decision-making. You will learn to generate various graph types, understand descriptive statistics, implement cluster analysis for data segmentation, and utilize AWS visualization tools including QuickSight to effectively communicate data insights to stakeholders and validate your analytical assumptions.

Chapter 7: Framing Business Problems as ML Problems- This chapter bridges the gap between business challenges and technical ML solutions. The chapter helps you assess when ML is appropriate, differentiate between supervised and unsupervised learning approaches, and select suitable models for various business scenarios through real-world case studies and best practices for problem definition, ensuring alignment between business objectives and technical implementation.

Chapter 8: Selecting Appropriate ML Models- This chapter provides comprehensive coverage of the ML model landscape, including XGBoost, logistic regression, decision trees, and neural networks such as RNNs and CNNs. You will develop intuition about model selection criteria based on data characteristics and problem types, while learning to leverage AWS tools and SageMaker's built-in algorithms for effective model implementation and comparison.

Chapter 9: Training ML Models- This chapter covers methodologies and best practices for effective model training, including data splitting strategies, optimization techniques, and compute resource selection. The chapter addresses GPU vs CPU considerations, Spark and non-Spark platforms, and provides guidance on updating and retraining strategies to maintain model relevance using SageMaker training jobs and distributed training capabilities.

Chapter 10: Hyperparameter Optimization- This chapter focuses on refining ML models for peak performance through systematic tuning approaches. You will learn regularization techniques including dropout and L1/L2 regularization, cross-validation methods, neural network architecture optimization, and tree-based model tuning. The chapter demonstrates how to leverage AWS solutions like SageMaker Automatic Model Tuning for efficient hyperparameter optimization at scale.

Chapter 11: Evaluating ML Models- This chapter centers on comprehensive model evaluation techniques to ensure optimal performance and avoid common pitfalls. The chapter covers detecting and handling bias and variance, understanding evaluation metrics such as AUC-ROC, precision, recall, and F1 score, and implementing both offline and online evaluation strategies using AWS tools for continuous model assessment and validation.

Chapter 12: Building ML Solutions for Performance and Scalability- This chapter discusses the creation of machine learning solutions that are high-performing, scalable, resilient, and fault-tolerant. You will explore monitoring with AWS CloudTrail and Amazon CloudWatch, deploying solutions across multiple regions and availability zones, creating and managing AMIs and Docker containers, implementing auto-scaling, and following AWS best practices for enterprise-grade ML deployments.

Chapter 13: Recommending and Implementing Appropriate ML Services- This chapter teaches you to choose and implement the most suitable AWS machine learning services for specific scenarios. The chapter covers AWS ML application services including Amazon Polly, Lex, and Transcribe, understanding service quotas, making build-versus-buy decisions with SageMaker built-in algorithms, and optimizing costs through strategic use of spot instances and AWS Batch for deep learning workloads.

Chapter 14: Applying AWS Security Practices to ML Solutions- This chapter focuses on implementing fundamental AWS security practices essential for production ML systems. You will learn about IAM roles and policies for ML workflows, S3 bucket security configurations, VPC networking for secure deployments, and encryption and anonymization techniques to protect sensitive data throughout the ML pipeline while maintaining compliance with organizational security requirements.

Chapter 15: Deploying and Operationalizing ML Solutions- This chapter covers the complete lifecycle of ML model deployment and operational management. The chapter addresses exposing and interacting with ML endpoints, implementing A/B testing strategies, establishing retraining pipelines, and debugging and troubleshooting techniques to ensure models continue performing optimally in production environments using SageMaker endpoints and monitoring capabilities.

Appendix- This chapter provides a comprehensive practice test that simulates the actual AWS Certified Machine Learning - Specialty exam experience. This chapter includes sample questions across all four domains, detailed explanations for correct and incorrect answers, and strategic guidance for exam preparation, helping you assess your readiness and identify areas requiring additional study before taking the certification exam.

Coloured Images

Please follow the link to download the
Coloured Images of the book:

https://rebrand.ly/503225

We have code bundles from our rich catalogue of books and videos available at https://github.com/bpbpublications. Check them out!

Errata

We take immense pride in our work at BPB Publications and follow best practices to ensure the accuracy of our content to provide an indulging reading experience to our subscribers. Our readers are our mirrors, and we use their inputs to reflect and improve upon human errors, if any, that may have occurred during the publishing processes involved. To let us maintain the quality and help us reach out to any readers who might be having difficulties due to any unforeseen errors, please write to us at:

errata@bpbonline.com

Your support, suggestions and feedback are highly appreciated by the BPB Publications' Family.

At www.bpbonline.com, you can also read a collection of free technical articles, sign up for a range of free newsletters, and receive exclusive discounts and offers on BPB books and eBooks. You can check our social media handles below:

Instagram

Facebook

Linkedin

YouTube

Get in touch with us at: business@bpbonline.com for more details.

Piracy

If you come across any illegal copies of our works in any form on the internet, we would be grateful if you would provide us with the location address or website name. Please contact us at business@bpbonline.com with a link to the material.

If you are interested in becoming an author

If there is a topic that you have expertise in, and you are interested in either writing or contributing to a book, please visit www.bpbonline.com. We have worked with thousands of developers and tech professionals, just like you, to help them share their insights with the global tech community. You can make a general application, apply for a specific hot topic that we are recruiting an author for, or submit your own idea.

Reviews

Please leave a review. Once you have read and used this book, why not leave a review on the site that you purchased it from? Potential readers can then see and use your unbiased opinion to make purchase decisions. We at BPB can understand what you think about our products, and our authors can see your feedback on their book. Thank you!

For more information about BPB, please visit www.bpbonline.com.

Join our Discord space

Join our Discord workspace for latest updates, offers, tech happenings around the world, new releases, and sessions with the authors:

https://discord.bpbonline.com

Table of Contents

CHAPTER 1
Creating Data Repositories for Machine Learning

Introduction

Machine learning (**ML**) is transforming the way we interact with technology, enabling systems to learn from data and make intelligent decisions without being explicitly programmed. From personalized recommendations and fraud detection to natural language processing and predictive analytics. At the core of every successful ML project lies one indispensable element: data. This chapter zeroes in on two foundational pillars essential for creating robust data repositories: identifying the myriad sources of data and selecting the optimal storage mediums to house this data. From understanding the content and location of primary data sources, such as user-generated data, to evaluating the strengths and use cases of various AWS storage solutions like Amazon S3, Amazon **Elastic File System** (**EFS**), and Amazon **Elastic Block Store** (**EBS**), this chapter equips you with the knowledge to architect data repositories that are not only scalable and secure but also precisely tailored to the needs of your ML applications.

Structure

The chapter covers the following topics:

- Introduction to data in ML
- Identifying data sources

- Analyzing data characteristics
- Determining storage mediums

Objectives

By the end of this chapter, readers will be able to identify and evaluate potential data sources for ML, understanding their content, location, and relevance. We will analyze data characteristics to inform the selection of appropriate storage solutions and choose the most suitable AWS storage mediums based on the specific needs of ML projects, considering factors like data type, access patterns, and scalability requirements. We will understand how to implement best practices for secure, cost-efficient, and compliant data storage on AWS and apply this knowledge to build real-world ML projects, ensuring a solid foundation for building scalable and robust data repositories.

Introduction to data in ML

In the enthralling world of ML, data is not just king; it is the very lifeblood that powers the algorithms, breathing intelligence into models that can predict, classify, and make decisions with astonishing accuracy. Data acts as the critical ingredient in concocting models that can foresee stock market trends, personalize your streaming service recommendations, or even diagnose diseases from medical images. You are now able to use your smartphone camera and identify plants or translate text in real-time, all of which is made possible through ML models trained on vast datasets of images and languages. Such practical applications underscore the quintessence of data: without diverse, high-quality datasets, ML models would be like ships without compasses adrift in a sea of potential, but lacking the direction needed to reach ground-breaking innovations.

As we explore the digital age, the exponential growth of data in all its forms has become a defining characteristic of our time. The latest statistics paint a staggering picture. According to the *International Data Corporation (IDC)*, the global datasphere is expected to grow to 175 zettabytes by 2025, a testament to the sheer volume of information generated, captured, and stored across the globe. This monumental growth is fueled by advancements in **Internet of Things** (**IoT**) devices, social media, high-resolution video content, and the increasing digitization of industries and personal lives. Each byte of this vast ocean of data holds potential insights for ML models, making the identification and strategic storage of data more crucial than ever.

The volume of data generated by various industry verticals has seen immense growth due to advancements in digital technology, the IoT, and increased internet usage worldwide, as illustrated in the following figure:

Figure 1.1: Top industry verticals generating huge amounts of data

Identifying this data, sifting through structured databases, unstructured social media posts, or semi-structured IoT sensor readings is the first step in harnessing its power. The challenge lies not only in collecting this data but in effectively storing it in ways that make it accessible and usable for ML projects. For instance, health care industries are leveraging **Electronic Health Records (EHRs)** to train ML models that can predict patient outcomes, improve diagnoses, and personalize treatment plans. This application requires meticulously organized and securely stored data to ensure patient privacy and compliance with regulations like the **Health Insurance Portability and Accountability Act (HIPAA)**.

In e-commerce, companies analyze customer behavior, preferences, and feedback from various sources to tailor recommendations, optimize supply chains, and enhance customer service. Here, the diversity of data, from transaction logs to customer service interactions, demands versatile storage solutions like *Amazon S3* for unstructured data or *Amazon RDS* for transactional data, ensuring scalability and high availability.

Furthermore, the advent of smart cities and autonomous vehicles underscores the importance of real-time data processing and storage. Traffic patterns, sensor data from vehicles, and environmental information must be stored in a manner that supports rapid access and analysis, often employing edge computing solutions alongside cloud storage to minimize latency.

The importance of identifying and categorically storing this data cannot be overstated. It enables organizations to not only make informed decisions and innovate but also to ensure ethical considerations are met in handling personal and sensitive information. As we continue to generate data at an unprecedented rate, the strategies we adopt for its identification, storage, and usage will dictate the trajectory of advancements in **machine learning (ML)** and **artificial intelligence (AI)**, shaping the future of technology and its impact on society.

Identifying data sources

The objective of identifying the location of data and understanding how it can be collected is crucial for building effective ML models. This process involves a nuanced understanding of various data types, such as user data, transactional data, and sensor data, and the methodologies employed to collect these data efficiently and ethically. Let us explore these components in detail.

Identifying location of data

The location of data will depend on the category of data, and the following are the important categories to be aware of:

- **User data**: Typically found in web applications, social media platforms, customer feedback forms, and online purchase histories.

- **Transactional data**: Located in e-commerce platforms, banking systems, and any digital platform where transactions occur. This data is usually stored in transactional databases or ledgers and can be accessed through database queries or transaction logs.

- **Sensor data**: Generated by IoT devices, smartphones, industrial equipment, and environmental sensors. A practical example includes smart home devices that continuously send data about temperature, humidity, or energy usage to a centralized server for analysis and optimization.

Collecting data

The following are the most common ways of collecting data:

- **Web scraping**: Employing bots or crawlers to collect data from websites. This is particularly useful for gathering user opinions, reviews, and product information from various online sources. *Amazon Kendra Web Crawler* is a very good example.

- **Application programming interfaces** (**APIs**): Leveraging APIs provided by platforms (like *Twitter*, *Facebook*, or *Google Maps*) to systematically collect data that includes the extraction of user posts, comments, and likes to analyze trends and sentiments. This method ensures structured data collection and is governed by the platform's data usage policies, ensuring ethical data usage.

- **Database queries**: Running **Structured Query Language** (**SQL**) queries on databases to extract transactional or operational data, which can then be used for trend analysis, financial forecasting, or customer behavior modeling. For example, an e-commerce platform might store transactional data in a **relational database management system** (**RDBMS**), where each transaction record details purchases, returns, and payment methods.

- **Direct collection from IoT devices**: This data is often streamed in real-time and requires technologies capable of handling big data streams, such as *Apache Kafka* or *Amazon Kinesis*. Utilizing **Message Queuing Telemetry Transport** (**MQTT**) or similar protocols to collect data directly from sensors or IoT devices in real-time, providing a continuous stream of data for analysis.

File formats for ML

Selecting the appropriate file format for storing and processing data is a critical step in preparing for ML workflows. The choice of format affects everything from data ingestion speed and storage efficiency to compatibility with ML tools and libraries. AWS services offer flexibility in handling a wide range of data formats, each suited for different types of tasks and stages in the ML lifecycle.

The following is an overview of commonly used file formats and their relevance in ML workflows:

- **Comma-separated values** (**CSV**) is a popular choice for structured, tabular data such as training datasets and feature sets. It is human-readable, easy to generate and parse, and widely supported by ML libraries like pandas and scikit-learn. However, it lacks support for hierarchical data and becomes inefficient when handling large or complex datasets due to its lack of compression and indexing capabilities.

- **JavaScript Object Notation** (**JSON**) is commonly used for semi-structured data from APIs or logs, especially when dealing with nested elements like metadata or sensor readings. It supports hierarchical structures and is widely compatible across programming languages, making it a flexible choice for many ML workflows. However, JSON can be verbose, and parsing large files may be slow without optimized tools or libraries.

- **Parquet** is a columnar storage format ideal for big data applications and large-scale model training, especially when using services like *Amazon Athena* or *AWS Glue*. It offers efficient compression and fast query performance, making it well-suited for analytics workloads. However, Parquet is less human-readable and usually requires a processing engine like *Apache Spark* for effective use.

- **Optimized row columnar** (**ORC**) is designed for high-performance data processing, particularly in *Amazon EMR* or *Hive-based workflows*. It provides high compression and faster read performance for large-scale datasets.

- **Avro** is well-suited for data serialization and streaming pipelines, particularly with tools like Kafka or AWS Kinesis. It uses a compact binary format and supports schema-based, row-oriented storage, making it efficient for message passing and data exchange. However, Avro is not human-readable and requires careful schema management to ensure compatibility across systems.

- **Image, audio, and video formats** like *JPEG*, *PNG*, *WAV*, and *MP4* are commonly used in deep learning models such as CNNs and RNNs. These formats are natively supported by frameworks like TensorFlow and PyTorch, enabling direct integration into ML pipelines. However, they typically require extensive pre-processing and transformation before being used for training or inference.

- **TFRecord** is a binary file format developed for TensorFlow, optimized for training large-scale deep learning models. It offers efficient storage and performance within TensorFlow pipelines, especially when working with large datasets. However, its use is limited outside the TensorFlow ecosystem due to a lack of broader compatibility.

Understanding when and how to use each of these file formats is essential for building efficient and scalable ML solutions on AWS. Whether you are streaming real-time data from IoT devices, querying historical data in S3, or feeding labeled images into a training pipeline, choosing the right format will help ensure performance, compatibility, and cost-efficiency throughout the ML workflow.

Types of data involved

The following are the types of data involved:

- **Structured data**: Highly organized and easily searchable, often stored in relational databases. Examples include customer information in a **customer relationship management** (**CRM**) system or transaction details in an e-commerce database.

- **Unstructured data**: Not organized in a pre-defined manner, making it harder to collect and interpret. Examples include text data from social media posts, images, and videos from user uploads.

- **Semi-structured data**: A mix between structured and unstructured data, such as JSON or **Extensible Markup Language** (**XML**) files from web APIs. For instance, sensor data might be transmitted in JSON format, containing both structured elements (like timestamps and device IDs) and unstructured elements (like complex sensor readings).

Analyzing data characteristics

In the dynamic and ever-evolving domain of big data, the comprehension and management of vast datasets necessitate a strategic framework, encapsulated by the seminal **7 Vs** of data. These critical dimensions are as follows:

- Volume
- Velocity
- Variety
- Veracity

- Value
- Variability
- Visualization and accessibility

The above core principles are used by data professionals to decipher the complexity of data. As navigators in the intricate world of information, data scientists and technology experts leverage these pillars to convert the extensive arrays of raw data into meaningful, actionable insights. Addressing the challenges presented by the immense volume of data generated continuously, the swift pace at which it flows, the diverse forms it assumes, and the imperative for accuracy and utility, the 7 Vs provide a structured approach to data analysis. This framework not only facilitates the efficient extraction of pertinent information but also ensures that data-driven decisions are both insightful and impactful. By adhering to these principles, organizations can adeptly maneuver through the intricacies of big data, unlocking its vast potential to drive innovation and inform strategic decisions. As we engage with the multifaceted aspects of big data, the 7 Vs serve as a guiding framework, steering efforts towards the realization of data's full potential in shaping future advancements.

Refer to the following table:

Type of V	Definition and impact	Handling strategies	Use cases
Volume	The sheer size of data collected can be massive and impact storage, processing, and analysis capabilities.	Use data compression, distributed storage systems, and scalable cloud solutions.	Analyzing social media posts for trends requires managing and processing large datasets.
Velocity	The speed at which data is generated and processed is crucial for real-time data applications.	Implement real-time processing frameworks (Apache Kafka, Spark Streaming); ensure rapid data storage performance.	Real-time monitoring of stock transactions for algorithmic trading.
Variety	The range of data types and sources includes structured, unstructured, and semi-structured data.	Utilize a mix of databases (NoSQL, RDBMS) and data integration tools for various data formats.	Integrating customer data from different sources for comprehensive analytics.
Veracity	The quality and accuracy of data affect the reliability of analyses and ML model predictions.	Data validation, cleansing, and enrichment processes to improve data quality.	Ensuring accurate patient data in healthcare applications for reliable diagnoses.

Value	The usefulness of data in deriving insights and making informed decisions highlights the need to focus on relevant data.	Use analytics and business intelligence tools to extract actionable insights; discard irrelevant data.	Using customer purchase history and preferences for personalized marketing campaigns.
Variability	Inconsistencies in data over time can complicate processing and analysis.	Develop adaptive models and data pipelines to accommodate data pattern changes.	Seasonal analysis of sales data to predict inventory needs.
Visualization and accessibility	How easily data can be accessed and visualized for analysis is crucial for data exploration and decision-making.	Leverage visualization tools (e.g., Amazon QuickSight, Tableau, Power BI) and ensure data is stored in accessible, secure formats.	Creating dashboards for business KPIs that pull data from multiple sources for real-time monitoring.

Table 1.1: *The 7 Vs of data*

Table 1.1 encapsulates the essence of understanding and managing data characteristics effectively for ML and data analytics projects. Each **V** represents a critical dimension of data that professionals must navigate to unlock the full potential of their data-driven initiatives.

Determining storage mediums

In the realm of ML and AI, the selection of appropriate storage mediums is a critical decision that profoundly influences the efficiency, scalability, and overall success of ML projects. As we embark on the journey of **determining storage mediums** for ML applications, particularly within the ecosystem of **Amazon Web Services (AWS)**, it is essential to approach this task with a blend of technical acumen and strategic foresight. This topic delves into the intricate process of selecting and optimizing storage solutions that not only accommodate the vast and varied nature of ML datasets but also align with the computational demands and data access patterns inherent to ML workflows.

The evolution of cloud computing and storage technologies has presented ML practitioners with a plethora of storage options, each with its unique characteristics, cost profiles, and performance metrics. From the highly scalable and durable **Amazon Simple Storage Service (Amazon S3)**, designed for data lake architectures, to the high-performance file systems offered by *Amazon FSx for Lustre*, and *Amazon EFS for smaller datasets*. Additionally, the advent of AWS Lake Formation further simplifies the setup and management of secure data lakes, enabling seamless access to clean and cataloged data for ML model training and inference.

As we navigate the complexities of determining storage mediums, it is imperative to consider factors such as data volume, velocity, and variety, alongside the requirements for data security, compliance, and cost-efficiency. Moreover, the integration of these storage solutions with Amazon SageMaker, AWS's fully managed service for building, training, and deploying ML models, highlights the importance of seamless data flow and accessibility in accelerating the ML model development lifecycle.

This exploration will not only highlight the technical specifications and ideal use cases for each AWS storage option but will also offer insights into best practices for lifecycle management, data storage optimization, and the strategic deployment of storage resources in support of ML objectives. Whether dealing with the ingestion and storage of real-time sensor data, managing large-scale datasets in a data lake, or ensuring low-latency access to training data, the careful determination of storage mediums stands as a cornerstone of effective ML architecture on AWS.

Determining storage mediums is a topic that demands a thoughtful and informed approach, marrying the technical capabilities of AWS storage services with the nuanced requirements of ML applications. Through this lens, we endeavour to equip ML practitioners with the knowledge and tools necessary to make informed storage decisions, paving the way for innovative, scalable, and cost-effective ML solutions.

Here is an in-depth look at the specified areas:

- **Amazon S3 as storage for a data lake**:
    - **Options and lifecycle configuration**: Amazon S3, serving as a centralized storage repository for data lakes, is critical for ML workflows in SageMaker. It provides a durable, scalable platform for storing training data, model artifacts, and output results.
    - **SageMaker integration benefits**: The direct integration between S3 and SageMaker facilitates easy access to datasets for training and inference, supporting various data formats essential for ML models. Amazon S3 data storage options offer a tailored, flexible solution for managing datasets within Amazon SageMaker workflows, catering to a wide range of ML project requirements from active model training to long-term dataset archiving. With services like S3 Standard for readily accessible data, essential for iterative model training and real-time analytics, to S3 Intelligent-Tiering, which automatically optimizes costs for datasets with unpredictable access patterns, SageMaker users can efficiently manage their ML data lifecycle. For datasets accessed less frequently but requiring quick retrieval when needed, S3 Standard-IA and S3 One Zone-IA provide cost-effective alternatives. Moreover, for the long-term storage of historical data, which might be used for trend analysis or compliance purposes within SageMaker projects, S3 Glacier and S3 Glacier Deep Archive offer secure, extremely low-cost storage solutions with flexible retrieval times. These diverse

S3 storage classes enable SageMaker users to streamline their ML workflows, ensuring data is stored in the most appropriate, cost-effective manner without compromising the performance and scalability of their ML models.

Table 1.2 is a summary of Amazon S3 data storage options, detailing their description, cost implications, latency characteristics, and practical use cases to provide a comprehensive overview tailored for quick reference:

S3 storage option	Description	Cost	Latency	Practical use case
S3 Standard	General-purpose storage for frequently accessed data.	Moderate, with higher costs for frequent access.	Low	Ideal for active content distribution and big data analytics.
S3 Intelligent-Tiering	Automatically moves data between two access tiers based on changing access patterns without performance impact.	Lower than Standard for infrequently accessed data, with a monitoring and automation fee.	Low to moderate	Suitable for data with unknown or changing access patterns.
S3 Standard-IA	Infrequently accessed data requires rapid access when needed.	Lower storage cost than Standard, but with retrieval fees.	Low	Perfect for long-term storage of data that is accessed less frequently.
S3 One Zone-IA	Similar to Standard-IA but stored in a single availability zone for cost savings.	Lower than Standard-IA, with a risk of data loss if the AZ is compromised.	Low	Ideal for secondary backup copies or storing data that can be recreated.
S3 Glacier	Low-cost storage option for archiving data that is rarely accessed and can tolerate retrieval times of several hours.	Very low storage cost, with additional retrieval fees based on speed.	High (minutes to hours)	Suitable for archiving compliance records and digital media archives.

S3 Glacier Deep Archive	The lowest-cost storage option for long-term archiving, where data retrieval times of 12 hours are acceptable.	Lowest storage cost, with retrieval fees.	Very high (12 hours)	Ideal for archiving data that may only need to be accessed once or twice a year

Table 1.2: *AWS storage options*

Table 1.2 offers a snapshot of the diverse range of Amazon S3 data storage options, helping users navigate the trade-offs between cost, latency, and access needs to select the most appropriate solution for their specific use cases, from active data analytics and content distribution to long-term data archiving.

- **Amazon FSx for Lustre**:
  - **High-performance file system for ML**: Amazon FSx for Lustre provides a high-performance file system optimized for workloads requiring fast processing of large datasets, such as complex simulations, genome sequencing, and ML/DL tasks.

  - **SageMaker integration benefits**: Amazon FSx for Lustre improves data transfer speed for Amazon SageMaker ML by eliminating the initial Amazon S3 download step. When FSx for Lustre is used as an input data source for SageMaker, ML training jobs are accelerated, leading to faster startup and training times. This integration also reduces the total cost of ownership by avoiding repetitive downloads of common objects for iterative jobs on the same dataset, thus saving on S3 request costs123.

    The high-performance file system provided by FSx for Lustre offers shared storage with sub-millisecond latencies, up to hundreds of GBs/s of throughput, and millions of IOPS, which significantly enhances the speed of data transfer and processing for SageMaker ML workloads.

- **Amazon EFS**:
  - **EFS for ML model training**: Amazon EFS offers a simple, scalable, elastic file system for Linux-based workloads. For ML tasks in SageMaker that require a shared file system, EFS is ideal for smaller datasets and scenarios where low latency is crucial.

  - **SageMaker integration benefits**: The integration of Amazon EFS with SageMaker allows for the direct interaction between SageMaker and Amazon EFS, reducing the start-up time by eliminating the data download step when using the file input mode.

- **Amazon FSx vs. Amazon EFS**: When deciding between Amazon FSx for Lustre and Amazon EFS for use with Amazon SageMaker, the choice hinges on the specific requirements of your ML workloads and where your training data resides. Amazon FSx for Lustre is the go-to option for scenarios necessitating rapid access to large datasets stored in Amazon S3, especially useful for ML model training that requires frequent access to the same data across multiple training jobs. Its ability to bypass initial S3 download steps significantly speeds up training processes and enhances workflow efficiency, making it ideal for iterative model training with various algorithms. Conversely, Amazon EFS is preferred for its scalability and high availability, supporting Linux-based applications and ML frameworks. It is particularly fitting when training data is already hosted on an EFS file system and there is a need for a shared environment, like in shared notebook systems within SageMaker, thanks to its seamless integration and ability to scale with data requirements. Ultimately, the decision between FSx for Lustre and EFS should align with the ML project's data access needs and training dynamics.

- **AWS Lake Formation**:

  o **Integration with Amazon SageMaker**: AWS Lake Formation simplifies the process of building, securing, and managing data lakes. Its integration with Amazon SageMaker allows for direct access to clean, secure, and cataloged data for ML model training, significantly reducing the time to procure datasets for ML projects.

  o **SageMaker integration benefits**: Automatically cataloging data makes it easier for data scientists to discover and prepare datasets for ML, enhancing productivity and model accuracy.

- **Amazon EBS volumes**

  o **Persistent Block Storage for ML**: Amazon EBS provides a high-performance block storage service suited for both transaction-intensive and throughput-intensive workloads on EC2, which can be leveraged by SageMaker for ML model training and inference.

  o **SageMaker integration benefits**: If you need persistent block storage that is highly available and reliable for your SageMaker notebook instances, Amazon EBS is a suitable choice.

    For example, if you require a specific size of storage volume that is scalable and can be easily attached to your SageMaker notebook instances, Amazon EBS is the preferred option.

The following table compares the various storage options available:

Storage option	Cost	Latency	Ideal use case scenario	Primary benefit
Amazon S3	Low cost for storage, costs for retrieval, and data transfer.	Varies from low (S3 Standard) to high (S3 Glacier).	Centralized data lake storage for large datasets; storing training data, model artifacts, and output results. Storing ML datasets in the most cost-effective storage class based on access patterns, e.g., frequent access (S3 Standard) vs. archival (S3 Glacier).	Highly scalable and durable, offering a cost-effective solution for massive datasets with integration ease into SageMaker for ML workflows.
Amazon FSx for Lustre	Higher than S3, based on performance requirements.	Low (sub-millisecond for compute instances).	Workloads requiring fast processing of large datasets, like complex ML model training with high I/O requirements.	Offers a high-performance file system optimized for fast processing of large datasets, crucial for time-sensitive ML tasks in SageMaker.
Amazon EFS	Higher cost for storage compared to S3, no data transfer costs within the same availability zone.	Low (milliseconds).	ML projects require a shared file system for smaller datasets with low-latency access across multiple instances.	Provides a simple, scalable file system with low latency, ideal for collaborative ML workflows and smaller datasets in SageMaker.
AWS Lake Formation	Variable, based on underlying storage and services used.	Depends on the underlying storage.	Building, securing, and managing data lakes for ML models.	Simplifies the creation and management of data lakes, providing secure and organized data for SageMaker without extensive setup.

Amazon EBS volumes	Moderate, depending on provisioned IOPS and storage size.	Very low (single to low double-digit milliseconds).	Persistent block storage for EC2 instances running high-performance databases or jobs with SageMaker.	Delivers high-performance block storage, suitable for intensive ML tasks requiring fast access to datasets or temporary storage of intermediate ML model computations.

Table 1.3: AWS storage options

Table 1.3 provides a snapshot of how each AWS storage option can be utilized in the context of ML with Amazon SageMaker, highlighting the strategic considerations for cost, latency, and use cases that guide the selection of a particular storage solution. The main reason for each choice reflects the optimal balance between performance requirements and cost-effectiveness, tailored to the specific needs of ML workflows.

Conclusion

As we conclude this foundational chapter on creating effective data repositories for ML, it is evident that the strategic identification, analysis, and storage of data represent a pivotal first step in developing impactful ML applications. By exploring the diverse sources and characteristics of data, from transactional records to real-time sensor streams, we can appreciate the multifaceted nature of the datasets that fuel modern AI innovations. Equipped with a structured framework to evaluate data volume, variety, velocity, and more through the lens of the 7 Vs, practitioners can adeptly navigate the intricacies of big data.

Most crucially, a nuanced understanding of AWS storage solutions empowers us to architect optimized data lakes and repositories tailored to the unique demands of ML workflows. Whether leveraging Amazon S3's scalability or FSx for Lustre's high throughput for model training, thoughtful storage decisions directly accelerate the development and deployment of performant, cost-efficient ML models. As we build the foundations for data-driven innovation, this chapter provides an indispensable guide for creating future-ready data repositories that can flexibly scale to meet the needs of emerging technologies.

With robust data practices in place, the stage is set to unleash ML's transformative potential, where real-world challenges can be solved through data-derived intelligence. By continuously honing our ability to harness data's power responsibly and securely, pioneering ML applications that elevate business objectives and enhance society become truly attainable.

In the next chapter, we will will learn about different data ingestion methods, including batch processing and real-time streaming, and understand how to select and implement appropriate solutions using AWS services such as Amazon Kinesis, EMR, AWS Glue, and Apache Flink. The chapter covers job scheduling strategies, pipeline orchestration, and best practices for managing data workflows in the cloud, ultimately enabling readers to design and implement efficient, scalable data ingestion solutions for their ML projects on AWS.

Multiple choice questions

1. **Which of the following is not one of the 7 Vs used to analyze data characteristics?**

    a. Variety

    b. Velocity

    c. Volume

    d. Vitality

2. **What term refers to the speed at which data is generated and processed?**

    a. Variety

    b. Veracity

    c. Velocity

    d. Value

3. **Which AWS storage service provides a high-performance shared file system suitable for ML workloads?**

    a. Amazon S3

    b. Amazon EFS

    c. Amazon EBS

    d. AWS Lake Formation

4. **Which of the following is an ideal use case for Amazon S3 Glacier Deep Archive?**

    a. Active ML model training data

    b. Frequently accessed e-commerce product images

    c. Daily database backups

    d. Long-term data archiving is accessed once a year

5. **What are two benefits of using Amazon FSx for Lustre for ML in SageMaker?**

    a. Persistent block storage, encryption

    b. Metadata cataloging, governance

    c. High throughput, eliminating S3 download

    d. Scalability, availability across zones

6. **Which service simplifies the building, securing, and management of data lakes?**

    a. Amazon S3

    b. Amazon EFS

    c. AWS Lake Formation

    d. Amazon FSx

7. **What are two common methods for collecting user data?**

    a. Web scraping, direct sensor data

    b. Database queries, transaction logs

    c. Batch processing, ETL

    d. Web scraping, APIs

8. **When should Amazon EBS volumes be used with SageMaker?**

    a. For data lake storage

    b. For long-term archival

    c. For a shared file system

    d. For persistent block storage

9. **Which S3 storage class is best suited for data that is frequently accessed?**

    a. S3 Glacier Deep Archive

    b. S3 Intelligent-Tiering

    c. S3 Standard

    d. S3 One Zone-IA

10. **What are two types of semi-structured data commonly used in ML?**

    a. Images, video

    b. XML, JSON

    c. Tables, graphs

    d. Text, audio

Answer key

1. d

2. c

3. b

4. d

5. c

6. c

7. d

8. d

9. c

10. b

Join our Discord space

Join our Discord workspace for latest updates, offers, tech happenings around the world, new releases, and sessions with the authors:

https://discord.bpbonline.com

CHAPTER 2

Implementing Data Ingestion Solutions

Introduction

In **machine learning (ML)** on AWS, the ability to effectively identify and implement data ingestion solutions is paramount. This chapter explores the process of data ingestion, a critical step in preparing for the **Amazon Web Services (AWS)** Certified Machine Learning - Specialty exam. Data ingestion, the initial step in the data preparation and analysis workflow, involves collecting data from various sources and moving it to a location where it can be accessed, used, and analyzed by applications. Given the diverse nature of data, ranging from real-time streaming data to large batches of historical data, understanding and selecting the appropriate data ingestion technique is crucial for building scalable and efficient ML systems.

This chapter will guide you through identifying different data job styles and job types, such as batch load and streaming, and how these affect the design and implementation of data ingestion pipelines. With AWS, you have access to a suite of services that facilitate the orchestration of data ingestion pipelines tailored for both batch-based and streaming-based ML workloads. We will explore Amazon Kinesis, Amazon Kinesis Data Firehose, Amazon EMR, AWS Glue, and Amazon Managed Service for Apache Flink, each offering unique features and capabilities to handle specific data ingestion needs.

Additionally, the ability to schedule and manage jobs efficiently plays a critical role in ensuring that data is available when needed, without overwhelming systems or incurring unnecessary costs. This chapter will provide insights into job scheduling strategies and best practices for managing data ingestion tasks in a cloud environment.

By the end of this chapter, you will be equipped with the knowledge to identify the most suitable data ingestion solutions for your ML projects, understand how to orchestrate efficient and scalable data pipelines, and implement job scheduling to streamline your data workflows on AWS.

Structure

The chapter covers the following topics:

- Introduction to data ingestion on AWS
- Data processing type
- Orchestrating data ingestion pipelines
- Understanding AWS services for data ingestion
- Scheduling jobs

Objectives

By the end of this chapter, readers will be able to identify suitable data job styles and types for different machine learning scenarios. They will gain comprehensive knowledge on orchestrating data ingestion pipelines using AWS services, offering insights into scheduling and managing data ingestion jobs efficiently on AWS. The chapter will include practical examples and exercises to apply the concepts learned in real-world scenarios, ultimately preparing readers for related topics in the AWS Certified Machine Learning - Specialty exam, with a focus on data ingestion solutions.

Introduction to data ingestion on AWS

Data ingestion is a crucial process in any data-driven application or system, and AWS provides a robust set of services and tools to streamline this process. In the context of AWS, data ingestion involves capturing, transferring, and storing data from various sources into AWS data stores, such as Amazon S3, Amazon Kinesis, or Amazon DynamoDB. This process ensures that data is readily available for downstream processing, analysis, and ML workloads. AWS offers a wide range of services, like AWS Data Migration Service, AWS Glue, Amazon Kinesis, and AWS Lambda, to facilitate data ingestion from on-premises databases, applications, and third-party sources. Additionally, AWS provides managed services like Amazon Athena and Amazon Redshift Spectrum, which allow querying and analyzing data directly from data lakes stored in Amazon S3. With its scalable, secure, and cost-effective solutions, AWS empowers organizations to ingest, store, and process large volumes of data efficiently, enabling them to derive valuable insights and make data-driven decisions.

Understanding data ingestion

Data ingestion is the process of obtaining and importing data for immediate use or storage in a database. It involves collecting data from various sources, which can include databases, **Software as a Service (SaaS)** platforms, cloud storage, and more, then moving it into a system where it can be analyzed, processed, and stored. In the context of AWS and ML, data ingestion is a foundational step that ensures the raw data collected from different sources is made ready for preprocessing, analysis, and model training.

The complexity of data ingestion varies based on the data volume, velocity, and variety, often referred to as the **three Vs** of big data. Volume refers to the amount of data, velocity to the speed at which it is generated and collected, and variety to the types and sources of data. Effective data ingestion strategies are capable of handling these aspects efficiently, ensuring data is accurately and quickly available for ML tasks.

Data ingestion in ML workflows

In ML workflows, the significance of data ingestion cannot be overstated. It directly impacts the quality of the model training, the efficiency of the data preprocessing, and ultimately, the accuracy and performance of the ML models. Proper data ingestion ensures:

- **Data availability**: Data is readily available in the required format for analysis, training, and inference.

- **Data quality**: Ensures high-quality data by allowing for initial cleaning and validation during the ingestion process.

- **Scalability**: Efficiently handles scaling data volumes and velocities, which is critical for ML applications as they evolve.

- **Timeliness**: Provides timely access to data, which is particularly crucial for applications requiring real-time processing and analytics.

Overview of AWS services for data ingestion

AWS offers a robust suite of services designed to simplify and automate the data ingestion process, catering to both batch and streaming data. Understanding these services and their best use cases is essential for architects, developers, and ML practitioners working on AWS. Here is a brief overview:

- **Amazon Kinesis Data Streams**: Ideal for real-time data streaming and processing. It can continuously capture gigabytes of data per second from hundreds of thousands of sources such as website clickstreams, database event streams, financial transactions, social media feeds, and IoT sensors.

- **Amazon Kinesis Data Firehose**: Automates the loading of streaming data into AWS data stores such as Amazon S3, Amazon Redshift, Amazon Elasticsearch Service, and Splunk, enabling near-real-time analytics with existing business intelligence tools and dashboards.

- **Amazon Elastic MapReduce (EMR)**: Provides a managed Hadoop framework that makes it easy, fast, and cost-effective to process vast amounts of data across dynamically scalable Amazon EC2 instances. You can use Amazon EMR to process data for analytics purposes and business intelligence workloads.

- **AWS Glue**: A fully managed **extract, transform, and load** (ETL) service that makes it easy for customers to prepare and load their data for analytics. AWS Glue is serverless, so there is no infrastructure to provision or manage.

- **Amazon Managed Streaming for Apache Kafka (MSK)**: A fully managed service that makes it easy to build and run applications that use Apache Kafka to process streaming data. MSK is optimized for data ingestion, distribution, and lightweight processing. It is highly available, secure, and integrated with AWS services like Amazon CloudWatch, AWS **Identity and Access Management (IAM)**, and Amazon VPC.

- **Amazon Managed Service for Apache Flink**: A fully managed service that simplifies complex and time-consuming tasks such as building and maintaining Apache Flink applications. Kinesis Data Analytics for Apache Flink excels in complex, real-time stream processing and analytics.

By leveraging these AWS services, organizations can build scalable, efficient, and flexible data ingestion pipelines that are essential for successful ML projects.

Data processing type

When it comes to data ingestion on AWS, organizations need to consider the appropriate data job styles and types based on their specific requirements and use cases. Two primary approaches emerge: batch loading and streaming. Batch loading involves ingesting large volumes of data periodically, typically from static sources like databases or file systems. This approach is suitable for scenarios where data processing can be delayed and performed in batches, such as analytics reports or historical data analysis. AWS services like AWS Glue and AWS Batch facilitate efficient batch data ingestion and processing. On the other hand, streaming data ingestion is ideal for real-time or near-real-time data processing, where data needs to be ingested continuously from sources like IoT devices, clickstreams, or application logs. AWS Kinesis Data Streams and Kinesis Data Firehose are designed for seamless streaming data ingestion, enabling organizations to capture, process, and analyze data as it arrives, unlocking opportunities for real-time analytics, anomaly detection, and event-driven architectures.

Batch load vs. streaming

Batch load and streaming are two fundamental methods used for data ingestion and processing, each with its own set of characteristics, advantages, and ideal use cases. Understanding the differences between these two approaches is crucial for selecting the right data processing strategy for your machine learning projects on AWS, as shown in the following figure:

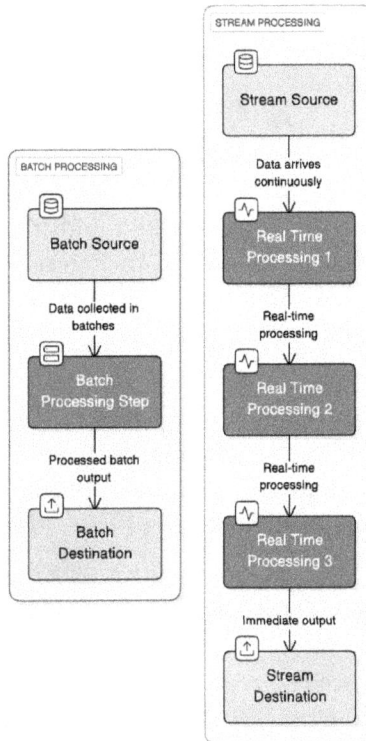

Figure 2.1: *Flow chart explaining the difference between batch load and streaming load*

Batch load

Batch load involves processing data in large, discrete chunks at specific intervals. This method collects data over a period of time and processes it all at once. Batch processing is typically scheduled and does not require immediate action on the data.

Some characteristics of batch load are:

- **Scheduled**: Batch jobs are often run on a regular schedule, such as hourly, daily, or weekly.

- **High throughput**: Capable of processing large volumes of data efficiently.

- **Latency**: There is a delay between data collection and data processing, as data is accumulated before being processed.

Some advantages of batch load are:

- **Simplicity**: Easier to implement and manage due to its scheduled nature.

- **Scalability**: Efficiently handles large volumes of data.

- **Cost-effective**: Can be more cost-effective for processing large datasets where real-time analysis is not critical.

Ideal use cases are:

- **Daily sales reports**: Businesses often need to generate comprehensive sales reports daily to track performance, identify trends, and make informed decisions. In this scenario, batch loading can be employed to ingest sales data from various sources (e.g., point-of-sale systems, e-commerce platforms) at the end of each day, consolidate it, and generate the required reports.

- **Monthly financial closings**: At the end of every month, organizations need to perform financial closings, which involve reconciling accounts, calculating month-end balances, and generating financial statements. Batch load can be used to extract data from multiple financial systems, accounting applications, and other relevant sources, enabling the consolidation and processing of this data in a batch mode to facilitate monthly financial closings.

- **Data warehousing updates**: Data warehouses are central repositories that consolidate data from various operational systems for analysis and reporting purposes. Batch load can be leveraged to periodically extract data from these operational systems (e.g., CRM, ERP, marketing automation tools) and load it into the data warehouse. This approach ensures that the data warehouse remains up-to-date with the latest information from different sources, enabling accurate and comprehensive reporting and analysis.

Streaming

Streaming, or stream processing, involves continuous ingestion and processing of data in real time as it is generated. This method allows for the immediate analysis and action based on live data streams.

Some characteristics of streaming are:

- **Real-time**: Data is processed immediately as it arrives, enabling near-instant analytics and decision-making.

- **Continuous**: Data is ingested and processed continuously, 24/7.

- **Low latency**: Minimal delay between data ingestion and processing.

Some advantages of streaming are:

- **Timeliness**: Enables immediate insights and actions, which is critical for time-sensitive applications.

- **Flexibility**: Can handle fluctuating volumes of data in real time.

- **Enhanced insights**: Provides the ability to analyze and respond to trends, patterns, and anomalies as they happen.

Ideal use cases are:

- **Real-time fraud detection**: In the realm of financial transactions, real-time fraud detection is crucial to safeguard against fraudulent activities. By leveraging streaming data processing, incoming transaction data can be analyzed in real-time, enabling the detection of suspicious patterns or anomalies as they occur. This allows for immediate action, such as blocking or flagging potentially fraudulent transactions, minimizing financial losses, and enhancing security.

- **Live dashboards and monitoring**: Streaming data processing plays a vital role in enabling live dashboards and monitoring systems. By ingesting and processing data streams from various sources, such as application logs, sensor data, or user interactions, these systems can provide real-time visualizations and insights. This empowers organizations to monitor their operations, infrastructure, or customer behavior in real-time, enabling timely decision-making and proactive response to emerging trends or issues.

- **Instant alerts and notifications**: In scenarios where time is of the essence, streaming data processing enables the generation of instant alerts and notifications. By continuously analyzing data streams, the system can detect predefined conditions or patterns that trigger alerts or notifications. These could range from monitoring critical systems for potential failures to tracking stock prices for investment opportunities. Instant alerts and notifications allow for immediate action, enhancing responsiveness and mitigating potential risks or losses.

Choosing between batch load and streaming

The choice between batch load and streaming depends on several factors, including the nature of the data, the requirements of the application, and the need for real-time analytics. *Table 2.1* highlights how batch processing is typically chosen for its simplicity and efficiency in handling large volumes of data when real-time processing is not necessary. In contrast, streaming is selected for applications requiring immediate data processing and analysis, where the timeliness of the insights is critical.

Aspect	Batch load	Streaming
Processing timing	Processes data in scheduled intervals or discrete chunks.	Processes data continuously in real-time as it arrives.
Latency	Higher latency (minutes to hours)	Low latency (seconds or milliseconds)
Data volume	Well-suited for large volumes of data.	Designed for continuous flows of smaller data units.
Complexity	Generally simpler to implement and manage.	More complex architecture and error handling.
Use cases	Daily reports, ETL jobs, and historical analytics.	Real-time dashboards, monitoring, and immediate alerts.
Resource efficiency	More resource-efficient for large batches.	It can require more consistent resource allocation.
Processing guarantee	Strong consistency and completeness guarantee.	May have challenges with exactly-once processing.
AWS services	AWS Glue, Amazon EMR, AWS Batch.	Amazon Kinesis Data Streams, Kinesis Data Firehose, and MSK.
Cost	Often, it is more cost-effective for large volumes.	It can be more expensive due to continuous processing.
Recovery	Easier recovery from failures (can reprocess batches)	Requires more sophisticated failure handling
Data freshness	Data insights are periodic	Data insights are immediate

Table 2.1: Batch and streaming load comparison

In AWS, services like AWS Glue and Amazon EMR are well-suited for batch processing tasks, while Amazon Kinesis Data Streams and Amazon Kinesis Data Firehose provide robust solutions for real-time data streaming and processing. Understanding the strengths and limitations of each approach allows architects and developers to design and implement the most effective data ingestion and processing architecture for their specific use cases.

Use cases and implications for ML

AWS offers a comprehensive suite of services tailored for both batch and real-time data ingestion, each designed to handle specific aspects of data volume, velocity, and variety efficiently. Understanding these services, categorized by their primary use cases, is crucial for building scalable and robust ML systems on AWS.

Services for batch data ingestion

Batch data ingestion involves processing data in discrete chunks, accumulated over a period. It is ideal for scenarios where real-time analysis is not critical. AWS provides several services for efficient batch data processing:

- **AWS Glue**: A managed ETL service that simplifies the preparation of data for analytics and ML. It is ideal for batch processing of data, enabling you to catalog, clean, enrich, and move data between data stores. AWS Glue can automate much of the effort involved in preparing data for ingestion and analysis.

- **Amazon EMR**: Offers a Hadoop framework for processing vast amounts of data quickly across resizable clusters of Amazon EC2 instances. It supports batch processing workloads by distributing data and processing across multiple machines and managing the orchestration.

Services for real-time data ingestion

Real-time data ingestion is essential for use cases that require immediate analysis and action, such as fraud detection, live dashboards, and instant alerts. AWS offers services that specialize in handling streaming data, such as:

- **Amazon Kinesis Data Streams**: Allows for the building of custom, real-time applications that process or analyze streaming data for specialized needs.

- **Amazon Kinesis Data Firehose**: Enables easier loading of streaming data into AWS data stores for near-real-time analytics with existing business intelligence tools.

- **Amazon MSK**: A fully managed service that facilitates building applications that process streaming data using Apache Kafka without managing the underlying infrastructure. It is highly suitable for high-volume, real-time data ingestion and processing tasks.

- **Amazon Managed Service for Apache Flink**: Provides a managed environment for deploying and managing Apache Flink applications, which are ideal for complex, real-time analytics and processing workloads. It simplifies the execution of high-performance, stateful computations over data streams.

The following table describes various AWS services that help with both batch and real-time workloads, and when to use each of them with an ideal use-case scenario:

AWS service	Data processing type	When to use	Ideal use case example
AWS Glue	Batch	When you need to prepare and transform datasets for analytics and ML without managing infrastructure.	ETL jobs for daily sales data aggregation from various sources.

Amazon EMR	Batch	For processing large datasets across resizable clusters of virtual servers using a broad ecosystem of Hadoop tools.	Analyzing historical stock price data for predictive modeling.
Amazon Kinesis Data Streams	Real-time	When your application requires custom processing of real-time streaming data.	Real-time monitoring of IoT sensor data for anomaly detection.
Amazon Kinesis Data Firehose	Real-time	For straightforward loading of streaming data into AWS data stores and analytics tools without needing to manage resources.	Streaming clickstream data analysis for website optimization.
Amazon Managed Streaming for Kafka	Real-time	When you need a managed Apache Kafka service for building high-throughput, distributed streaming applications.	Real-time processing of financial transactions for fraud detection.
Amazon Managed Service for Apache Flink	Real-time	For complex, real-time analytics and processing with a managed Apache Flink service.	Analyzing streaming social media data for sentiment analysis.

Table 2.2: Batch and real-time AWS services: when to use them and ideal use case scenarios

The preceding table categorizes AWS services by their suitability for batch or real-time data ingestion, providing guidance on when each service is best used, along with an example of an ideal use case. Understanding these distinctions is crucial for selecting the right AWS service for your machine learning and data analytics projects.

By categorizing AWS services into batch and real-time data ingestion, architects and developers can more easily select the appropriate tools for their specific ML workloads. This organized approach not only aids in designing efficient data ingestion pipelines but also helps with the AWS Certified Machine Learning—Specialty exam by providing a clear understanding of the services' best use cases and functionalities.

Orchestrating data ingestion pipelines

In ML, the orchestration of data ingestion pipelines plays a pivotal role in ensuring the seamless flow of data from various sources to the destination, where it can be processed and analyzed effectively. This critical process not only demands a deep understanding of the technical aspects of AWS services but also the operational proficiency to integrate them into cohesive workflows that align with ML objectives. Whether dealing with batch-based or streaming-based ML workloads, AWS offers a comprehensive suite of services that empower organizations to ingest, process, and analyze data with unparalleled efficiency, reliability, and scalability.

Principles of data pipeline orchestration

Batch-based workloads play a crucial role in processing and analyzing data that accumulates over time. AWS offers a robust set of services specifically designed to streamline the ingestion and processing of data in discrete batches. With services like AWS Glue and Amazon EMR, organizations can effectively orchestrate their batch-based ML pipelines, ensuring efficient data preparation, transformation, and scalable processing across resizable clusters of Amazon EC2 instances. For scenarios that demand real-time data processing and analysis, such as streaming-based ML workloads, AWS provides a comprehensive ecosystem of services tailored to handle continuous data streams. The Amazon Kinesis suite, including services like Amazon Kinesis Data Streams, Kinesis Data Firehose, and Kinesis Data Analytics, empowers organizations to ingest, process, and derive insights from data in motion. With the ability to apply SQL queries and machine learning algorithms directly on streaming data, these services enable immediate decision-making and proactive response to emerging patterns or anomalies.

Batch-based ML workloads

Tools and strategies for batch-based ML workloads, AWS services like AWS Glue and Amazon EMR, and Apache Airflow are pivotal. AWS Glue simplifies the process of ETL jobs, allowing for easy data preparation for analytics and ML. Amazon EMR offers a managed Hadoop framework that efficiently processes vast amounts of data across resizable clusters of Amazon EC2 instances. Apache Airflow, often integrated with AWS via **Amazon Managed Workflows for Apache Airflow (MWAA)**, is a powerful orchestration tool that helps manage, schedule, and monitor complex workflows across Glue, EMR, and other services.

Imagine an e-commerce platform aiming to analyze customer behavior and sales trends. The data, stored in various sources like databases and logs, needs to be ingested and processed, details, as follows:

1. **Data collection with AWS Glue**: Begin by using AWS Glue to crawl the existing databases to catalog the data. AWS Glue can automate the extraction of data from these sources, transforming it into a suitable format for analysis.

2. **Batch processing with Amazon EMR**: Leverage Amazon EMR to process this data. For instance, you can run Spark jobs on EMR to analyze sales trends, customer segmentation, and product performance. This batch processing can be scheduled during low-traffic hours to optimize costs and resources.

3. **Workflow orchestration with Apache Airflow**: Use Apache Airflow to orchestrate the entire data pipeline, from data extraction with AWS Glue to batch processing with EMR, ensuring tasks are executed in the correct sequence and enabling retry logic, alerts, and dependencies.

The following are the best practices:

- Automate ETL workflows with AWS Glue to streamline data preparation and loading.

- Utilize Amazon EMR for heavy-duty data processing tasks, taking advantage of its scalability and flexibility.

- Use Apache Airflow to orchestrate workflows, ensuring modular, repeatable, and fault-tolerant execution.

- Monitor and optimize the performance of batch jobs using Amazon CloudWatch and AWS CloudTrail to ensure cost-efficiency and reliability.

Streaming-based ML workloads

For tools and strategies, or real-time data processing, Amazon Kinesis is the go-to AWS service, providing the ability to collect, process, and analyze data streams in real time. Amazon Kinesis Data Firehose simplifies data loading into AWS data stores, while Amazon Kinesis Data Analytics allows for the processing of streaming data using standard SQL.

Practical example: Real-time fraud detection

Consider a financial institution that needs to detect fraudulent transactions in real time. The institution receives a continuous stream of transaction data that must be analyzed instantly to flag any potential fraud.

Refer to the following:

1. **Data streaming with Amazon Kinesis Data Streams**: Use Amazon Kinesis Data Streams to collect real-time transaction data from various sources. This enables the immediate capture and processing of data as it arrives.

2. **Real-time processing with Amazon Kinesis Data Analytics**: Apply SQL queries or machine learning algorithms directly on the streaming data using Amazon Kinesis Data Analytics. For fraud detection, you might employ anomaly detection algorithms that analyze transaction patterns and flag unusual activities for further investigation.

The following are the best practices:

- Leverage Amazon Kinesis Data Firehose for effortless data streaming into AWS storage services, ensuring that data is readily available for real-time analytics and ML.

- Employ Amazon Kinesis Data Analytics to perform real-time data processing and analysis, enabling immediate insights and actions.

- Ensure scalability and reliability by monitoring streaming pipelines with Amazon CloudWatch and adjusting resources as needed to handle varying data volumes.

By understanding the concepts and techniques outlined in this chapter, you will be well-equipped to tackle the challenges of data ingestion in AWS, a critical competency for the AWS Certified Machine Learning—Specialty exam. This knowledge will empower you to design and implement efficient, scalable data pipelines that serve as the backbone of sophisticated ML systems, paving the way for innovative applications and insights.

Understanding AWS services for data ingestion

Navigating the AWS Certified Machine Learning - Specialty exam requires a solid understanding of the various AWS services for data ingestion. These services are foundational for creating efficient, scalable ML workflows:

- **Amazon Kinesis**: Real-time data streaming
- **Amazon Kinesis Data Firehose**: Simplifying data loading
- **Amazon EMR**: Processing large datasets
- **AWS Glue**: Serverless data integration
- **Amazon Managed Service for Apache Flink**: Advanced stream processing

Let us explore these services in detail, providing practical tips to leverage them effectively in your ML projects and to ace the exam.

Real-time data streaming

At the core of AWS's real-time data streaming capabilities lies Kinesis Data Streams, a powerful service that enables the continuous ingestion and processing of data from diverse sources. Whether it is log files, IoT sensor data, or live video streams, Kinesis Data Streams provides a robust foundation for building scalable and reliable data pipelines. By understanding the key concepts such as data producers, streams, shards, and consumers, you can harness the full potential of this service, enabling real-time processing, analysis, and decision-making in a wide range of applications.

Concepts of Kinesis data streams

To effectively leverage the capabilities of Kinesis Data Streams, it is essential to understand the key components that make up its architecture. These include data producers, which are the sources that send data records to the stream, the streams themselves, which are logical groupings of data records composed of shards that determine the overall throughput capacity, and consumers, which are the applications or services that process the data from the stream:

- **Data producers**: Data producers are the sources of data that send records to your Kinesis Data Stream. These can range from simple log files generated by applications, data from IoT devices, or live video streams. Understanding how to configure data producers to reliably send data to your stream is fundamental.

- **Streams**: A stream is a logical grouping of data records. Each stream is composed of one or more shards, which are the base throughput units of Kinesis Data Streams. Each shard has a capacity limit, so the number of shards determines the overall capacity of the stream.

- **Consumers**: Consumers are applications or services that process the data from your stream. They can be custom applications built on the **Kinesis Client Library (KCL)**, AWS Lambda functions triggered by Kinesis, or other AWS services like Amazon Kinesis Data Analytics and Amazon Kinesis Data Firehose.

Creating and using a data stream

To put the concepts of Kinesis Data Streams into practice, it's essential to understand the steps involved in setting up and utilizing a stream for real-time data processing. This includes creating the stream itself, defining its capacity through shards, configuring data producers to send data to the stream, and implementing consumers to process and analyze the incoming data in real-time:

- **Create a Kinesis Data Stream**: Start by creating a Kinesis Data Stream in the AWS Management Console. Define the number of shards based on your throughput requirements. Remember, each shard can support up to 1 MB/s data input and 2 MB/s data output.

- **Send data to your stream**: Use the AWS SDK in your preferred programming language to create a data producer. This could involve writing a simple script that simulates IoT sensor data or log files being sent to your stream at regular intervals.

- **Process data in real-time**: Implement a consumer using the Kinesis Client Library or configure an AWS Lambda function to be triggered by your stream. Practice processing and analyzing this data in real-time, perhaps by calculating aggregates or filtering records based on certain criteria.

Scaling your stream

While setting up a Kinesis Data Stream is crucial, ensuring its scalability and performance are equally important, especially for applications with dynamic data volumes. This involves understanding how to adjust the shard count based on throughput requirements, leveraging the resharding process to split or merge shards as needed, and continuously monitoring key metrics using Amazon CloudWatch to proactively scale the stream's capacity:

- **Shard count adjustment**: Understand how to calculate the number of shards needed based on your data throughput requirements. Remember, if your data input rate exceeds 1 MB/s or your output rate exceeds 2 MB/s per shard, you will need to add more shards to your stream.

- **Resharding**: Familiarize yourself with the process of resharding, which involves splitting and merging shards in your stream to adjust the capacity. This can be critical for applications that experience variable data volumes.

- **Monitoring and scaling**: Practice monitoring your stream's performance using Amazon CloudWatch metrics. Look for metrics like IncomingBytes, IncomingRecords, ReadProvisionedThroughputExceeded, and WriteProvisionedThroughputExceeded to decide when to adjust your shard count.

In preparation for the exam, focus on scenarios that require you to evaluate and adjust the throughput of a Kinesis Data Stream by managing the shard count. Be able to articulate how you would scale a stream up or down based on changing data volumes or processing requirements.

Example: Handling seasonal traffic for an e-commerce platform:

- **Scenario**: An e-commerce platform experiences significant increases in traffic during holiday seasons, leading to a spike in data volume as user interactions, transactions, and log data surge.

- **Evaluation**: Monitor the incoming data metrics using Amazon CloudWatch. If you notice the IncomingBytes and IncomingRecords metrics approaching or exceeding 1 MB/s and 1,000 records/s per shard, respectively, it is time to consider scaling up.

- **Adjustment**: Calculate the required shard count to accommodate the peak load by dividing the peak incoming data rate by the shard capacity (1 MB/s for data, 1,000 records/s for records). For example, if you anticipate a peak load of 5 MB/s, you would need at least 5 shards to handle the data without throttling.

- **Scaling up**: Increase the shard count through the AWS Management Console or AWS CLI before the peak season begins. Monitor the metrics closely to ensure that the additional shards are sufficient to handle the increased load.

Simplifying data loading

Amazon Kinesis Data Firehose is the cornerstone service for effortlessly loading streaming data into AWS data stores, analytics services, and other destinations. It automates the complexities of reliably and securely capturing, transforming, and loading streaming data, enabling near real-time analytics with minimal effort. Kinesis Data Firehose is designed to handle massive streams of data from countless sources, making it an essential tool for data-driven applications.

Concepts of Kinesis Data Firehose

Amazon Kinesis Data Firehose is a fully managed service that simplifies the process of capturing, transforming, and loading streaming data into various AWS data stores and analytics tools. At its core, it revolves around three key components: data producers, which are the sources sending data to Firehose; delivery streams, which act as the conduits for data flow from producers to destinations; and consumers, which are the downstream services or tools that leverage the ingested data for real-time analytics and processing:

- **Data producers**: Data producers in the context of Amazon Kinesis Data Firehose include a wide range of sources, such as website clickstreams, application logs, and IoT sensor data. These producers send data directly to Kinesis Data Firehose, which then automatically loads the data into the chosen destinations.

- **Delivery streams**: A delivery stream is the core component of Kinesis Data Firehose. It is the conduit through which data flows from producers to destinations such as Amazon S3, Amazon Redshift, Amazon Elasticsearch Service, and Splunk. Unlike Kinesis Data Streams, Kinesis Data Firehose does not require manual shard management, as it automatically scales to match the input data flow.

- **Consumers**: In the Kinesis Data Firehose context, consumers are essentially the downstream AWS services or analytics tools that utilize the data once it has been loaded into the target destination. These can include data analysis and visualization tools that perform real-time analytics on the ingested data.

Automating data loading

To harness the power of Kinesis Data Firehose for seamless data ingestion and transformation, it is crucial to understand the steps involved in setting up and configuring a delivery stream. This includes creating the stream itself, specifying the data source and destination, optionally applying data transformations or filtering rules using AWS Lambda, and ultimately leveraging AWS analytics and visualization tools to monitor and analyze the ingested data:

1. **Create a Kinesis Data Firehose delivery stream**: Begin by setting up a delivery stream in the AWS Management Console. Choose your data source and specify the destination, such as Amazon S3 for data storage or Amazon Redshift for analysis.

2. **Configure data transformation**: Optionally, apply data transformation and filtering rules within Kinesis Data Firehose. This can involve converting data formats or enriching the data before it reaches the destination, using AWS Lambda for custom processing logic.

3. **Monitor and analyze data**: Once your data is automatically loaded into the destination, use AWS analytics and visualization tools to monitor and analyze your data. For instance, query your data in Amazon S3 using Amazon Athena or visualize it with Amazon QuickSight for insights.

Simplifying data loading

As you prepare for the AWS Certified Machine Learning—Specialty exam, it is essential to understand how Kinesis Data Firehose can simplify the process of loading streaming data into various AWS data stores and analytics services. This includes mastering the configuration of delivery streams, leveraging AWS Lambda for data transformations, and monitoring key performance metrics to ensure optimal operation. One practical example that highlights the power of Kinesis Data Firehose is streamlining log analysis for web applications, where application logs can be automatically captured, transformed, and loaded into Amazon S3 for near real-time analysis using services like Amazon Athena.

Refer to the following:

- **Understand delivery stream configuration**: Know how to configure a delivery stream, including setting up data transformation, choosing a destination, and configuring retry and backoff settings for failed delivery attempts.

- **Data transformation**: Be familiar with the process of using AWS Lambda for transforming data within Kinesis Data Firehose, including common use cases like log format conversion or data enrichment before loading.

- **Monitoring and optimization**: Practice using Amazon CloudWatch to monitor Kinesis Data Firehose metrics such as IncomingRecords, DeliveryToS3.Success, DeliveryToRedshift.Success, etc., to ensure your delivery stream is performing optimally and to troubleshoot any issues.

Example: Streamlining log analysis for a web application:

- **Scenario**: A web application generates extensive logs that need to be analyzed in near real-time to monitor user activity and system health.

- **Setup**: Configure a Kinesis Data Firehose delivery stream to capture logs from the application. Transform the logs into a query-able format using AWS Lambda and load them directly into Amazon S3.

- **Analysis**: Use Amazon Athena to perform ad-hoc queries on the logs stored in S3, enabling the team to gain insights into user behavior and system performance without manual data handling.

This approach demonstrates the power of Amazon Kinesis Data Firehose in simplifying the data loading process, making it an invaluable topic for AWS Certified Machine Learning - Specialty exam candidates to master.

Processing large datasets

As organizations grapple with the ever-increasing volumes of data, Amazon EMR emerges as a powerful solution for processing and analyzing large datasets efficiently. This managed Hadoop framework allows you to leverage a wide range of open-source tools and frameworks, such as Apache Spark and Hadoop, to perform tasks ranging from batch processing to real-time analytics. By understanding the core concepts of EMR, including clusters, data processing tasks, and storage options, you can harness the full potential of this service to derive valuable insights from your data.

Concepts of Amazon EMR

At the heart of Amazon EMR lies the concept of clusters, which are the core computational units designed to process data efficiently. These clusters consist of a collection of EC2 instances, including a master node that orchestrates the distribution of data and tasks, as well as multiple core and task nodes that perform the heavy lifting. EMR's versatility extends beyond just clusters, as it supports a wide range of data processing tasks, from batch processing to interactive queries and real-time analytics, allowing users to leverage the most appropriate tool for their specific needs. Moreover, EMR offers flexible data storage options, enabling direct processing of data stored in Amazon S3, HDFS, Amazon DynamoDB, or any other Hadoop-compatible file system. The details are as follows:

- **Clusters**: EMR cluster is a collection of EC2 instances (nodes) running big data frameworks. Clusters are the core computational units of Amazon EMR, designed to process data efficiently. Each cluster is composed of one master node that manages the distribution of data and tasks among other nodes, and multiple core and task nodes that do the heavy lifting.

- **Data processing tasks**: EMR supports a variety of big data processing tasks, from batch processing to interactive queries and real-time analytics. This flexibility allows users to use the best tool for their specific data processing needs.

- **Data storage and file systems**: EMR can directly process data stored in Amazon S3, HDFS, Amazon DynamoDB, or any other Hadoop-compatible file system, enabling flexible data storage options.

Processing large datasets

To truly harness the power of Amazon EMR for processing large datasets, it is essential to understand the practical steps involved in setting up and running data processing jobs on the platform. This includes creating an EMR cluster tailored to your specific requirements, ensuring your data is stored in a location accessible by EMR (typically Amazon S3), and leveraging the various tools and frameworks available to run transformations, aggregations, analyses, and even complex tasks like machine learning model training on your large datasets:

1. **Create an EMR cluster**: Start by launching an EMR cluster from the AWS Management Console. Choose the appropriate instance types and number of instances based on your processing requirements and budget. Select the software options, including Hadoop, Spark, or other applications, according to your data processing needs.

2. **Prepare your data**: Ensure your data is stored in a location accessible by EMR, typically in Amazon S3. Use **EMR File System** (**EMRFS**) to seamlessly process data in S3 with Hadoop and Spark.

3. **Run data processing jobs**: Submit your data processing jobs using EMR steps or directly interact with the software on your cluster using SSH. You can run transformations,

aggregations, and analyses on large datasets. For example, use Apache Spark to perform complex data processing tasks like machine learning model training on large datasets.

Scaling and optimization

As you prepare for the AWS Certified Machine Learning - Specialty exam, it is crucial to develop a deep understanding of scaling and optimization techniques for Amazon EMR clusters. This encompasses concepts such as dynamically resizing clusters to match workload demands, leveraging cost-effective Spot Instances for compute capacity, employing auto-scaling features like EMR Managed Scaling, and implementing performance tuning strategies. Practical examples that showcase the application of these techniques, such as the scenario involving a digital marketing agency optimizing their batch processing workloads using Spot Instances, can further solidify your comprehension of designing and implementing efficient EMR solutions:

- **Cluster resizing**: Understand how to dynamically resize your clusters by adding or removing nodes to match your workload requirements. This feature helps in optimizing the cost and performance of data processing tasks.

- **Spot instances**: Familiarize yourself with the use of Amazon EC2 Spot Instances within EMR clusters to reduce costs. Spot Instances can significantly lower the cost of running data processing jobs by using unused EC2 capacity.

- **Cost optimization**: Learn how to use EMR Managed Scaling to automatically resize your clusters and minimize costs without compromising on performance. Also, be aware of different pricing options and best practices for cost management in EMR.

- **Performance tuning**: Be prepared to discuss strategies for tuning the performance of EMR clusters, including choosing the right instance types, optimizing the distribution of data across nodes, and configuring the software settings for optimal processing speed.

Example: Batch processing of user data for marketing insights:

Scenario: A digital marketing agency wants to analyze large datasets of user interactions collected from various online platforms to gain insights into user behavior and preferences. The analysis includes data cleansing, aggregation, and complex machine learning model training. The datasets are processed weekly, and the agency seeks to minimize the computational costs without compromising the time-to-insight.

Decision to use spot instances:

- **Batch processing nature**: The batch processing nature of the workload, which does not require constant availability of compute resources, makes it ideal for Spot Instances. The agency schedules the EMR jobs to run during off-peak hours when Spot Instance prices are typically lower, further reducing costs.

- **Fault tolerance and flexibility**: The data processing tasks are designed to be fault-tolerant. They can be paused and resumed or restarted without significant loss of progress. This characteristic is crucial because Spot Instances can be terminated by AWS on short notice. The agency uses EMR's capability to checkpoint workloads and save intermediate results to Amazon S3, ensuring that they can quickly recover and continue processing from the last saved state if Spot Instances are reclaimed.

Implementation:

- **Cluster configuration**: When setting up the EMR cluster, the agency selects a mix of On-Demand and Spot Instances. They use On-Demand Instances for the master node to ensure it remains uninterrupted, and Spot Instances for core and task nodes where the data processing and analytics tasks are executed.

- **Cost-control strategies**: The agency sets a maximum price for Spot Instances that they are willing to pay, which is below the On-Demand rate but high enough to ensure they acquire the necessary compute capacity quickly. They also use EMR Managed Scaling to automatically adjust the number of Spot Instances in the cluster based on the workload, ensuring cost-efficiency without manual intervention.

- **Monitoring and management**: They closely monitor Spot Instance termination notices and cluster performance metrics via Amazon CloudWatch. This allows them to make informed decisions on whether to bid for more Spot Instances or switch some workloads temporarily to On-Demand Instances if Spot capacity becomes scarce or prices rise.

Outcome:

By leveraging Spot Instances for their EMR workloads, the digital marketing agency significantly reduces their data processing costs while still completing their batch analytics tasks within the desired timeframe. This approach allows them to allocate more budget towards other initiatives, enhancing their overall marketing strategy's effectiveness.

Exam tip:

Understanding when and how to use Spot Instances with Amazon EMR is valuable for the AWS Certified Machine Learning - Specialty exam. Focus on scenarios where workloads are flexible, fault-tolerant, and where interruptions can be managed without severe consequences. Demonstrating knowledge of cost optimization strategies without sacrificing performance is crucial for designing efficient AWS solutions.

On-Demand Instances are used for the master node to ensure it remains uninterrupted, and Spot Instances for core and task nodes, where the data processing and analytics tasks are executed.

Serverless data integration

AWS Glue is a fully managed, serverless data integration service that makes it simple to discover, prepare, and combine data for analytics, ML, and application development. AWS Glue provides a scalable, flexible platform that handles all aspects of data integration, so you can focus on your data rather than on managing infrastructure.

Concepts of AWS Glue

AWS Glue simplifies the process of data preparation and management for analytics workloads. It provides the ability to connect to and ingest data from various sources, maintain a centralized data catalog, and orchestrate ETL jobs. Understanding these core components is crucial for leveraging AWS Glue effectively in data engineering pipelines.

- **Data sources**: Data sources in AWS Glue refer to the various origins of data that you can connect to, including databases, data warehouses, and data lakes stored across AWS services like Amazon S3, Amazon RDS, and Amazon Redshift. Understanding how to connect to and ingest data from these sources is key to leveraging AWS Glue effectively.

- **Data catalog**: The AWS Glue Data Catalog is a central repository to store structural and operational metadata for all your data assets, making it easier to manage and search for data across AWS. It serves as a unified metadata store integrated with Amazon Athena, Amazon EMR, and Amazon Redshift Spectrum, facilitating seamless data discovery and management.

- **ETL jobs**: ETL jobs in AWS Glue are used to prepare and transform data for analytics. You can author jobs in the AWS Management Console using visual tools or code directly in languages like PySpark or Scala. AWS Glue automatically generates the code to execute these transformations at scale.

Using AWS Glue for data integration

Putting the core components of AWS Glue into action is essential to fully leverage its capabilities for data engineering tasks. This involves connecting to and cataloging various data sources, creating and executing ETL jobs to transform and load data, and continuously monitoring and optimizing these ETL workflows for optimal performance.

1. **Connecting to data sources**: Begin by defining your data sources in the AWS Glue Data Catalog. You can use crawlers to discover and catalog data from Amazon S3, JDBC-connected databases, or Amazon DynamoDB tables.

2. **Creating and running ETL jobs**: Use the AWS Glue Studio visual interface to create an ETL job. Define your source, transformations, and target without writing any code. For complex transformations, you can manually script in PySpark using the AWS Glue scripts editor.

3. **Monitoring and optimizing ETL workflows**: After defining and running your ETL jobs, monitor their performance and execution metrics in the AWS Glue Console. Use CloudWatch logs for detailed debugging information and job run history to optimize job performance and reduce execution time.

Leveraging AWS Glue for scalable data integration

As you prepare for the AWS Certified Machine Learning - Specialty exam, it is crucial to develop a deep understanding of how AWS Glue can be leveraged for scalable and efficient data integration. This includes mastering best practices around the Data Catalog, optimizing ETL job performance, and ensuring proper security and access control mechanisms. By recognizing scenarios that align with AWS Glue's capabilities, such as data preparation, cataloging, and serverless ETL workflows, you can effectively demonstrate your expertise in building robust data pipelines, a critical skill for successful machine learning implementations.

Refer to the following:

- **Data Catalog best practices**: Understand how to leverage the Data Catalog for efficient data management and governance. Know how to use crawlers to automate the discovery, cataloging, and classification of your data.

- **ETL job optimization**: Be familiar with strategies to optimize ETL job performance, such as choosing the right data partitions, optimizing transformation scripts, and utilizing job bookmarks to process incremental data efficiently.

- **Security and access control**: Know how to secure your data in AWS Glue by managing permissions with AWS IAM, encrypting data at rest and in transit, and using resource-based policies to control access to the Data Catalog.

Exam strategy: For questions that align with these scenarios, consider how AWS Glue's features and capabilities address the requirements. Understanding AWS Glue's role within the AWS ecosystem for data integration and ETL processes will be crucial for selecting it as the correct answer in relevant exam questions.

Here are some tips to help you spot these questions:

- **Data preparation and ETL workflows**: Questions that describe scenarios involving the extraction of data from various sources, transformation of this data into a format suitable for analysis or machine learning and loading it into a data store for querying or further processing are prime candidates for AWS Glue solutions.

- **Serverless data integration needs**: Look for mentions of the need for serverless solutions to manage data integration tasks without provisioning or managing infrastructure. AWS Glue's serverless nature makes it ideal for such scenarios.

- **Data cataloging and discovery**: If a question involves organizing, searching, and cataloging data across multiple AWS services and data stores, AWS Glue's Data

Catalog is likely the solution. This is especially true when the scenario emphasizes the importance of a metadata repository that integrates with other AWS analytics and database services.

- **Complex data sources**: Questions that highlight challenges with connecting to and processing data from diverse sources, including relational databases, data warehouses, and data lakes on AWS, suggest the use of AWS Glue. The service's ability to crawl data sources and automatically create schemas is a strong indicator.

- **Scalable and flexible ETL jobs**: Scenarios that require scalable ETL jobs capable of transforming and moving large volumes of data efficiently may hint at AWS Glue. This is particularly evident if there is an emphasis on managing and orchestrating these jobs without dealing with the underlying compute resources.

- **Incremental data processing**: If a question discusses processing new or incremental data as it arrives or changes, consider AWS Glue. Look for mentions of job bookmarks, which allow AWS Glue ETL jobs to track data processed between job runs, efficiently handling incremental loads.

- **Integration with AWS analytics services**: Scenarios where there's a need to prepare and transform data for analytics with AWS services like Amazon Redshift, Amazon Athena, or Amazon QuickSight likely point towards AWS Glue, especially if there's a mention of using a centralized schema repository.

By understanding AWS Glue's serverless data integration capabilities, you can efficiently prepare and transform data for analytics and machine learning, a critical skill for the AWS Certified Machine Learning - Specialty exam. Understanding how to navigate and optimize AWS Glue will empower you to build scalable, efficient data pipelines, making it easier to derive insights and value from your data assets.

Advanced stream processing

Amazon Managed Service for Apache Flink is an AWS service that simplifies building and running scalable, complex stream processing applications. Apache Flink is an open-source framework and engine for processing data streams. Amazon Managed Service for Apache Flink allows you to deploy, operate, and scale Apache Flink applications with less overhead and without managing the underlying infrastructure, enabling real-time processing of streaming data.

Concepts of Apache Flink

Apache Flink is a powerful open-source framework for distributed stream processing and batch data analysis. At the core of Flink lies a set of fundamental concepts that govern how data processing applications are designed, executed, and managed within the Flink ecosystem. Understanding these concepts, such as jobs, operators, task managers, and job managers, is essential for leveraging Flink's capabilities effectively and building robust, scalable data processing pipelines:

- **Jobs**: In Apache Flink, a stream processing application is defined as a job. A job consists of the business logic that defines how data is processed, transformed, and stored. Each job is composed of one or more operations that can be parallelized across the Flink cluster.

- **Operators**: Operators are the building blocks of a Flink application. They define the data processing functions, such as filtering, mapping, aggregating, or joining data streams. Operators can be chained together to form complex data processing pipelines.

- **Task managers and job managers**: Apache Flink applications run on a distributed cluster consisting of Task Managers and a Job Manager. The Job Manager coordinates the distribution of jobs and recovery from failures, while Task Managers execute the tasks of a job in parallel.

Building a stream processing application

While understanding the core concepts of Apache Flink is essential, putting that knowledge into practice is key to unlocking the true potential of this powerful stream processing framework. AWS provides the Amazon Managed Service for Apache Flink, which simplifies the deployment and execution of Flink applications, allowing you to specify the necessary resources, configure parallelism levels, and seamlessly process streaming data in real-time while monitoring and optimizing performance as needed.

- **Deploy on Amazon Managed Service for Apache Flink**: Use the AWS Management Console or AWS CLI to deploy your Flink application. Specify the resources needed for your application, such as CPU and memory, and configure the parallelism level to define how many tasks should be executed concurrently.

- **Process streaming data in real-time**: Once deployed, your Flink application will start processing streaming data in real-time. You can monitor the application's performance and adjust resources or the parallelism level as needed to optimize processing speed and efficiency.

Scaling and monitoring your application

As you prepare for the AWS Certified Machine Learning - Specialty exam, it is crucial to understand how to effectively scale and monitor Apache Flink applications deployed on AWS. This includes managing parallelism levels, utilizing monitoring tools like Amazon CloudWatch, and ensuring resilience and fault tolerance through Flink's checkpointing mechanisms. Additionally, being able to distinguish between the appropriate use cases for Apache Flink versus Amazon Kinesis is a valuable skill, as it demonstrates your ability to select the right tool for the job based on factors such as complexity, control requirements, deployment environments, and cost considerations:

- **Managing parallelism**: Understand how to adjust the parallelism level in your Flink application to scale up or down based on the processing requirements. Higher parallelism levels can increase throughput but may require more resources.

- **Application monitoring**: Familiarize yourself with monitoring your Flink application using Amazon CloudWatch. Key metrics to monitor include CPU and memory utilization, throughput, and application latency. Monitoring these metrics can help identify bottlenecks and optimize application performance.

- **Resilience and fault tolerance**: Know how Apache Flink handles fault tolerance through its checkpointing and save point mechanisms. Being able to configure and manage checkpoints for stateful stream processing is critical for developing resilient applications.

Exam tip:

Choosing between Apache Flink and Amazon Kinesis depends on various factors, including the specific requirements of your data processing tasks, the environment in which your applications are deployed, and the level of control and customization you need. Here is a guide on when to choose Apache Flink over Amazon Kinesis:

Choose Apache Flink when:

- **Complex Event Processing is required**: If your application needs to perform **complex event processing (CEP)**, such as detecting patterns or sequences within the data stream, Apache Flink's CEP capabilities are more advanced and flexible compared to the basic data processing capabilities of Amazon Kinesis.

- **Customizable and fine-grained control**: Apache Flink offers a high degree of control over the stream processing pipeline, including state management, windowing, and time semantics. This is beneficial for complex applications requiring custom logic and optimizations.

- **Cross-platform deployment**: If you require a stream processing solution that can run not only on AWS but also on other cloud platforms or on-premises, Apache Flink provides the flexibility to deploy your applications across different environments.

- **Need for a unified batch and stream processing**: Flink is designed from the ground up to handle both batch and real-time stream processing with a single technology. If your use case involves comprehensive analytics that blend real-time and historical data processing, Flink's unified model can be advantageous.

Choose Amazon Kinesis when:

- **Tight integration with AWS services**: If your ecosystem is primarily AWS-based, Kinesis offers seamless integration with other AWS services like AWS Lambda, Amazon S3, Amazon Redshift, and Amazon DynamoDB. This can simplify architecture and reduce development effort.

- **Managed service**: For teams with limited operational capacity or those preferring not to manage infrastructure, Amazon Kinesis provides a fully managed service. This means AWS handles the scaling, availability, and maintenance of your data streams.

- **Quick setup and simplicity**: If the stream processing requirements are relatively straightforward and the primary need is to collect, process, and analyze streaming data in real-time without the need for complex event processing or custom state management, Kinesis can be easier to set up and use.

- **Cost considerations**: Depending on your specific use case and processing volume, Amazon Kinesis might offer a more cost-effective solution, especially if you can leverage its pay-as-you-go pricing model without needing the extensive features and control that Flink provides.

In summary, choose Apache Flink when you need advanced stream processing features, complex event processing, cross-platform support, and a unified model for handling both real-time and batch processing. Opt for Amazon Kinesis for simpler use cases requiring seamless integration with AWS, managed service benefits, quick setup, and potentially lower costs for certain workloads.

Scheduling jobs

In the context of AWS ML workflows, scheduling jobs efficiently is critical for handling data ingestion, processing, and analysis tasks. Proper job scheduling helps optimize resource utilization, reduce operational costs, and ensure timely data availability for ML model training and inference. AWS offers a variety of tools and services designed to automate and streamline the scheduling of jobs, from data ingestion to complex ML workflows. This section explores the strategies, tools, and best practices for job scheduling in AWS, focusing on how they can be applied to ML projects.

Strategies for job scheduling

Effective job scheduling is essential for orchestrating the various tasks involved in machine learning workflows. This involves mapping dependencies, leveraging AWS automation services, and optimizing for cost and performance:

- **Understand job dependencies and priorities**: Before implementing job scheduling, it is important to map out the dependencies between different tasks. Some jobs may need to be completed before others can start, while others may be independent and can run concurrently. Prioritizing jobs based on their importance and impact on the overall ML workflow is crucial.

- **Leverage AWS automation services**: AWS provides several services that automate the scheduling and execution of jobs. Utilizing these services can help minimize manual intervention, reduce errors, and ensure jobs are executed at the right time.

- **Optimize for cost and performance**: Consider the cost implications of running jobs at different times and on various AWS resources. Scheduling jobs during off-peak hours and leveraging spot instances or reserved instances for compute-intensive tasks can lead to significant cost savings.

Tools for job scheduling in AWS

Orchestrating machine learning workflows often involves coordinating various tasks and processes across different AWS services. AWS provides several powerful tools for job scheduling and workflow management; each tailored to specific use cases:

- **AWS Lambda**: AWS Lambda allows you to run code in response to triggers such as modifications in data or changes in system state. It is ideal for executing small, quick jobs in response to events. For ML workflows, Lambda can be used to preprocess data, initiate model training jobs, or automate deployment tasks.

- **Amazon CloudWatch Events and EventBridge**: These services enable you to schedule automated actions that respond to system events. For example, you can set up a rule to trigger a Lambda function for data preprocessing every time new data is uploaded to an S3 bucket.

- **AWS Step Functions**: Step Functions is a powerful service for managing complex workflows. It allows you to orchestrate multiple AWS services into serverless workflows. For ML projects, Step Functions can coordinate data ingestion, preprocessing, model training, evaluation, and deployment tasks, ensuring that each step is executed in the correct order and managing error handling.

- **AWS Batch**: Specifically designed for batch processing jobs, AWS Batch efficiently runs hundreds to thousands of batch computing tasks. It dynamically provisions the optimal quantity and type of compute resources based on the volume and specific requirements of the batch jobs submitted.

- **Apache Airflow (via Amazon MWAA)**: Apache Airflow is an open-source workflow orchestration tool that excels in managing and scheduling complex, dependency-driven workflows. With **Amazon Managed Workflows for Apache Airflow** (**MWAA**), users can deploy Airflow easily on AWS. It is particularly well-suited for ML workflows that require advanced scheduling, retry logic, branching, and cross-service orchestration. Airflow's **Directed Acyclic Graph** (**DAG**) structure makes it easy to visualize and control multi-step pipelines involving services like S3, Glue, SageMaker, and EMR.

Best practices for job management

While leveraging AWS tools for job scheduling streamlines machine learning workflows, it is essential to implement best practices. These include robust error handling, monitoring and logging, secure access control, and continuous optimization of scheduling strategies.

- **Implement error handling and retries**: Ensure your job scheduling setup includes robust error handling and retry mechanisms. This is crucial for minimizing the impact of transient failures and ensuring the resilience of your ML workflows.

- **Monitoring and logging**: Utilize Amazon CloudWatch to monitor the execution of scheduled jobs and log their outcomes. This provides visibility into the performance of your ML workflows and helps in identifying and troubleshooting issues early.

- **Security and access control**: Use AWS IAM to control access to AWS resources involved in scheduled jobs. Assign specific IAM roles and policies to each job to adhere to the principle of least privilege.

- **Continuous optimization**: Regularly review your job scheduling strategy and its execution. As your ML workflows evolve, you may need to adjust schedules, optimize resource allocation, or update the logic of your jobs to maintain efficiency and cost-effectiveness.

By effectively leveraging AWS tools and services for job scheduling, ML practitioners and data engineers can automate and optimize their workflows, from data ingestion to model deployment. This not only streamlines operations but also enables teams to focus more on strategic tasks, such as model development and optimization, rather than on infrastructure management.

Conclusion

Effective data ingestion is the foundation of any machine learning workflow on AWS. This chapter covered key ingestion strategies, tools like AWS Glue, Kinesis, and EMR, and best practices for building scalable, cost-efficient data pipelines. You also explored job scheduling and orchestration tools to ensure reliable, timely data flow. With these skills, you're equipped to design robust ML pipelines that align with AWS best practices.

These foundational skills position you to architect high-performing ML data pipelines with confidence.

In the next chapter, we will explore how to extract meaningful intelligence from your data to drive impactful machine learning outcomes.

Multiple choice questions

1. **Which AWS service allows you to easily collect, process, and analyze video and data streams in real time?**

    a. Amazon Kinesis

    b. AWS Glue

    c. Amazon EMR

    d. Amazon Athena

2. **What is the core component of Amazon Kinesis Data Firehose that serves as the conduit for streaming data to flow from producers to destinations?**

   a. Delivery streams

   b. Data catalogs

   c. Crawlers

   d. ETL jobs

3. **Which service provides a managed Apache Hadoop framework to process vast amounts of data quickly across resizable clusters of EC2 instances?**

   a. Amazon Redshift

   b. Amazon EMR

   c. Apache Spark

   d. AWS Glue

4. **Which of the following concepts is NOT directly associated with Amazon EMR?**

   a. EMRFS

   b. Delivery streams

   c. HDFS

   d. DynamoDB

5. **Which AWS service allows you to discover, prepare, transform, and combine data for analytics and machine learning without managing infrastructure?**

   a. Amazon Athena

   b. AWS Glue

   c. Amazon EMR

   d. AWS Lake Formation

6. **What AWS Glue capability automatically crawls diverse data sources to extract schemas and populate the metadata catalog?**

   a. Resource-based policies

   b. Crawlers

   c. Serverless nature

   d. Data encryption

7. **Which Apache Flink concept refers to the building blocks that define the data processing operations within a stream processing application?**

   a. State backends

   b. Operators

c. Job managers

d. Task slots

8. **What is an advantage of using Amazon Kinesis for data ingestion over Apache Kafka?**

   a. Tighter integration with AWS services

   b. Ability to handle more complex data processing needs

   c. Advanced queue management features

   d. Open source codebase

9. **When ingesting large volumes of batch data, which AWS service simplifies the process of preparing the data for analytics and ML?**

   a. Amazon Athena

   b. AWS Glue

   c. Amazon Redshift

   d. Apache Spark

10. **To optimize costs for Amazon EMR workloads, when is it advisable to use EC2 Spot Instances?**

    a. For fault-intolerant data processing jobs requiring constant uptime

    b. For real-time stream processing applications needing uninterrupted resources

    c. For batch processing jobs that are flexible, resilient, and can handle interruptions

    d. For master nodes, which must remain available to manage the Hadoop cluster

Answer key

1. a
2. a
3. b
4. b
5. b
6. b
7. b
8. a
9. b
10. c

CHAPTER 3
Transforming Data into Insights

Introduction

In the journey of mastering AWS **Machine Learning** (**ML**), understanding how to transform raw data into actionable insights is paramount. This chapter focuses on the critical process of data transformation, utilizing AWS's powerful tools and services. The essence of ML lies in its ability to make predictions or decisions based on data; thus, preparing this data in a way that machines can easily interpret is a fundamental step.

Structure

This chapter covers the following topics:

- Understanding data transformation needs
- Data transformation techniques
- AWS Glue and its role in data transformation
- Handling ML-specific data
- Big data processing frameworks overview
- Handling large datasets using SageMaker and EMR
- Optimizing data for ML algorithms

- Best practices in data transformation for ML
- Data transformation in action

Objectives

This chapter is designed to bridge the gap between theoretical knowledge and practical application, ensuring you are well-prepared to handle the challenges of data transformation in your ML projects on AWS. By the end of this chapter, you will gain the knowledge to transform raw data into a format ready for ML analysis using AWS. Further, you will be able to understand the significance of data quality and structure in the context of ML algorithms. It is recommended to get some hands-on experience with AWS services designed for data transformation tasks. This will help you apply these concepts in real-world scenarios effectively. By the end of this chapter, you will learn the nuances of transforming data effectively, ensuring it is primed for insightful analysis with AWS tools like AWS Glue, Amazon EMR, and more.

Understanding data transformation needs

Data transformation is a crucial step in ML, involving converting raw data into a format that is easily analyzed by ML algorithms. This process can include normalizing scales, handling missing values, and encoding categorical data to numerical values, thereby making the data more digestible for models. A practical example of this is dealing with customer data from different countries, where currency values might need to be standardized to a single currency or dates formatted uniformly. This standardization enables algorithms to accurately identify patterns and relationships in the data, leading to more reliable predictions. Data transformation is not just about cleaning data but optimizing it for analysis, ensuring that ML models can learn from it effectively and efficiently.

Preparing data for ML models is foundational for achieving accurate and efficient outcomes. This process involves cleaning data to remove inaccuracies and inconsistencies, normalizing data to ensure uniformity in scale and format, and encoding categorical variables to be model-friendly. A practical example is predictive modeling for credit risk; inaccurate or incomplete data can lead to misclassification of an applicant's risk profile. Similarly, for image recognition tasks, images are standardized in size and resolution to improve model training efficiency. Proper preparation enhances model performance, reduces computational cost, and increases the reliability of predictions, making it a critical step in the ML pipeline.

Data transformation techniques

Data transformation techniques are essential in the **extract, transform, load (ETL)** process, facilitating the preparation of data for ML models. This involves extracting data from various sources, transforming it into a suitable format, and loading it into a system for analysis. Techniques include:

1. Normalization to ensure data is on the same scale.

2. Handling missing values through imputation.

3. Encoding categorical variables into numerical formats, and feature engineering, where new features are created from existing data.

These steps are critical for cleaning, integrating, and structuring data, ensuring it is optimized for effective ML model training and prediction accuracy.

Different data transformation techniques

Different data transformation techniques are as follows:

- **Normalization and standardization**:

  o **Description**: Normalization is the process of scaling data to a specific range, typically between 0 and 1, which helps in handling disparities in units and scales across different features. Standardization, on the other hand, involves rescaling data so that it has a mean of 0 and a standard deviation of 1. Both techniques ensure that different features or variables are on a similar scale, facilitating better comparison and analysis.

  o **Practical application**: Normalization: Consider the heights of students in a class ranging from 4 feet to 6 feet. To normalize these heights, we can use the formula: *Normalized height = (Actual height - Minimum height) / (Maximum height - Minimum height)*. So, if a student's height is 5 feet, the minimum height is 4 feet, and the maximum is 6 feet, their normalized height would be *(5 - 4) / (6 - 4) = 0.5*. After normalization, all heights are between 0 and 1. Standardization (or Z-score normalization)—rescales data to have a mean of 0 and a standard deviation of 1. For instance, with student grades ranging from 50 to 100, with an average of 75 and a standard deviation of 10, we can standardize them using: *Standardized grade = (Actual grade - Mean grade) / Standard deviation*. If a student's grade is 80, their standardized grade would be *(80 - 75) / 10 = 0.5*. Positive standardized grades indicate performance better than average, while negative scores mean below average.

- **Encoding categorical variables**:

  o **Description**: Categorical data encoding is essential for converting non-numeric labels into numerical form. Techniques include One-Hot Encoding, where each category value is converted into a new categorical column and assigned a 1 or 0, and Label Encoding, where each category is assigned a unique integer.

  o **Practical application**: In a dataset of customer preferences with categorical features like gender (Male, Female) and membership type (Standard, Premium,

VIP), one-hot encoding can be used to transform these categories into a binary matrix, facilitating the use by ML algorithms.

- **Imputation of missing values**:
  - **Description**: Imputation involves replacing missing data with substituted values, and the choice of method depends on factors like the amount and pattern of missing data, correlation with other features, complexity of relationships, and class distributions. Simple techniques like mean/median/mode imputation or arbitrary value imputation may suffice for random missing data with a small amount of missing values, while advanced techniques like regression imputation, **k-nearest neighbors** (**KNN**) imputation, multiple imputation, imputation with additional information (e.g., time series or spatial data), and imputation with ML models (e.g., decision trees, random forests, neural networks) are better suited for larger amounts of missing data, correlated features, nonlinear relationships, or varying class distributions. It is important to evaluate the impact of different imputation methods on downstream analyses or model performance using techniques like cross-validation or holdout testing, as improper imputation can introduce bias or distort the underlying data patterns, negatively affecting model performance.

  - **Practical application**: Let us consider a dataset containing customer information, including age, income, and credit score, which will be used to build an ML model for loan approval predictions. Upon initial data exploration, you notice that some customers have missing values for income or credit score. To address this, you could try different imputation techniques. For instance, you could use mean imputation to replace missing income values with the mean income of the dataset, or regression imputation to predict missing credit scores based on other available features like age and income. Alternatively, if you have additional information like the customer's occupation or employment history, you could leverage that data to impute missing values more accurately using techniques like imputation with additional information or ML models. However, if the amount of missing data is substantial or the missing data mechanism is complex, you might consider using multiple imputation, which generates multiple imputed datasets and combines the results to account for uncertainty in the missing data process.

- **Feature engineering**:
  - **Description**: Feature engineering involves creating new features from existing data to improve model performance. This can include interaction terms, polynomial features, and aggregations.
  - **Practical application**: In a sales prediction model, creating a new feature that captures the interaction between advertising spend and seasonality might reveal patterns that are not apparent from the individual features alone.

- **Data scaling**:

    o **Description**: Apart from normalization and standardization, other scaling techniques like min-max Scaling and robust scaling ensure that the features of a dataset are on a similar scale. This is particularly useful for models that compute distances between data points.

    o **Practical application**: For a dataset with features like age and income, where income varies over a much wider range than age, robust scaling could be used to reduce the impact of outliers in the income feature.

- **Discretization and binning**:

    o **Description**: Discretization involves converting continuous features into discrete values, often into bins. This can be useful for reducing the sensitivity of the outcome to small fluctuations in the dataset or for transforming the data distribution to better meet the assumptions of the ML algorithm.

    o **Practical application**: Age, a continuous variable, could be binned into discrete categories such as 18-25, 26-35, etc., to analyze consumer behavior in marketing datasets.

- **Handling outliers**:

    o **Description**: Outlier detection and treatment are crucial for preventing extreme values from distorting the model. Techniques range from trimming (removing outliers) to transformation methods like log transformation.

    o **Practical application**: In financial fraud detection, outlier treatment can help in identifying transactions that deviate significantly from the norm, which could be indicative of fraudulent activity.

- **Dimensionality reduction**:

    o **Description**: Techniques like **principal component analysis (PCA)** and **linear discriminant analysis (LDA)** are used to reduce the number of input variables in a dataset, helping in alleviating the curse of dimensionality and improving model performance.

    o **Practical application**: In image recognition tasks, PCA can reduce the dimensionality of the feature space without losing significant information, thus speeding up the training process.

The application of these data transformation techniques plays a vital role in enhancing the performance of ML models. By carefully preprocessing data, leveraging the strengths of each method, and applying them judiciously within the context of specific ML tasks, practitioners can significantly improve the accuracy and efficiency of their models. The key lies in understanding the nature of the dataset at hand and selecting the appropriate techniques that align with the goals of the analysis, thereby unlocking deeper insights and driving value from the data.

AWS Glue and its role in data transformation

AWS Glue is a fully managed ETL service that makes it easy for customers to prepare and load their data for analytics. By providing a simple interface for data preparation, AWS Glue simplifies the process of ETL and automates much of the manual coding typically required to transform data. Here is a detailed look at AWS Glue, touching on its features, benefits, and how it fits into the AWS ecosystem for those preparing for the AWS ML specialty certification test:

- **Alternative interfaces for data preparation**: In addition to traditional AWS Glue, AWS now offers AWS Glue Studio and AWS Glue DataBrew as alternative tools for data transformation workflows. AWS Glue Studio provides a newer visual interface for building, running, and monitoring ETL jobs with minimal code, while AWS Glue DataBrew enables no-code data preparation through a visual interface targeted at data analysts and scientists. These tools make it easier to build and manage ETL pipelines without writing code.

- **Automatic schema discovery**: Upon pointing AWS Glue to your data source, it automatically performs schema discovery. This involves scanning your data, identifying data formats, and suggesting schemas and transformations, thus eliminating the need for manual data exploration and schema definition. This feature accelerates the ETL process by automatically generating ETL scripts for data transformation, enrichment, and loading.

- **Code generation**: AWS Glue generates customizable Python or Scala code for your ETL jobs, which can be further refined and modified. This auto-generated code is designed to run on AWS Glue's managed Spark environment, optimizing data processing tasks for performance and scalability. The ability to customize the generated code provides flexibility, allowing you to tailor ETL processes to meet specific data transformation requirements. In addition, AWS Glue now supports running Ray jobs within ETL workflows, enabling efficient scaling of Python workloads using the Ray framework. This provides an alternative to Spark for certain data transformation tasks, especially those that benefit from Ray's lightweight, distributed processing model.

- **Integration with popular data stores**: AWS Glue's ability to integrate seamlessly with a wide range of AWS and third-party data stores enhances its versatility. It supports data sources like *Amazon S3, relational databases on Amazon RDS, Amazon DynamoDB,* and *Amazon Redshift,* among others. This wide range of integrations facilitates the extraction and loading of data from various sources, enabling complex data transformation workflows.

- **Developer endpoints**: Developer endpoints in AWS Glue provide an interactive environment for coding and testing ETL scripts. By connecting an IDE or notebook to a developer endpoint, you can interactively develop, debug, and test your ETL scripts before deploying them as AWS Glue jobs. This feature significantly improves the development workflow and accelerates the ETL script development process.

- **Flexible scheduling**: AWS Glue offers flexible scheduling options for running ETL jobs, including triggers based on schedules, event conditions, or on-demand execution. This flexibility ensures that ETL workflows can be precisely aligned with business requirements, allowing for efficient data processing pipelines that operate according to specific operational or analytical needs.

Understanding these key features of AWS Glue in detail provides a solid foundation for leveraging the service in ML and analytics projects.

Exam tip: Glue bundled vs. ML transformations.

AWS Glue bundled transformations offer a broad suite of tools for data cleaning and preparation suitable for analytics and reporting. ML transformations go a step further by preparing data specifically for ML purposes. Understanding the distinction and how to apply each type of transformation effectively is crucial for leveraging AWS services to build scalable, efficient, and powerful ML solutions. This knowledge is particularly relevant for individuals preparing for the AWS ML specialty certification, as it encompasses both the data engineering and modeling aspects of ML on AWS.

Table 3.1 outlines some of the ML-specific transformations available in AWS Glue. These transformations leverage the power of AWS Glue for data preparation tasks that are commonly required before ML model training and inference.

The table highlights key ML-specific transformations in AWS Glue that facilitate the preparation of data for ML tasks. These transformations are instrumental in ensuring data is in the right state for ML model training and inference, contributing significantly to the success of ML projects on AWS.

Transformation	Description	Purpose
Find matches	Utilizes ML to identify and deduplicate similar records across datasets.	**Data cleaning**: Improves data quality by removing duplicates, which is essential for accurate ML model training.
Apply mapping	Transforms source data schema into the target data schema by mapping source columns to target columns.	**Data structuring**: Ensures data conforms to the required format for ML models, facilitating easier data ingestion.

Filter	Applies a custom SQL-like query to filter data based on specific conditions.	**Data selection**: Filters out irrelevant or unnecessary data, focusing on subsets important for ML analysis.
Join	Combines data from two or more datasets based on a common key.	**Data enrichment**: Enhances datasets by combining features from different sources, providing a richer dataset for ML models.
Relationalize	Flattens nested JSON and XML structures into relational formats.	**Data normalization**: Transforms semi-structured or unstructured data into a structured format suitable for ML processing.
Drop null fields	Removes fields (columns) that are entirely null from the dataset.	**Data cleaning**: Simplifies the dataset and improves processing efficiency by eliminating irrelevant features.
Split rows	Splits a dataset into two datasets based on a specified condition.	**Data segmentation**: Enables targeted analysis or model training on specific segments of the data.

Table 3.1: Data transformation techniques

AWS Glue Data Catalog functions as a central metadata repository that allows you to manage, access, and discover data across AWS services efficiently. It plays a crucial role in the AWS ecosystem, especially for data engineering and analytics workloads, including ML projects. Here is an in-depth look at how the AWS Glue Data Catalog operates, along with a practical example to illustrate its use.

Functioning of AWS Glue Data Catalog

AWS Glue Data Catalog is a fully managed metadata repository that serves as a central hub for organizing, discovering, and managing data assets across AWS services. It offers a comprehensive suite of features designed to streamline data management, enhance data accessibility, and ensure secure, efficient operations in cloud-based data environments:

- **Metadata storage**: The Data Catalog stores metadata about your data assets, such as database and table definitions, job definitions, and other control information. This metadata helps in organizing and locating data stored across AWS data storage services.

- **Schema management**: It supports schema versioning and history, allowing you to track and manage changes to your data schema over time. This is particularly useful for data lakes where the schema can evolve.

- **Data discovery**: The Data Catalog makes data discovery easier by providing a unified view of all your data assets across AWS. You can search and filter data assets based on various attributes like name, type, or custom tags.

- **Integration with AWS services**: It integrates seamlessly with other AWS services such as *Amazon Athena, Amazon Redshift Spectrum,* and *Amazon EMR,* enabling these services to directly query and access data listed in the Data Catalog.

- **Security and access control**: The Data Catalog leverages **AWS Identity and Access Management (IAM)** to control access to the data assets. This ensures that only authorized users and services can discover and access the metadata.

- **Serverless and managed**: Being a fully managed service, it removes the overhead of setting up, managing, and scaling the infrastructure typically required for managing metadata.

Practical example of using AWS Glue Data Catalog for a data lake

Scenario: A company wants to build a data lake on Amazon S3 to consolidate various types of data (structured, semi-structured, and unstructured) from different sources for analytics and ML purposes.

The following figure is an illustration of a high-level architecture diagram:

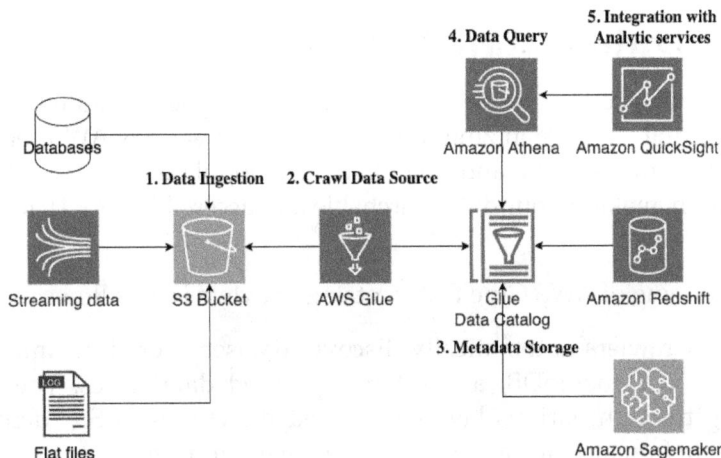

Figure 3.1: *AWS Glue and Integration with Data Lake*

The steps are as follows:

1. **Data ingestion**: The company ingests data into Amazon S3 buckets from various sources like databases, streaming data, and flat files.

2. **Crawl data sources**: They set up AWS Glue crawlers to scan the data stored in S3 buckets. The crawlers automatically detect and infer schemas from the data.

3. **Metadata storage**: The inferred schemas and other metadata are stored in the AWS Glue Data Catalog. Each data source can be categorized into different databases and tables within the Data Catalog, mimicking a traditional database catalog.

4. **Data discovery and querying**: With the data cataloged, data analysts and scientists can easily discover available data through the AWS Glue Data Console or by querying the Data Catalog directly. They can use services like Amazon Athena to run SQL queries on the data stored in S3 without moving the data.

5. **Integration with analytics and ML services**: The metadata in the Data Catalog is used by Amazon Redshift Spectrum or Amazon QuickSight for querying large datasets in S3. It can also be utilized by Amazon SageMaker for building and training ML models, where SageMaker can access and understand the structure of the data through the Data Catalog.

6. **Outcome**: The AWS Glue Data Catalog enables the company to efficiently manage and access its data lake's metadata, simplifying data discovery, analysis, and the building of ML models on top of its vast data assets in S3.

This example showcases how the AWS Glue Data Catalog serves as the backbone for managing metadata in a scalable, secure, and accessible manner, facilitating a wide range of data-driven projects, including comprehensive analytics and ML initiatives.

AWS Glue Data Catalog crawlers

AWS Glue Data Catalog crawlers are powerful tools designed to automate the process of discovering, classifying, and organizing data stored across various AWS services. They scan your data sources, extract schema and metadata, and populate the AWS Glue Data Catalog with this information, making your data searchable and accessible for ETL jobs, analytics, and ML.

The detailed functioning of AWS Glue Data Catalog crawlers is as follows:

1. **Discovery**: Crawlers automatically discover datasets stored in Amazon S3, Amazon RDS, Amazon DynamoDB, and other supported data stores. They are capable of navigating through various layers of nested directories in S3, identifying different types of data formats such as *CSV, JSON, Parquet*, and *Avro*.

2. **Classification**: Upon discovery, crawlers classify the data based on its format and schema. This classification process involves determining the structure of your data, including table definitions and data types for each column. AWS Glue comes equipped with built-in classifiers, but you can also create custom classifiers to handle unique or proprietary data formats.

3. **Schema generation and versioning**: Crawlers generate schemas for the discovered data and create table definitions in the AWS Glue Data Catalog. If a crawler runs and detects changes to the underlying data structure, it can version the schema, allowing you to track schema evolution over time.

4. **Automation and scheduling**: Crawlers can be scheduled to run at specific intervals, ensuring your Data Catalog remains up-to-date as your data changes. This scheduling capability is essential for dynamic datasets that are updated frequently.

5. **Integration with AWS services**: Once data sources are cataloged, the metadata is readily available for use across various AWS services, including Amazon Athena for SQL queries, Amazon Redshift for data warehousing, Amazon EMR for big data processing, and AWS Glue ETL jobs for data transformation.

Data lake crawling with AWS Glue Data Catalog

Imagine a company with a data lake stored in Amazon S3, consisting of diverse datasets in multiple formats, including sales transactions, customer feedback, and operational logs. The following are the important steps involved in data lake crawling using AWS Glue crawler:

1. **Setting up the crawler**: The company sets up an AWS Glue crawler, pointing it to their S3 buckets containing the data lake. The crawler is scheduled to run nightly to reflect any new data ingested into the data lake during the day.

2. **Discovery and classification**: The crawler scans the S3 buckets, identifies the different data formats, and classifies each dataset according to its format and structure.

3. **Schema generation**: For each classified dataset, the crawler generates a schema, identifying the tables and fields within each dataset, and adds this information to the AWS Glue Data Catalog.

4. **Data Catalog update**: The Data Catalog is now updated with the latest structure of the data lake, including any new datasets added during the day.

5. **Analytics and ML**: With the updated Data Catalog, data analysts and scientists can easily discover and access the data using Amazon Athena for ad-hoc queries or Amazon SageMaker for building ML models.

This example illustrates how AWS Glue Data Catalog crawlers facilitate data management and accessibility, enabling seamless analytics and ML workflows.

AWS Glue best practices

AWS Glue best practices with practical examples enhance the understanding and provide actionable insights for implementation. Here are the best practices enriched with examples:

- **Optimize data storage for ETL processing:**
  - **Use columnar storage formats:** For a dataset of customer transactions stored in CSV format, converting it to Parquet can significantly reduce the time and cost associated with reading the data for analytics. This is because Parquet allows for efficient compression and encoding schemes.
  - **Partition data:** If you have a dataset with a date column, partitioning the data by year, month, or day can allow AWS Glue and other AWS services to read only the relevant partitions for a query, reducing the amount of data scanned.

- **Efficiently handle data processing:**
  - **Incremental data loads:** Instead of reprocessing the entire dataset each time, track the last processed timestamp and only process records added or modified after that timestamp in subsequent ETL jobs.
  - **Utilize pushdown predicates:** If you are processing log data and only interested in error logs, apply a pushdown predicate to filter for logs where `log_level = ERROR` before the data is read into memory, minimizing the volume of data processed.

- **Leverage AWS Glue Data Catalog:**
  - **Central metadata repository:** Use the Data Catalog to manage metadata for datasets stored in S3, allowing analysts to easily discover and query data using services like *Amazon Athena* without needing to know the underlying storage details.
  - **Automate schema recognition:** Set up a crawler to run daily on a new S3 bucket where sales data is uploaded. The crawler automatically infers the schema of new files and updates the Data Catalog, streamlining the integration of this data into your analytics workflows.

- **Optimize AWS Glue jobs:**
  - **Job bookmarks:** For daily sales data processing, enable job bookmarks to track previously processed files, ensuring that each Glue job only processes new or updated files since the last run, thereby optimizing processing time and resource use.
  - **Parallelism and worker types:** If processing large datasets, choose the G.1X worker type and adjust the number of DPUs to parallelize the job effectively, reducing the job completion time.

- **Debugging and monitoring:**
  - **Error handling:** In your ETL script, include try-catch blocks around operations known to potentially fail, such as network calls, and log these exceptions to CloudWatch for analysis.

- o **Use CloudWatch Logs**: Set up monitoring and alerts for specific error messages or performance metrics in CloudWatch Logs to proactively address issues with ETL jobs.

- **Security best practices**:

  - o **Fine-grained IAM policies**: Create an IAM role specifically for a Glue job that accesses customer data, granting permissions only to the necessary S3 buckets and KMS keys, following the principle of least privilege.

  - o **Encrypt data at rest and in transit**: Configure AWS Glue to use AWS KMS keys for encrypting data stored in S3 buckets and ensure that data is encrypted in transit using SSL when moving between AWS Glue and data sources.

- **Cost optimization**:

  - o **Monitor job metrics**: Use the AWS Glue console to review job run metrics, identifying stages in your ETL process that consume disproportionate resources, and optimize those stages.

  - o **Manage resource allocation**: For non-time-sensitive workloads, consider scheduling AWS Glue jobs during off-peak hours and using spot instances for compute resources to lower costs.

Implementing these best practices with the provided examples will help you utilize AWS Glue more effectively, ensuring that your data processing workflows are optimized for performance, cost, and security.

Exam tip: Use AWS Glue when working with large-scale data transformation tasks that require complex ETL pipelines and integration with a data catalog. Choose AWS Lambda for lightweight, event-driven tasks such as simple file format conversions, data validation, or real-time data triggers that do not require Spark or parallelized processing. Lambda is ideal for low-latency use cases with shorter execution times, while Glue is better suited for batch processing of large datasets.

Handling ML-specific data

Focusing more on ML-specific data formats and structures, it is essential to understand the unique challenges and opportunities these data types present in ML projects.

Learn to work with ML-specific data formats and structures. ML-specific data formats include structured data (like *CSV, JSON*), semi-structured data (like *XML, HTML*), and unstructured data (like text, images, videos). Each of these data types requires specific handling to prepare them for ML models effectively:

- **Structured data**: Structured data is highly organized and easily understandable by ML algorithms. Formats such as **comma-separated values** (**CSV**) and **JavaScript**

Object Notation (JSON) are commonly used in ML projects for their simplicity and effectiveness in representing data in a tabular form. For ML tasks, structured data is usually the starting point for data preprocessing, including normalization, feature selection, and dimensionality reduction.

- **Semi-structured data**: Semi-structured data, while not as organized as structured data, still contains tags or markers to separate semantic elements and enforce hierarchies of records and fields. **eXtensible Markup Language (XML)** and **Hyper Text Markup Language (HTML)** are examples of semi-structured data. Processing semi-structured data for ML involves parsing the data to extract useful information and convert it into a format that ML algorithms can work with, such as converting HTML content into text for **natural language processing (NLP)** tasks.

- **Unstructured data**: Unstructured data is the most complex type for ML-specific tasks. This includes data like text, images, videos, and audio. Each of these types requires distinct preprocessing steps:

  o **Text**: NLP techniques such as tokenization, stemming, and lemmatization are applied to text to prepare it for ML models.

  o **Images**: Image data requires preprocessing steps like resizing, normalization, and augmentation before it can be used for training **convolutional neural networks (CNNs)**.

  o **Videos**: Video data processing might involve frame extraction, motion detection, and temporal feature extraction.

  o **Audio**: Audio files are transformed into spectrograms or feature vectors through processes like Fourier transforms or **mel-frequency cepstral coefficients (MFCCs)** extraction.

Data structures for ML

Beyond formats, the structure of data plays a crucial role in ML. Data structuring for ML involves organizing data into features and labels for supervised learning tasks or into features alone for unsupervised learning tasks. This often means transforming raw data into a clean, organized format like a data frame, where each row represents a sample, and each column represents a feature.

Examples of frequently used data structures in ML workloads are as follows:

- **Arrays and matrices**: Fundamental data structures for representing numerical data and facilitating mathematical operations.

- **Sparse matrices and vectors**: Efficient representation of high-dimensional data with many zero values, commonly used in text mining and recommendation systems.

- **Hash tables and dictionaries**: Associative arrays for storing key-value pairs, used for feature encoding and fast lookup.

- **Trees**: Hierarchical data structures with nodes and branches, used in decision tree algorithms and modeling hierarchical data.

- **Graphs**: Consist of nodes and edges, representing complex relationships and dependencies between entities, used in network analysis and graph neural networks.

- **Queues and stacks**: Linear data structures with specific insertion and removal orders, helpful in tree and graph traversal algorithms.

- **Tensors**: Multidimensional arrays that generalize matrices, extensively used in deep learning for representing and processing high-dimensional data.

In summary, handling ML-specific data formats and structures requires a comprehensive understanding of the data types involved and the appropriate preprocessing and structuring techniques. By effectively managing these data types, ML practitioners can ensure that their models have access to high-quality, well-structured data, leading to more accurate and effective ML outcomes.

Big data processing frameworks overview

Let us embark on an intuitive journey through the foundational technologies of MapReduce, Apache Hadoop, Spark, and Hive, focusing on their relevance in handling large datasets, especially in the context of ML. These technologies are pillars in the data processing and analytics domain, providing scalable solutions for managing vast amounts of data: A common scenario in ML projects.

- **MapReduce:** MapReduce is a programming model designed for processing large datasets across distributed clusters in a parallel manner. It simplifies data processing on large scales by dividing the task into small chunks, processing them independently, and then combining the results. The process consists of two main steps:

  1. **Map step**: Each data chunk is processed to produce key-value pairs.

  2. **Reduce step**: All pairs with the same key are combined or reduced to a single tuple.

     o **When to use**: MapReduce is ideal for tasks that need to process vast amounts of data in batch mode, such as aggregating web log data or preprocessing for ML algorithms.

- **Apache Hadoop:** Apache Hadoop is an open-source framework that supports data-intensive distributed applications. It is built on the MapReduce programming model and provides a reliable shared storage (Hadoop Distributed File System) and analysis system.

o **When to use**: Hadoop is best used when you have large datasets that cannot fit into a single server's memory. Its distributed file system facilitates storing and processing data across multiple machines.

- **Apache Spark**: Apache Spark is an open-source, distributed computing system that offers an interface for programming entire clusters with implicit data parallelism and fault tolerance. Spark is designed for both batch and real-time analytics, making it more versatile than Hadoop.

  o **When to use**: Spark is ideal for iterative algorithms required in ML and data streaming tasks. It is known for its speed and ability to handle real-time data processing.

- **Apache Hive**: Apache Hive is a data warehouse software project built on Hadoop, facilitating data summarization, query, and analysis. Hive allows users to query data using HiveQL, a language similar to SQL.

  o **When to use**: Hive is particularly useful for running ad-hoc queries on large datasets and performing data mining tasks. It is a good choice when you need to interact with data stored in HDFS using a query language.

Handling large datasets using SageMaker and EMR

When handling large datasets for ML workloads on AWS, leveraging the scalable and distributed computing capabilities of AWS services becomes crucial. Amazon SageMaker, a fully managed ML service, provides a variety of features and integrations to tackle big data challenges effectively. One approach is to use SageMaker's built-in data preprocessing and feature engineering capabilities, which can distribute the workload across multiple instances, enabling efficient processing of large datasets.

Another powerful tool within the SageMaker ecosystem is SageMaker Data Wrangler, which provides a visual interface for data preparation. It allows users to import, clean, transform, and export data without writing code. Data Wrangler integrates with popular data sources like *Amazon S3, Redshift,* and *Snowflake,* and includes built-in data visualization and feature engineering capabilities. This makes it especially useful for analysts and data scientists who prefer a no-code or low-code approach to exploring and transforming data at scale.

Additionally, SageMaker can seamlessly integrate with Amazon Athena, a serverless interactive query service, to analyze data stored in Amazon S3 using standard SQL queries. This integration allows you to preprocess and extract relevant features from massive datasets stored in S3 without the need for complex ETL pipelines. Furthermore, SageMaker can leverage Amazon EMR (Elastic MapReduce) clusters for distributed data processing using frameworks like *Apache Spark* or *Hadoop*. EMR clusters can scale up or down automatically based on the workload, providing cost-effective and scalable data processing for ML workloads. By combining these AWS services, you can efficiently handle large datasets, preprocess and extract features in a distributed manner, and seamlessly feed the processed data into SageMaker for model training and deployment.

MapReduce, Hadoop, Spark, and Hive each play a critical role in the ecosystem of data processing and analytics, especially within the realm of ML. Knowing when and how to use these technologies, along with their importance in ML workflows, can significantly contribute to your success in the AWS Certified ML - Specialty certification exam. Each technology has its unique strengths, and together, they provide a robust toolkit for handling the challenges of big data in ML projects.

Optimizing data for ML algorithms

Embarking on an ML journey unveils the vast landscape of data: A terrain both rich and complex. At the heart of crafting algorithms that can learn and predict with astonishing accuracy lies the art of data optimization. This process is akin to refining raw ore into precious metals; it is about transforming the crude, unprocessed data into a form that is not just digestible but delectable for ML models.

Techniques to optimize data

The techniques employed in this transformation are diverse, each serving a unique purpose, from cleansing the data of its impurities to enhancing it with features that are akin to intricate carvings on metalwork, adding value and insight. Following is a Tableau that unfolds the myriads of techniques at your disposal, illustrating not just when and why to use them, but also their advantages, potential pitfalls, and real-world applications. This guide is your map through the data optimization landscape, designed to navigate you toward achieving the pinnacle of ML efficacy. It also shows different optimization techniques and guidelines on when to use them and when not to use them, along with some practical examples:

Technique	Description	When to use	Pros	Cons	Example
Data cleaning and preprocessing	Removing noise and correcting inconsistencies.	Almost every ML project	Improves accuracy	Time-consuming	Removing duplicate entries, filling missing values
Feature engineering	Creating new features from existing data.	Enhance the dataset	Improves performance	Requires knowledge	Extracting the day of the week from a date field

Dimensionality reduction	Reducing the number of variables.	Large number of features	Reduces costs	Loss of information	Applying PCA to reduce feature dimensions
Data augmentation	Increasing the dataset size artificially.	Deep learning tasks	More robust models	May introduce noise	Flipping images in image recognition tasks
Normalization and standardization	Scaling feature values without distorting differences.	Scale features equally	Essential for convergence	Not suitable for all data	Standardizing features to have a zero mean and unit variance
Handling missing data	Filling in or removing missing data entries.	Datasets with missing values	Enables the use of incomplete datasets	Can introduce bias	Imputing missing values with the median or mode
Balancing datasets	Adjusting class proportions to be more uniform.	Imbalanced classes	Improves minority class performance	Can lead to overfitting	Oversampling the minority class or undersampling the majority class
Encoding categorical variables	Converting categories into numbers.	Categorical data needs to be numerical	Enables the use of non-numerical data	Increases dimensionality	One-hot encoding for categorical variables

Table 3.2: Data optimization techniques

This overview serves as a beacon for those venturing into the realm of ML, providing clarity and direction in optimizing data for the algorithms that drive our future.

Best practices in data transformation for ML

Data quality is a multifaceted concept in ML that refers to the accuracy, completeness, consistency, and relevance of data used for training ML models. It is the cornerstone of any ML project, as the data fed into algorithms directly influences their ability to learn, predict, and perform tasks effectively. Understanding the impact of data quality on ML model performance is critical for developing robust, accurate, and efficient ML systems.

Impact of data quality on ML model performance

The following are the important best practices in data transformation for ML workloads:

- **Ensure data cleanliness**: Start by cleaning your data to remove inaccuracies, duplicates, and irrelevant information. This includes identifying and correcting errors, handling missing values strategically, and removing outliers that could skew your ML model's performance.

- **Normalize and standardize data**: Many ML algorithms perform better when numerical input data is scaled to a standard range. Normalization (scaling data between 0 and 1) and standardization (shifting the distribution to have a mean of zero and a standard deviation of one) are crucial steps to ensure that all features contribute equally to the model's prediction.

- **Feature engineering**: Transform raw data into features that better represent the underlying problem to the predictive models, resulting in improved model accuracy on unseen data. This could involve creating new features from existing ones, selecting the most relevant features, or encoding categorical variables into numerical values.

- **Dimensionality reduction**: Use techniques like **principal component analysis (PCA)** or **linear discriminant analysis (LDA)** to reduce the number of random variables under consideration, removing redundant and irrelevant data, and making the training process more efficient.

- **Data augmentation**: Especially in fields like image and speech recognition, augmenting your data by creating modified versions of existing data points can significantly increase the diversity of your training set, leading to more robust models.

- **Utilize appropriate data transformation tools**: Tools such as AWS Glue for ETL processes, Apache Spark for handling large-scale data processing, or Pandas in Python for data manipulation and analysis, can significantly streamline the data transformation process.

- **Handling time-series data**: For time-series data, ensure proper sequence alignment and consider windowing techniques to capture temporal dependencies, which are crucial for forecasting tasks.

- **Data versioning**: Data is the new code or algorithm; keep track of different versions of datasets and transformations applied. This practice is invaluable for reproducibility, debugging, and understanding the impact of changes in data preprocessing on model performance.

- **Automate data pipelines**: As data sources and volumes grow, automating the data transformation process becomes essential. Automation ensures that data flows seamlessly from ingestion to preprocessing to feeding into ML models, saving time and reducing errors.

- **Continuous monitoring and updating**: ML models can drift over time due to changes in underlying data patterns. Regularly monitor, evaluate, and update your data transformation pipelines to ensure they remain relevant and effective.

By adhering to these best practices, data scientists and ML practitioners can enhance the quality and utility of their data, paving the way for the development of high-performing, reliable, and insightful ML models. Each step, from cleaning to augmentation, plays a critical role in sculpting the raw data into a form that not only feeds into ML algorithms but does so in a way that maximizes the model's ability to learn, adapt, and predict.

Data transformation in action

Here are practical implementation examples for each of the best practices specific to understanding the impact of data quality on ML model performance:

- **Ensure data cleanliness**:

  Example: In a credit card fraud detection system, removing duplicate transactions, handling missing values (e.g., imputing missing credit card limits with the mean or median), and identifying and correcting errors (e.g., transactions with negative amounts) can significantly improve the accuracy of the ML model.

- **Normalize and standardize data**:

  Example: When building a recommendation system for movies, features like movie duration, user age, and rating scores may have different scales. Normalizing these features to a common range (e.g., 0-1) or standardizing them to have a mean of 0 and a standard deviation of 1 can ensure that the ML model treats all features equally during training.

- **Feature engineering**:

  Example: In a predictive maintenance system for industrial machinery, creating new features like time since last maintenance or running hours per day from raw sensor data can provide more meaningful insights to the ML model, improving its ability to predict equipment failures accurately.

- **Dimensionality reduction**:

  Example: In a gene expression analysis project, where there are thousands of gene expression values for each sample, applying PCA can reduce the dimensionality of the data by identifying the most important principal components, making the ML model training more efficient and potentially improving its predictive performance.

- **Data augmentation**:

  Example: When training an image recognition model for self-driving cars, augmenting the dataset by introducing variations like flipping, rotating, or adding noise to the existing images can help the model better generalize to real-world scenarios, improving its robustness and accuracy.

- **Utilize appropriate data transformation tools**:

  Example: For a large-scale data transformation pipeline in a retail analytics project, using Apache Spark can enable efficient parallel processing of massive datasets, while Pandas in Python can be used for exploratory data analysis and prototyping data transformations.

- **Handling time-series data**:

  Example: In a stock price prediction model, ensuring proper sequence alignment of historical stock prices and applying windowing techniques to capture temporal dependencies (e.g., using LSTM or GRU neural networks) can significantly improve the model's forecasting accuracy.

- **Data versioning**:

  Example: When developing a credit risk scoring model, maintaining versioned datasets and transformation pipelines can help track changes made to data preprocessing steps, enabling easier debugging, reproducibility, and understanding the impact of data changes on model performance.

- **Automate data pipelines**:

  Example: In a large e-commerce company with continuous data streams from various sources (e.g., customer interactions, inventory updates, sales data), automating the data transformation pipeline using tools like *AWS Glue* or *Apache Airflow* can ensure that the ML models are always trained on the latest, preprocessed data.

- **Continuous monitoring and updating**:

  Example: For a predictive maintenance model deployed in a manufacturing plant, regularly monitoring the model's performance and updating the data transformation pipeline to account for changes in sensor data patterns (e.g., due to equipment upgrades or environmental factors) can help maintain the model's accuracy over time.

Conclusion

This chapter provides a comprehensive overview of the critical process of data transformation in ML, with a focus on AWS tools and services. This chapter emphasizes the importance of effective data transformation in preparing raw data for ML analysis. It covers various techniques, from basic data cleaning to advanced feature engineering, and highlights the significance of tools like *AWS Glue* and *Amazon EMR* for handling large datasets. The discussion on optimizing data for ML algorithms and best practices in data transformation underscores the impact of data quality on model performance. Through practical examples and real-world applications, the chapter demonstrates how proper data transformation can significantly enhance the accuracy and efficiency of ML models. Ultimately, it reinforces that mastering data transformation techniques is crucial for successfully implementing ML projects on AWS.

In the next chapter, you will gain a comprehensive understanding of data analysis and data preparation techniques essential for ML projects.

Multiple choice questions

1. **Which of the following is a primary feature of AWS Glue?**
   a. Providing a managed Apache Spark environment for data processing
   b. Automating the ETL process
   c. Storing and managing metadata about data sources
   d. Performing real-time data processing

2. **What is the purpose of AWS Glue Data Catalog crawlers?**
   a. To execute ETL jobs on data sources
   b. To automatically discover, classify, and catalog data sources
   c. To generate code for data transformation
   d. To schedule and trigger ETL workflows

3. **Which AWS Glue transformation is suitable for removing duplicate records across datasets?**
   a. ApplyMapping
   b. Filter
   c. FindMatches
   d. Relationalize

4. **In the context of data transformation for ML, what is the purpose of feature engineering?**
   a. Reducing the dimensionality of the dataset
   b. Cleaning and removing irrelevant data
   c. Creating new features from existing data to improve model performance
   d. Normalizing the data to a common scale

5. **Which technique is commonly used to handle class imbalance in a dataset for ML?**

   a. Normalization

   b. Dimensionality reduction

   c. Oversampling or undersampling

   d. Data augmentation

6. **Which AWS service is designed for distributed processing of large datasets using the MapReduce programming model?**

   a. AWS Glue

   b. Amazon EMR

   c. Amazon Redshift

   d. Amazon SageMaker

7. **What is a key advantage of Apache Spark over Apache Hadoop for ML workloads?**

   a. Spark provides distributed storage capabilities

   b. Spark is better suited for batch processing

   c. Spark offers in-memory computing for faster data processing

   d. Spark is more cost-effective than Hadoop

8. **Which data transformation technique can be used to convert categorical variables into numerical format?**

   a. Normalization

   b. Dimensionality reduction

   c. Imputation

   d. Encoding

9. **What is the purpose of dimensionality reduction techniques like PCA in data transformation?**

   a. Handling missing values in the dataset

   b. Creating new features from existing data

   c. Reducing the number of features in the dataset

   d. Normalizing the data to a common scale

10. **Which AWS Glue component is responsible for managing metadata about data sources and enabling data discovery across AWS services?**

    a. AWS Glue jobs

    b. AWS Glue crawlers

    c. AWS Glue Data Catalog

    d. AWS Glue triggers

Answer key

1. b
2. b
3. c
4. c
5. c
6. b
7. c
8. d
9. c
10. c

Join our Discord space

Join our Discord workspace for latest updates, offers, tech happenings around the world, new releases, and sessions with the authors:

https://discord.bpbonline.com

CHAPTER 4

Data Sanitization and Preparation

Introduction

In the vibrant field of **machine learning (ML)**, the journey towards building effective models begins with a foundational step: a thorough understanding and meticulous preparation of your data. This chapter, delineated into two principal sections, understanding data and sanitizing data, serves as a compass to navigate through this critical phase. The essence of this chapter is to illuminate the path from raw, unstructured data to a polished dataset, ready for the analytical rigor of ML algorithms.

Understanding your data deeply and preparing it meticulously are not just steps in the ML workflow; they are the bedrock upon which the integrity and success of your projects rest. This chapter equips you with the statistical tools to explore and comprehend your dataset nuances and the practical skills to cleanse and refine your data, addressing challenges such as missing values, outliers, and unlabeled data. Through a blend of theory and AWS-centric practical examples, you will master the art and science of making your data ML-ready.

Structure

The chapter covers the following topics:

- Introduction to data understanding
- Handling unstructured data on AWS

- Descriptive statistics and data exploration
- Identifying and handling missing or corrupt data
- Data preprocessing steps
- Data encryption and security services
- Navigating labeled data challenges

Objectives

By the end of this chapter, you will gain a comprehensive understanding of data analysis and data preparation techniques essential for ML projects.

Preparing data for ML models is foundational for achieving accurate and efficient outcomes. This process involves understanding data and cleaning data to remove inaccuracies and inconsistencies, normalizing data to ensure uniformity in scale and format, and encoding categorical variables to be model-friendly. A practical example is in predictive modeling for credit risk; inaccurate or incomplete data can lead to misclassification of an applicant's risk profile. Similarly, for image recognition tasks, images are standardized in size and resolution to improve model training efficiency. Proper preparation enhances model performance, reduces computational cost, and increases the reliability of predictions, making it a critical step in the ML pipeline.

You will learn core statistical concepts, descriptive statistics, and data exploration methods to uncover valuable insights from your dataset. Additionally, you will develop proficiency in data sanitization, normalization, scaling, and addressing labeled data challenges. Finally, you will learn how to leverage AWS tools such as SageMaker Ground Truth and Amazon Mechanical Turk to streamline data labeling and preparation processes, ensuring high-quality datasets for your ML models.

Introduction to data understanding

Data understanding is a crucial first step in any ML or data science project. It involves gaining comprehensive knowledge and insights about the data at hand, which is essential for making informed decisions throughout the modeling process. Failure to properly understand the data can lead to flawed assumptions, inaccurate models, and unreliable results.

The primary goal of data understanding is to develop a thorough comprehension of the data's characteristics, structure, quality, and potential issues or limitations. This process involves exploring the data through various techniques, such as statistical analysis, visualization, and domain knowledge application.

Here are some key aspects of data understanding:

- **Data provenance**: Understanding the source, origin, and collection methods of the data is crucial. This information provides context and helps identify potential biases or limitations inherent in the data.

- **Data description**: Examining the data's attributes, types, and values is essential for gaining a basic understanding of the data. This includes identifying categorical, numerical, and textual data, as well as understanding the relationships between different variables.

- **Data quality**: Assessing the quality of the data is a fundamental step in data understanding. This involves identifying missing values, outliers, inconsistencies, and other data quality issues that may impact the modeling process.

- **Data distribution**: Exploring the distribution of the data, both for individual variables and their relationships, can reveal valuable insights. This includes examining central tendencies, dispersion, skewness, and other statistical properties.

- **Domain knowledge**: Incorporating domain-specific knowledge and expertise is essential for interpreting the data accurately and extracting meaningful insights. Subject matter experts can provide valuable guidance and context for understanding the data.

Effective data understanding not only lays the foundation for successful modeling but also helps identify potential challenges or limitations early in the process. By thoroughly comprehending the data, data scientists and ML engineers can make informed decisions about data preprocessing, feature engineering, and model selection, ultimately increasing the likelihood of building accurate and reliable models.

In the context of the AWS ML certification exam, candidates should demonstrate a solid understanding of data exploration techniques, statistical methods, and best practices for gaining insights from data. This knowledge is crucial for addressing the exam objectives related to data sanitization, preparation, and handling challenges such as missing or corrupt data.

Handling unstructured data on AWS

In many ML applications, raw data is unstructured, meaning it does not fit neatly into rows and columns like tabular data. Common types of unstructured data include:

- **Text documents**: Emails, reviews, social media posts, logs

- **Images**: Photographs, scans, satellite imagery

- **Audio**: Voice recordings, music

- **Video**: Surveillance, instructional content

Before using unstructured data in ML models, it must often be cleaned, preprocessed, and transformed into structured or semi-structured formats.

Common file formats for unstructured data:

- **Text**: `.txt`, `.json`, `.csv`, `.log`
- **Image**: `.jpg`, `.png`, `.bmp`, `.tiff`
- **Audio**: `.wav`, `.mp3`, `.flac`
- **Video**: `.mp4`, `.mov`, `.avi`

AWS Services for handling unstructured data:

- **Amazon S3**: Primary storage location for all unstructured data types.
- **Amazon Textract**: Extracts structured data from scanned documents or PDFs.
- **Amazon Comprehend**: Performs NLP tasks like sentiment analysis, entity recognition, and topic modeling on text.
- **Amazon Rekognition**: Processes image and video data for face detection, object recognition, and activity detection.
- Amazon Transcribe: Converts speech (audio) to text using **Automatic Speech Recognition (ASR)**.
- **Amazon SageMaker Data Wrangler**: NEW supports visual transformations of semi-structured and unstructured text data, allowing you to clean, normalize, and engineer features through a no-code UI.
- **AWS Glue and AWS Glue DataBrew**: Useful for transforming semi-structured outputs (like JSON from NLP) into tabular form.

Best practices:

- Use metadata and tags to add structure to files stored in Amazon S3 (e.g., tagging images by category or date).
- Convert audio/video to transcripts using Amazon Transcribe or Rekognition to enable further text-based analysis.
- Combine services: For example, use Textract to extract table data from a document and then process it using AWS Glue or SageMaker for modeling.
- Use Parquet or JSON as intermediate file formats when transforming unstructured outputs for downstream ML pipelines.

By leveraging the appropriate AWS services and understanding which formats to use, unstructured data can be efficiently prepared and integrated into ML workflows.

Descriptive statistics and data exploration

Before exploring advanced data preparation techniques, it is crucial to gain a comprehensive understanding of your dataset. Descriptive statistics and data exploration play a pivotal role in uncovering the underlying characteristics, patterns, and potential issues within your data. This section will equip you with practical techniques to analyze and explore your data effectively:

- **Descriptive statistics**: It provides a concise summary of your data's central tendency, dispersion, and distribution. These measures offer valuable insights into the nature of your variables, enabling you to make informed decisions during the data preparation process.

  Let us explore three key aspects of your data: central tendency, dispersion, and distribution, and how they can be applied to real-world scenarios, such as analyzing customer data for an e-commerce business:

  o **Central tendency**: Measures such as mean, median, and mode help you understand the typical or central values of your data. For example, calculating the mean age of customers can provide a quick overview of your target audience's age range. In a dataset containing customer information for an e-commerce business, you can calculate the mean age of customers to understand the typical age range of your target audience.

  o **Dispersion**: Measures like variance, standard deviation, and range, quantify the spread or variability of your data. High variability may indicate the presence of outliers or diverse subgroups within your dataset. For the same e-commerce dataset, you can calculate the standard deviation of order values to understand the variability in order sizes. High variability may indicate the presence of outliers or diverse customer segments.

  o **Distribution**: Measures such as skewness and kurtosis reveal the shape and symmetry of your data's distribution. Highly skewed or heavy-tailed distributions may require special handling or transformations during the data preparation stage. Analyzing the skewness and kurtosis of the income distribution in the e-commerce dataset, you can identify if the distribution is skewed (for example, if there are more customers with lower or higher incomes) or if it has heavy tails (indicating the presence of extreme income values).

- **Data exploration**: It goes beyond descriptive statistics by providing visual and interactive techniques to uncover patterns, relationships, and potential issues within your dataset. Visualizations such as histograms, scatter plots, and box plots are powerful tools for exploring and understanding your data. They can reveal outliers, multimodal distributions, and relationships between variables. For the e-commerce dataset, you can create a histogram of order values to identify any multimodal distributions or outliers. Additionally, you can create a scatter plot of order value versus customer lifetime value to explore their relationship. Correlation analysis measures the strength and direction of the relationship between variables. Strong correlations may indicate the presence of multicollinearity (multicollinearity is a situation where the predictor or independent variables in a statistical model are highly related or correlated with each other. This makes it difficult to determine the unique contribution of each predictor variable to the outcome variable or dependent variable), which can be addressed during the data preparation stage. In the e-commerce dataset, you can perform correlation analysis between variables like age, income, and order frequency to identify potential multicollinearity issues, which may require addressing during the data preparation stage. Handling categorical variables often requires special attention during data exploration techniques such as bar plots, contingency tables, and chi-square tests, which can reveal patterns and associations within these variables. This contingency table allows us to examine the relationship between gender and preferred mode of transportation. For instance, we can see that more females preferred the bus compared to males, while more males preferred bicycles compared to females. Statistical tests, such as the chi-square test, can be performed on this contingency table to determine if the observed differences in frequencies are statistically significant.

By leveraging descriptive statistics and data exploration techniques, you can gain valuable insights into your dataset, identify potential issues, and make informed decisions during the data preparation process. These techniques lay the foundation for effective data sanitization, formatting, and preprocessing, ultimately leading to more accurate and reliable ML models.

Identifying and handling missing or corrupt data

In the real world, data is rarely pristine. It often contains missing values, corrupted entries, or outliers that can negatively impact the performance of ML models. Therefore, it is crucial to identify and handle these issues before proceeding with data modeling.

Identifying missing data

Missing data can occur due to various reasons, such as equipment malfunction, human error, or data collection issues. Pandas, a powerful data manipulation library in Python, provides several methods to identify and handle missing data.

Example:
```python
import pandas as pd
# Load data into a DataFrame
data = pd.read_csv('data.csv')
```

```
# Check for missing values
print(data.isnull().sum())
```

The `isnull().sum()` method will print the count of missing values for each column in the DataFrame. If any column has a significant number of missing values, you may need to decide whether to drop those rows or columns or impute the missing values.

Handling missing data

Once you have identified the missing data, you can choose from various strategies to handle it, such as dropping rows or columns, imputing with a constant value, or using advanced techniques like mean or median imputation or k-nearest neighbor imputation.

Example (mean imputation):

```python
# Impute missing values with column mean
data = data.fillna(data.mean())
```

Various data imputation techniques, along with practical examples, pros, and cons:

- **Mean/Median/Mode imputation:**
  - **Description:** Missing values are replaced with the mean (for continuous variables), median (for continuous variables, robust to outliers), or mode (for categorical variables) of the respective variable or column.
  - **Example:** Suppose you have a dataset containing the ages of students, and some values are missing. You can replace the missing values with the mean age of all students.
  - **Pros:**
    - Simple and easy to implement.
    - Preserves the original dataset size and distribution.
  - **Cons:**
    - Can distort the distribution of the variable, especially if there are a large number of missing values.
    - Introduces a single value for all missing values, which may not be representative of the true missing value.
    - Does not consider the relationships between variables.

- **Regression imputation**:
  - **Description**: Missing values are imputed using a regression model that predicts the missing values based on the other variables in the dataset.
  - **Example**: In a dataset containing information about houses (e.g., size, number of bedrooms, location, etc.) and their prices, you can use a regression model to predict the missing prices based on the other available features.
  - **Pros**:
    - Takes into account the relationships between variables.
    - Can be more accurate than mean/median imputation, especially when dealing with non-random missing data.
  - **Cons**:
    - Requires sufficient data and strong relationships between variables to build an accurate regression model.
    - Can be computationally intensive for large datasets.
    - Assumes a linear relationship between variables, which may not always be the case.
- **K-nearest neighbors (KNN) imputation**:
  - **Description**: KNN imputation is a non-parametric method that imputes missing values based on the k most similar observations (neighbors) in the dataset. The missing value is imputed by taking the average or weighted average of the values from the k nearest neighbors.
  - **Example**: In a customer segmentation dataset with missing values for income, you can impute the missing income values based on the KNN, considering other features like age, occupation, and spending habits.
  - **Pros**:
    - Non-parametric method, making no assumptions about the distribution of the data.
    - Can capture complex relationships and patterns in the data.
    - Handles both continuous and categorical variables effectively.
    - Preserves the distribution and relationships within the dataset.
  - **Cons**:
    - Computationally expensive, especially for large datasets or high-dimensional data.

- Sensitive to the choice of distance metric and the value of k.

- May not perform well if there are large gaps or sparse regions in the data.

- Can be influenced by the presence of outliers or noise in the data.

- **Multiple imputation**:

  - **Description**: This technique involves creating multiple imputed datasets, analyzing each one separately, and then combining the results using rules of statistical inference.

  - **Example**: In a medical study with missing data on patient outcomes, you can create multiple imputed datasets, analyze each one separately using statistical models, and then combine the results to obtain more accurate and unbiased estimates.

  - **Pros**:

    - Accounts for the uncertainty associated with missing data.

    - Provides valid statistical inferences.

    - Can handle arbitrary missing data patterns.

  - **Cons**:

    - Computationally intensive and complex to implement.

    - Requires specialized software or packages.

    - May require strong assumptions about the missing data mechanism.

- **Predictive mean matching (PMM)**:

  - **Description**: PMM is a semi-parametric imputation method that combines the strengths of regression imputation and hot-deck imputation. It imputes missing values by finding the nearest neighbors based on predicted values from a regression model and then randomly selecting an observed value from the nearest neighbors.

Note: **Multiple imputation uses statistical models to generate imputed values, while predictive mean matching imputes by directly borrowing observed values from similar cases.**

The choice between the two methods depends on the specific characteristics of the missing data and the goals of the analysis.

  - **Example**: In a healthcare dataset with missing values for cholesterol levels, you can use PMM to impute the missing values based on a regression model that predicts cholesterol levels using other variables like age, BMI, and blood pressure, and then randomly select an observed cholesterol value from the nearest neighbors.

- o **Pros**:
  - Preserves the distribution and relationships within the dataset.
  - Can handle both continuous and categorical variables.
  - Provides more realistic imputed values compared to regression imputation.

- o **Cons**:
  - Computationally more intensive than simple imputation methods.
  - Requires careful selection of the regression model and distance metric.
  - May not perform well if there are large gaps or sparse regions in the data.

- **Stochastic regression imputation**:
  - o **Description**: Stochastic regression imputation is an extension of regression imputation that introduces random noise to the imputed values. This helps preserve the variability and distribution of the data.

  - o **Example**: In a dataset containing employee salaries and their job characteristics, you can use stochastic regression imputation to impute missing salaries based on a regression model that considers job title, experience, and education, while adding random noise to the imputed values to maintain the variability in salaries.

  - o **Pros**:
    - Preserves the variability and distribution of the data.
    - Takes into account the relationships between variables.
    - Can be more accurate than simple regression imputation.

  - o **Cons**:
    - Requires careful selection of the regression model and the level of added noise.
    - Can introduce additional noise or uncertainty to the imputed values.
    - May not be appropriate for certain types of data (e.g., categorical variables).

- **Imputation with ML models**:
  - o **Description**: This approach involves training ML models, such as decision trees, random forests, or neural networks, to predict the missing values based on the available data.

- o **Example**: In a dataset containing customer data and purchase histories, you can train an ML model (e.g., a random forest regressor) to predict the missing values for customer income based on other features like age, location, and purchase patterns.

- o **Pros**:
  - Can capture complex non-linear relationships between variables.
  - Can handle both continuous and categorical variables.
  - Potentially more accurate than traditional imputation methods, especially with large and complex datasets.

- o **Cons**:
  - Requires sufficient data and feature engineering.
  - Can be computationally intensive, especially for complex models.
  - Interpretability of the imputed values may be limited, depending on the model used.
  - Potential for overfitting if not properly tuned and validated.

It is important to note that the choice of imputation technique depends on various factors, such as the amount and pattern of missing data, the type of variables (continuous or categorical), the size of the dataset, and the assumptions about the missing data mechanism. It is often recommended to try multiple imputation techniques and evaluate their performance using appropriate metrics or cross-validation techniques.

The following table describes the proper use case scenario of each of the above techniques and when they should be used:

Technique	Use case scenario (applicable)	Use case scenario (not recommended)
Mean/Median/Mode imputation	A small to moderate amount of missing data, when preserving the original dataset size and distribution, is important.	A large number of missing values, or when the missing data pattern is not random.
Regression imputation	When there are strong relationships between variables, and the missing data pattern is not completely random.	Weak or no relationships between variables, or when the assumptions of linear regression are violated.

Technique	Use case scenario (applicable)	Use case scenario (not recommended)
K-nearest neighbors imputation	When dealing with complex relationships and patterns in the data, preserving the distribution and relationships is important.	Large datasets or high-dimensional data, where computational cost is a concern.
Multiple imputation	When dealing with arbitrary missing data patterns, valid statistical inferences are required.	Small datasets or when the assumptions about the missing data mechanism are not met.
Predictive mean matching	When preserving the distribution and relationships within the dataset is important, borrowing observed values is preferred.	Sparse or large gaps in the data, or when the regression model and distance metric are not carefully selected.
Stochastic regression imputation	When preserving the variability and distribution of the data is important, taking into account relationships between variables is desired.	Categorical variables, or when the added noise may not be appropriate for the data.
Imputation with ML models	Large and complex datasets with non-linear relationships, and when higher accuracy is required.	Small datasets, or when the interpretability of the imputed values is crucial.

Table 4.1: Use case scenario related to various techniques of handling missing data

Identifying corrupt data

Corrupt data can take many forms, such as inconsistent data formats, invalid values, or outliers. Pandas provides utilities to identify and handle these issues.

Example (identifying outliers):

```python
# Compute z-scores for each column
z_scores = np.abs(data - data.mean()) / data.std()
# Identify outliers (e.g., z-score > 3)
outliers = (z_scores > 3).sum()
print(outliers)
```

Handling corrupt data

Once you have identified corrupt data, you can choose to either remove it or correct it, depending on the nature of the issue and the amount of data available.

Example (removing rows with outliers):

```python
# Remove rows with outliers
data = data[(z_scores < 3).all(axis=1)]
```

Throughout this process, it is essential to document your decisions and the steps taken to handle missing or corrupt data, as it can impact the performance and interpretability of your ML models.

In addition to Pandas, AWS provides various services and tools to assist with data preparation, such as AWS Glue for data integration and AWS Data Wrangler for data transformation and exploration.

By following these steps and utilizing the appropriate tools, you can ensure that your data is clean and ready for modeling, ultimately improving the accuracy and reliability of your ML models.

Data preprocessing steps

Data preparation is a crucial step in the ML pipeline, as it directly impacts the performance and accuracy of your models. In this section, we will explore various techniques for formatting, normalizing, augmenting, and scaling data to ensure it is ready for modeling.

Data formatting

Data formatting refers to the process of converting raw data into a structured format that can be easily consumed by ML algorithms. This can involve tasks such as:

- **Handling different data types**: ML algorithms often require data to be in a specific format, such as numerical or categorical. You may need to convert data types accordingly, for example, converting text data into numerical representations using techniques like one-hot encoding or label encoding. Let us consider a dataset containing customer information for an e-commerce platform, including features like age (numerical), income (numerical), product category (categorical), and purchase date (timestamp). To prepare this data for modeling, we might need to convert the product category feature into a numerical representation using one-hot encoding. For instance, if the product category feature has three unique values (electronics, clothing, and books), we would create three new binary columns, with a value of 1 indicating the presence of that category for a particular customer, and 0 otherwise.

- **Handling dates and timestamps**: Date and time data can be tricky to work with, as they may require special handling or conversion to a numerical format. For example, you might need to extract specific components like year, month, or day from a timestamp and treat them as separate features. In the same customer dataset, we might need to convert the purchase date feature from a timestamp into separate numerical features for year, month, and day. This can be useful for capturing seasonal or cyclical patterns in customer behavior. For instance, if a customer's purchase date is '2022-06-15 10:30:00', we would create three new features: purchase year with a value of 2022, purchase month with a value of 6, and purchase day with a value of 15.

- **Handling categorical data**: Categorical data, such as product categories or customer segments, may need to be encoded into a numerical format that ML algorithms can understand. Common techniques include one-hot encoding, label encoding, or target encoding.

- **One-hot encoding**: In our customer dataset, let us assume we have a categorical feature called customer segment with four unique values: premium, standard, basic, and loyal. To apply one-hot encoding, we would create four new binary columns, one for each category. For a given customer, the column corresponding to their segment would be 1, and the rest would be 0. For example, if a customer belongs to the premium segment, their encoded representation would be: **[1, 0, 0, 0]**. If another customer belongs to the loyal segment, their encoded representation would be: **[0, 0, 0, 1]**. One-hot encoding is a suitable approach when there is no inherent ordering or hierarchy among the categories.

- **Label encoding**: Let us consider a different categorical feature in our dataset called product condition, which can take values like new, used, or refurbished. With label encoding, we would assign a unique numerical value to each category, such as **new = 0**, **used = 1**, and **refurbished = 2**. This approach assumes an ordinal relationship among the categories, where new is considered better than used, which is better than refurbished. However, it is important to be cautious when using label encoding, as the algorithm may assume an inappropriate ordinal relationship if one does not exist.

- **Target encoding**: In our customer dataset, we might have a categorical feature called city representing the location of each customer. Instead of using one-hot or label encoding, which can lead to a high-dimensional sparse matrix, we can apply target encoding. This technique replaces each category with a target statistic, such as the mean of the target variable (e.g., annual spending) for that category. For example, if customers in the city of New York have an average annual spending of $5,000, and customers in Los Angeles have an average annual spending of $6,500, we would replace New York with 5000 and Los Angeles with 6500 in our dataset. This approach can help capture the relationship between the categorical feature and the target variable while reducing the dimensionality of the data.

Data normalization

It is the process of rescaling numerical features to a common range, typically between zero and one. This is important because many ML algorithms are sensitive to the scale of the input features, and features with different scales can have a disproportionate impact on the model's performance.

Two common normalization techniques are:

- **Min-max normalization**: This technique rescales the features to a range between zero and one by subtracting the minimum value and dividing by the range (maximum - minimum). This is useful when you want to preserve the relative distances between data points. Suppose we want to train a model to predict customers' annual spending based on their age and income features. However, these features have different scales, like age typically ranges from 18 to 80, while income could range from $20,000 to $500,000 or more. To prevent the income feature from dominating the model due to its larger scale, we can apply min-max normalization. Let us assume the minimum age in our dataset is 20, and the maximum is 75, while the minimum income is $25,000, and the maximum is $250,000. We would normalize the age feature as normalized *age = (age - 20) / (75 - 20)*, and the income feature as *normalized income = (income - 25000) / (250000 - 25000)*. After normalization, both features would fall within the range of zero to one, preventing any feature from having a disproportionate impact on the model.

- **Z-score normalization**: This technique centers the data around a mean of 0 and scales it to a standard deviation of 1. This can be useful when you want to treat all features equally, regardless of their original scales. In the customer dataset, let us assume that the age feature has a mean of 40 and a standard deviation of 12, while the income feature has a mean of $80,000 and a standard deviation of $40,000. To standardize these features, we would apply the following transformations: standardized *age = (age - 40) / 12*, and standardized *income = (income - 80000) / 40000*. After standardization, both features would have a mean of 0 and a standard deviation of 1, ensuring that they are treated equally by the ML algorithm regardless of their original scales.

Data augmentation

It is a technique used to artificially increase the size of your training data by creating new, synthetic data points from existing ones. This can be particularly useful when you have a limited amount of labeled data, as it can help prevent overfitting and improve model generalization. Common data augmentation techniques include:

- **Image augmentation**: For image data, you can apply transformations such as rotation, flipping, cropping, or adding noise to create new training examples. Suppose you are working on a project to develop an ML model for classifying different types of fruits. You have a dataset of 10,000 labeled images, consisting of various fruits like apples, oranges, bananas, and strawberries. While this dataset is a good starting point, it may not be sufficient to capture all the possible variations in real-world scenarios, such as changes in lighting conditions, angles, or scale. To augment your dataset, you can apply the following transformations:

- o **Rotation**: Geometric transformations include rotation. You can rotate the images by different angles, such as 90°, 180°, or 270°. This helps the model learn to recognize objects from different orientations.

- o **Flipping**: Flip the images horizontally or vertically. For example, flipping an image of an apple horizontally could help the model recognize the fruit from different perspectives.

- o **Scaling**: Scale the images up or down by a certain factor, simulating different distances from the camera or object sizes.

- o **Cropping**: Crop portions of the images, simulating partial occlusion or zoomed-in views of the objects.

- o **Brightness and contrast**: These adjustments increase or decrease the brightness of the images, simulating different lighting conditions or exposure levels. Contrast adjusts the contrast of the images, making certain features more or less pronounced.

- o **Noise and blur**: Add random Gaussian noise to the images, mimicking sensor noise or other types of noise that may be present in real-world scenarios. Gaussian blur: apply a Gaussian blur to the images, simulating out-of-focus or defocused regions.

- o **Color transformations**: Adjust the hue, saturation, and value channels of the images, simulating different color conditions or filtering effects. By applying these transformations to your existing dataset, you can generate a vast number of new, augmented images. For example, if you apply a combination of rotations (0°, 90°, 180°, 270°), horizontal and vertical flips, and brightness adjustments (±20%) to each of your 10,000 original images, you could potentially end up with hundreds of thousands of new training examples. These augmented images can then be used to train your ML model, helping it become more robust and generalize better to real-world scenarios.

Image augmentation can significantly improve the performance of computer vision models, particularly when working with limited or imbalanced datasets. It is important to note that not all augmentation techniques may be appropriate or useful for every task or dataset. You should carefully consider the characteristics of your data and the specific problem you are trying to solve when selecting and applying augmentation techniques.

- **Text augmentation**: Text augmentation is a technique used to artificially increase the size and diversity of a text dataset by generating new, synthetic samples from existing ones. This can be particularly useful in **natural language processing** (**NLP**) tasks, such as text classification, sentiment analysis, or language modeling, where large amounts of labeled data are required to train accurate models. Suppose you are working on a project to develop an ML model for sentiment analysis of product reviews. You have a dataset of 20,000 labeled reviews, where each review is classified as either positive or negative. While this dataset is a good starting point, it may not capture all the possible variations in language and writing styles that can be found in real-world product reviews. To augment your dataset, you can apply the following text augmentation techniques:

  o **Synonym replacement**: It refers to identifying certain words or phrases in the reviews and replacing them with their synonyms. For example, in the review, the product is excellent and easy to use; you could replace excellent with outstanding or superb. This technique helps introduce lexical variations and can make the model more robust to different word choices and writing styles.

  o **Random word insertion/deletion**: This involves randomly inserting or deleting words from the reviews, simulating common errors or variations in natural language. For example, in the review, *I highly recommend this product to everyone.* You could insert the word really before highly, or delete the word to, resulting in I highly recommend this product to everyone. This technique can help the model become more resilient to noise and variations in text data.

  o **Sentence shuffling**: This applies when handling multiple sentences. You can shuffle the order of the sentences, creating new variations of the same review. For example, if a review states: *The product is easy to use. It has great features. I love this product.*, You could shuffle the sentences to create a new review, like *I love this product. The product is easy to use. It has great features.*

  o **Back translation**: This involves translating the text from the original language to one or more intermediate languages and then translating it back to the original language. This can introduce paraphrasing and lexical variations, as well as potential errors or noise that can be found in real-world translated text. For example, you could translate an English review to French, then to German, and then back to English, resulting in a slightly different version of the original review.

Text augmentation can significantly improve the performance of NLP models, particularly when working with limited or imbalanced datasets. As with any augmentation technique, it is important to carefully consider the characteristics of your data and the specific problem you are trying to solve when selecting and applying text augmentation techniques. Additionally, you should ensure that the augmented data remains consistent with the overall distribution and semantics of the original dataset.

- **Audio augmentation**: Audio augmentation is a technique used to artificially increase the size and diversity of an audio dataset by applying various transformations to existing audio samples. This can be particularly useful in tasks such as speech recognition, music classification, or audio event detection, where large amounts of labeled data are required to train accurate models. Suppose you are working on a project to develop an ML model for speech recognition in noisy environments, such as in-car voice assistants or smart home devices. You have a dataset of 50,000 labeled audio clips, consisting of various spoken phrases recorded in a controlled environment with minimal background noise. While this dataset is a good starting point, it may not accurately represent the diverse range of real-world conditions in which your speech recognition model will be expected to perform. To improve the robustness and generalization of your model, you can apply the following audio augmentation techniques:

  o **Background noise addition**: Add various types of background noise to your existing audio samples, simulating real-world environments like traffic, construction sites, or crowded indoor spaces. Examples of background noise that could be added include car engine sounds, construction machinery, ambient chatter, or music. This technique can help the model learn to recognize speech in the presence of different types of background noise.

  o **Time stretching and pitch shifting**: This involves applying time stretching to your audio samples, making them either slower or faster without changing the pitch. Additionally, you can apply pitch shifting, which changes the pitch of the audio while keeping the duration the same. These techniques can help the model become more robust to variations in speech rates and pitches, which can occur due to differences in speakers, accents, or emotional states.

  o **Reverberation and room simulation:** It can simulate different room acoustics or reverberation effects by convolving your audio samples with impulse responses captured from various environments, such as small rooms, large halls, or outdoor spaces. This technique can help the model learn to recognize speech in different acoustic environments, accounting for factors like room size, materials, and speaker-microphone distances.

  o **Volume adjustment**: Adjust the volume of your audio samples either by increasing or decreasing the amplitude to simulate different recording levels or distances from the microphone. This can help the model become more resilient to variations in volume levels, which can occur in real-world scenarios. By applying these augmentation techniques to your existing dataset, you can generate a vast number of new, augmented audio samples that better represent the diverse range of conditions your speech recognition model may encounter. For example, if you apply a combination of background noise addition, time stretching, pitch shifting, and reverberation to each of your 50,000 original audio clips, you could potentially end up with millions of new training examples. These augmented audio samples can then be used to train your speech recognition model, helping it become more robust and generalize better to real-world noisy environments.

Audio augmentation can significantly improve the performance of speech recognition and other audio-based models, particularly when working with limited or imbalanced datasets. As with any augmentation technique, it is important to carefully consider the characteristics of your data and the specific problem you are trying to solve when selecting and applying audio augmentation techniques. Additionally, you should ensure that the augmented data remains consistent with the overall distribution and acoustics of the original dataset.

Data scaling

Data scaling involves transforming numerical features to a consistent scale, which is crucial for many ML algorithms. Scaling ensures that features with different ranges do not disproportionately influence the model. Common scaling techniques include:

- **Standard scaling**: This technique transforms the data with a mean of 0 and a standard deviation of 1. It is useful when your data follows a normal distribution or when you want to preserve outliers. For example, in a customer dataset with age and income features, you might apply standard scaling as follows:

  scaled_age = (age - mean(age)) / std(age)

  scaled_income = (income - mean(income)) / std(income)

- **Min-max scaling**: This method scales the data to a fixed range, typically between 0 and 1. It is useful when you want to preserve zero values in sparse data or when you need bounded values. Using the same example:

  scaled_age = (age - min(age)) / (max(age) - min(age))

  scaled_income = (income - min(income)) / (max(income) - min(income))

- **Robust scaling**: This technique uses statistics that are robust to outliers, such as the median and interquartile range. It is particularly useful when your data contains significant outliers. For instance:

  scaled_age = (age - median(age)) / IQR(age)

  scaled_income = (income - median(income)) / IQR(income)

Choosing the appropriate scaling method depends on your data characteristics and the requirements of your ML algorithm. Proper scaling can significantly improve model performance and convergence speed.

File formats for ML workflows

Choosing the right data file format plays a critical role in the performance, cost, and scalability of ML workflows. File formats affect how fast data can be read, how much storage is required, and what types of operations are possible.

Here is a comparison of commonly used file formats:

File format	Type	Compression	Schema support	Best use cases	AWS compatibility
CSV	Row-based	No (native)	No	Simplicity, small datasets, tabular exports	Amazon S3, AWS Glue, SageMaker
JSON	Semi-structured	No (native)	No	Log data, nested attributes, APIs	S3, Glue, Athena, SageMaker
Parquet	Columnar	Yes	Yes	Large-scale analytics, ML preprocessing, ETL jobs	S3, Athena, Redshift, Glue, SageMaker
ORC	Columnar	Yes	Yes	Hadoop-based processing, high compression	S3, EMR, Hive
Avro	Row-based	Yes	Yes	Streaming data, schema evolution	Kinesis, Kafka, Glue
Image formats (JPG, PNG)	Binary	Yes (lossy / lossless)	N/A	Computer vision tasks	S3, SageMaker
Audio formats (WAV, MP3)	Binary	Yes	N/A	Speech recognition, NLP	S3, Transcribe, SageMaker

Table 4.2: Comparison of common file formats used in ML workflows

Key considerations:

- Use Parquet for large, structured datasets in ML pipelines; it is optimized for columnar reads and compresses well.

- Use CSV when simplicity and compatibility are priorities, though it is not optimal for performance.

- Use JSON for nested or hierarchical data, such as API responses or logs.

- Use Avro when working with streaming data or needing schema evolution.

- For unstructured formats like images or audio, choose file types (e.g., .jpg, .wav) that balance quality and size, and preprocess using tools like SageMaker Data Wrangler or AWS Glue.

Exam tip:

Parquet is preferred in most AWS ML pipelines due to its compressed, columnar format, making it ideal for Athena, Glue, and SageMaker ingestion. CSV, though common, can become inefficient at scale due to a lack of compression and schema metadata.

Data encryption and security services

In ML workflows, data privacy and protection are critical, especially when working with sensitive information such as financial records, healthcare data, or user activity logs. Encryption helps ensure that data remains secure both at rest and in transit, preventing unauthorized access and maintaining compliance with standards like HIPAA, GDPR, and SOC 2.

The following are different types of encryption:

- **Encryption at rest**: Protects stored data on disk (e.g., in S3, RDS, EBS).

- **Encryption in transit**: Secures data while being transferred between services using protocols like HTTPS or TLS.

Key AWS services for data encryption are as follows:

- **AWS Key Management Service (KMS)**: A fully managed service that makes it easy to create and control cryptographic keys used for encrypting your data. KMS integrates with nearly all AWS services, including S3, Glue, Redshift, SageMaker, and RDS.

- **Amazon S3 Server-Side Encryption (SSE)**: Enables automatic encryption of objects in S3 buckets using either AWS-managed keys (SSE-S3), customer-managed KMS keys (SSE-KMS), or customer-provided keys (SSE-C).

- **Amazon SageMaker**: Supports encryption of both training data and model artifacts using KMS. You can specify a KMS key when creating SageMaker notebooks, training jobs, or model endpoints.

- **AWS Glue and Glue Data Catalog**: Allow encryption of metadata and ETL job data using KMS. You can configure Glue jobs to encrypt temporary data stored during processing.

- **AWS CloudTrail and CloudWatch**: Support encryption of logs and audit trails, useful for tracking data access and maintaining compliance.

Best practices for securing data in ML pipelines:

- Always encrypt sensitive data in S3 using SSE-KMS for fine-grained control and auditability.

- Use VPC endpoints and private links to avoid sending data over the public internet.

- Enable SageMaker encryption when dealing with regulated data or customer PII.

- Rotate and manage your KMS keys regularly and enforce strict IAM permissions.

- Use CloudTrail to log all KMS usage and CloudWatch to monitor access patterns.

By using the above services and adhering to best practices, you can build secure and compliant ML pipelines on AWS without sacrificing performance or scalability.

Navigating labeled data challenges

Having sufficient labeled data is crucial for training accurate and reliable models. However, obtaining high-quality labeled data can be a significant challenge. In this section, we will explore strategies to mitigate labeled data challenges and leverage tools like Amazon Mechanical Turk and Amazon Ground Truth to augment your dataset.

Refer to the following:

- **Identifying labeled data challenges**:
  - **Insufficient data**: If you have a limited amount of labeled data, your model may struggle to generalize well and achieve high accuracy.
  - **Imbalanced data**: When one class is significantly underrepresented compared to others, models can become biased toward the majority class.
  - **Noisy or mislabeled data**: Incorrect labels can lead to training issues and poor model performance.
  - **Skewed data distribution**: If your data does not reflect the real-world distribution, your model may exhibit bias or fail to generalize properly.

- **Mitigation strategies**:
  - **Data augmentation**: This technique involves creating new, synthetic data points by applying transformations (such as rotations, flips, or noise injections) to existing data. This can help increase the size and diversity of your dataset.
  - **Transfer learning**: If you have limited labeled data in your domain, you can leverage pre-trained models on larger datasets from related domains and fine-tune them on your specific task.
  - **Semi-supervised learning**: This approach combines a small amount of labeled data with a larger set of unlabeled data to improve model performance.
  - **Active learning**: Instead of labeling all data upfront, active learning iteratively selects the most informative data points for labeling, reducing the overall labeling effort.

- o **Data cleaning and denoising**: Identifying and removing mislabeled or noisy data points can improve the quality of your dataset and lead to better model performance.

- **Amazon Mechanical Turk (MTurk)**: MTurk is a crowdsourcing marketplace that allows you to outsource tasks, including data labeling, to a distributed workforce. You can leverage MTurk for labeled data challenges as described earlier.

- **Amazon ground truth**: Amazon Ground Truth is a service that makes it easy to build high-quality training datasets for ML models. It provides access to a high-quality workforce and offers built-in workflows and tools to efficiently create and manage labeling jobs. These are as follows:

  - o **Creating labeling Jobs**: Define your data labeling task, such as image classification, text classification, or object detection, using ground truth's predefined task types or custom workflows.

  - o **Managing workforce**: Ground truth provides access to a skilled workforce, including MTurk workers and third-party vendors, ensuring high-quality labeling.

  - o **Quality control**: It offers built-in quality control mechanisms, such as automated data validation, worker qualification tests, and consensus-based labeling, to ensure data quality.

  - o **Integration with AWS**: Services seamlessly integrate with other AWS services like Amazon S3, Amazon SageMaker, and AWS Lambda, allowing you to streamline your ML workflows.

Example: Suppose you are building an ML model to classify text documents into different categories. You can leverage Amazon Ground Truth to create a text classification labeling job. Ground truth will handle the task of distributing the documents to qualified workers, implementing quality control measures, and consolidating the labeled data for you to use in training your model. By understanding labeled data challenges and employing strategies like data augmentation, transfer learning, semi-supervised learning, active learning, and data cleaning, you can mitigate the impact of limited or low-quality labeled data.

Additionally, leveraging tools like Amazon Mechanical Turk and Amazon Ground Truth can help you scale your labeling efforts and acquire high-quality labeled data cost-effectively and efficiently.

Conclusion

This chapter has covered the essential aspects of data sanitization and preparation in ML. We explored data understanding, handling missing or corrupt data, preprocessing techniques, and strategies for managing labeled data. Tools like Amazon Mechanical Turk and Ground

Truth were introduced to enhance data quality and quantity. Proper data sanitization and preparation are crucial for optimal model performance, making this process a fundamental step in successful ML projects.

In the next chapter, we will use the sanitized and prepared data to perform feature engineering, a critical step in the ML pipeline, enabling models to learn effectively from the data provided.

Multiple choice questions

1. **You are working on a project to develop an ML model for predicting customer churn in a telecommunication company. Your dataset contains customer information such as age, income, tenure, and service usage, but you notice that a significant portion of the income values are missing. Which imputation technique would be most appropriate in this scenario?**
   a. Mean imputation
   b. Regression imputation
   c. K-nearest neighbors imputation
   d. Multiple imputation

2. **You are tasked with building a computer vision model to classify different types of fruits. However, your dataset is limited, and you want to increase the size and diversity of your training data. Which technique would be most suitable for this task?**
   a. Text augmentation
   b. Audio augmentation
   c. Image augmentation
   d. Data normalization

3. **In an e-commerce project, you have a dataset containing customer information, including a categorical feature called customer segment with values like premium, standard, basic, and loyal. Which encoding technique would be most appropriate for this feature?**
   a. One-hot encoding
   b. Label encoding
   c. Target encoding
   d. Z-score normalization

4. **You are working on a project to develop an ML model for sentiment analysis of product reviews. Your dataset contains 20,000 labeled reviews, but you want to**

increase the size and diversity of your training data. Which text augmentation technique would be most suitable for introducing lexical variations?

    a. Synonym replacement

    b. Random word insertion or deletion

    c. Sentence shuffling

    d. Back-translation

5. You are developing a speech recognition model for in-car voice assistants. Your dataset consists of 50,000 labeled audio clips recorded in a controlled environment. To improve the robustness of your model, which audio augmentation technique would be most appropriate for simulating different acoustic environments?

    a. Background noise addition

    b. Time stretching and pitch shifting

    c. Reverberation and room simulation

    d. Volume adjustments

6. You are working on a project to develop an ML model for credit risk assessment. Your dataset contains customer information such as income, employment status, and credit history. However, you notice that some of the credit history values are corrupted or inconsistent. Which technique would be most appropriate for identifying and handling corrupt data?

    a. Descriptive statistics

    b. Data visualization

    c. Z-score outlier detection

    d. Correlation analysis

7. You are tasked with building an ML model to classify images of handwritten digits. Your dataset is imbalanced, with significantly fewer examples of certain digits compared to others. Which strategy would be most effective in mitigating this labeled data challenge?

    a. Data augmentation

    b. Transfer learning

    c. Semi-supervised learning

    d. Active learning

8. You are working on a natural language processing project, and you need to label a large amount of text data for training your ML model. Which AWS service would be most suitable for outsourcing this labeling task to a skilled workforce?

    a. Amazon Mechanical Turk

    b. Amazon Ground Truth

    c. AWS Glue

    d. AWS Data Wrangler

9. You are developing an ML model to predict housing prices based on various features such as square footage, number of bedrooms, and location. Your dataset contains a mix of continuous and categorical variables. Which data preparation technique would be most appropriate for handling categorical variables like location?

    a. Min-max normalization

    b. Z-score normalization

    c. One-hot encoding

    d. Data augmentation

10. You are working on a project to develop an ML model for anomaly detection in network traffic data. Your dataset contains numerical features such as packet size, latency, and throughput, but the scales of these features vary widely. Which normalization technique would be most appropriate for ensuring that no single feature dominates the model due to its scale?

    a. Min-max normalization

    b. Z-score normalization

    c. One-hot encoding

    d. Target encoding

Answer key

1. b

2. c

3. a

4. a

5. c

6. c

7. a

8. b

9. c

10. b

CHAPTER 5

Feature Engineering

Introduction

Feature engineering is a critical step in the ML pipeline, enabling models to learn effectively from the data provided. In this chapter, we will delve into the techniques and methodologies required to identify, extract, and transform features from various data sources. Whether dealing with text, speech, images, or public datasets, mastering feature engineering will enhance our ability to build robust ML solutions on the AWS Cloud.

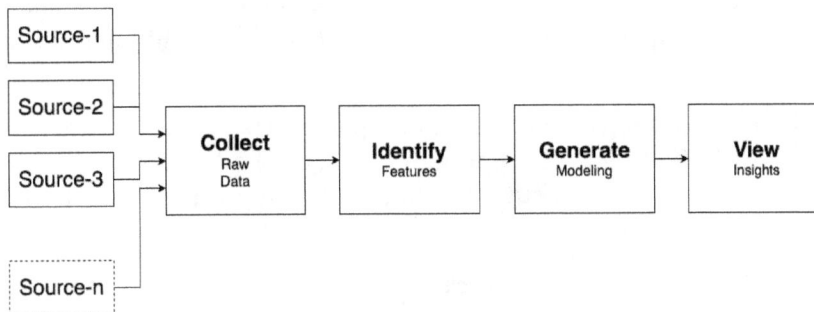

Figure 5.1: *ML process flow*

Figure 5.1 shows the high-level overview of how the identification of features fits in the overall ML process. The source data is collected as raw data, which is then refined and processed to identify the key features. The features are then used to generate the ML model, which is used to generate insights.

Structure

This chapter covers the following topics:

- Definition and importance of feature engineering
- ML pipeline
- Identifying and extracting features from text data
- Identifying and extracting features from speech data
- Identifying and extracting features from an image
- Identifying and extracting features from numerical data
- Comparing feature engineering techniques

Objectives

By the end of this chapter, you will have a comprehensive understanding of feature engineering, grasping its significance in the context of ML and recognizing how effective feature engineering can enhance model performance. You will master techniques for feature extraction by learning to identify and extract relevant features from text, speech, and image data while utilizing public datasets for feature extraction and model training. Additionally, you will analyze and apply various feature engineering techniques, including implementing binning to categorize continuous variables, performing tokenization for NLP tasks, detecting and handling outliers to improve data quality, and generating synthetic features to enrich datasets. Moreover, you will apply one-hot encoding for categorical variables and leverage dimensionality reduction techniques, such as **principal component analysis (PCA)**, to simplify datasets and optimize model performance.

By achieving these objectives, you will be well-prepared to tackle feature engineering-related questions on the AWS Certified ML - Specialty (MLS-C01) exam. This preparation will not only help you pass the certification but also equip you with practical skills for real-world ML tasks.

By the end of this chapter, you will have the skills to prepare data for ML models and optimize and improve their performance.

Definition and importance of feature engineering

Feature engineering is a crucial step in the ML pipeline. It involves the process of selecting, modifying, or creating features from raw data to improve the performance of ML models. Features are the input variables that the model uses to make predictions. Effective feature engineering can significantly enhance the model's predictive accuracy and ability to generalize to new data. The quality of the features directly impacts the quality of the model. Good features can simplify the problem the model is trying to solve, making it easier for the model to identify patterns in the data. Poor features, on the other hand, can obscure these patterns and lead to poor model performance. Feature engineering helps in:

- Reducing model complexity
- Improving model accuracy
- Enhancing the interpretability of the model
- Decreasing training time

Feature engineering requires a blend of domain expertise, creativity, and technical skills to extract the most relevant features from the data. By improving the quality of features, practitioners can build more accurate, robust, and interpretable ML models. As the field evolves, automated feature engineering tools are making it easier to implement and scale these techniques, but the human touch remains indispensable for achieving the best results.

ML pipeline

Understanding the role of feature engineering within the broader ML pipeline is crucial for grasping its importance. Let us break down a typical ML pipeline to see where feature engineering fits in and why it is indispensable:

- **Data collection**: This is the initial step where raw data is gathered from various sources. These sources can include databases, online repositories, sensors, or any other means of collecting data relevant to the problem at hand.

- **Data cleaning**: Once the data is collected, it must be cleaned. This involves removing or correcting erroneous data, handling missing values, and ensuring the data is in a usable format. Clean data is essential for the success of subsequent steps.

- **Feature engineering**: This step involves creating new features and transforming existing ones to better represent the underlying patterns in the data. It is the process of turning raw data into meaningful inputs for ML algorithms. Techniques such as binning, tokenization, handling outliers, creating synthetic features, and reducing dimensionality fall under this category.

- **Model training**: In this step, the processed data (with engineered features) is used to train ML models. The goal is to enable the algorithms to learn from the data and make accurate predictions or classifications.

- **Model evaluation**: After training, the model's performance is assessed using various metrics and validation techniques. This step ensures that the model is reliable and performs well on unseen data.

- **Model deployment**: Finally, the trained and validated model is deployed into production. This involves integrating the model into an application or system where it can provide real-time predictions or insights.

Feature engineering is the third step in this pipeline and serves as the backbone of the model training process. Properly engineered features are critical because they provide the necessary structure and context that ML algorithms need to learn effectively. Without well-engineered features, even the most sophisticated models may struggle to make accurate predictions, rendering the entire process less effective.

In summary, feature engineering transforms raw data into a format that highlights the relevant information for ML models. It ensures that the subsequent steps, model training, evaluation, and deployment, are built on a strong foundation, leading to better performance and more reliable outcomes.

Identifying and extracting features from text data

Feature extraction from text data is a fundamental task in **natural language processing** (**NLP**) and text mining. Text data is inherently unstructured, making it challenging to process and analyze directly. Feature extraction techniques transform this unstructured text into a structured format that ML models can use. These techniques include tokenization, vectorization, and more advanced methods like word embeddings and **Term Frequency-Inverse Document Frequency (TF-IDF)**.

Tokenization

Tokenization is the process of breaking down text into smaller units called tokens, which can be words, subwords, or characters.

Example: The sentence *Feature engineering is crucial* can be tokenized into [**Feature, engineering, is, crucial**].

Bag of Words

Bag of Words (BoW) is a simple representation where text is represented as the frequency of words within a document, disregarding grammar and word order.

Example: For the sentences *I love dogs* and *I love cats*, the BoW representation might be {"I": 2, "love": 2, "dogs": 1, "cats": 1}.

TF-IDF:

Term frequency (TF) tells us how often a word appears in a document compared to all the words in that document. The formula is:

TF(t,d) = (number of times "t" appears in "d")/(total number of words in "d")

t - term

d - document

For example, in report 1: Volcanoes are dangerous and erupt with lava.

The total number of words in *report 1* from above is 7, and *volcanoes* appear 1 time.

TF(volcanoes) = 1/7 = 0.14

Inverse Document Frequency (IDF) tells us how rare or special a word is across all documents. The formula is:

IDF(t) = log ((total number of documents)/(1+number of documents containing the term))

> Note: **The +1 in the denominator is added to avoid division by zero when a term does not appear in any document. This technique, called smoothing, ensures that every term gets a defined IDF score, even if it is absent in the dataset.**

In our example, there are 3 reports, and volcanoes only appear in *report 1*. Total reports are 3, and reports with volcanoes are 1.

IDF(volcanoes) = log (3/(1+1)) = log 3/2 = 0.18

Combine TF and IDF (TF-IDF), and now, we multiply the TF and IDF values to find out how important *volcanoes* are in report 1.

TF-IDF = TF x IDF = 0.14*0.18 = 0.0252

To understand the above TF-IDF value, we need to compare it against a term that is very common across different reports. Let us assume the term that appears in reports 1 and 2.

TF = 1/7 = 0.14

IDF = log (3/(1+2)) = log 3/3 = log 1 = 0

TF-IDF = 0.14*IDF = 0 (not an important word)

By using TF-IDF, we can focus on the words that matter most in understanding the document, like *volcanoes* and *lava*. Words like *and* get filtered out because they do not add much meaning.

Word embeddings

Word embeddings are dense vector representations of words learned using neural networks. They capture semantic relationships between words and allow models to understand similarity and context.

Traditional embedding techniques include:

- **Word2Vec, GloVe, and FastText**: These generate static embeddings, where each word has a single vector regardless of its context. For example, the word *bank* will have the same vector whether it is used in a **river bank** or a **bank account**.

Modern contextual embeddings, on the other hand, assign different vectors to the same word based on its context in the sentence. These models significantly improve performance across NLP tasks:

- **Bidirectional Encoder Representations from Transformers (BERT)**: Pre-trained on large text corpora, BERT captures word meaning based on surrounding words using a bidirectional transformer architecture.

- **Robustly Optimized BERT (RoBERTa)**: A variant of BERT with optimized training for better performance on downstream tasks.

Example: In BERT, the word *light* in *light the candle* and *travel light* will be represented differently to reflect their meaning in each context.

These embeddings are especially effective for tasks such as named entity recognition, sentiment analysis, and question answering.

Tip: **You can use modern libraries like Hugging Face Transformers to easily implement BERT, RoBERTa, and other state-of-the-art models for contextual embeddings.**

N-grams

N-grams are contiguous sequences of n items from a given text. They help in capturing the context and local structure of text.

Example: For the sentence *Feature extraction is essential*, bigrams (2-grams) are [**Feature extraction, extraction is, is essential**].

Part-of-speech tagging

Definition: POS tagging involves labeling each word in a sentence with its part of speech (e.g., noun, verb, and adjective).

Example: In the sentence, *Feature engineering is important*, *Feature* (noun), *engineering* (noun), *is* (verb), *important* (adjective).

Named entity recognition

Named entity recognition (NER) identifies and classifies entities in text into predefined categories like names of people, organizations, locations, etc.

Example: In the sentence, *Elon Musk founded SpaceX*, *Elon Musk* is a person, and *SpaceX* is an organization.

Sentiment analysis

Sentiment analysis determines the emotional tone behind a body of text, which can be positive, negative, or neutral.

Example: The review: *The movie was fantastic!* has a positive sentiment.

Tools and libraries

The following are some popular tools and libraries that help accelerate the process of handling NLP tasks:

- **Natural Language Toolkit (NLTK)**: A comprehensive library for NLP tasks in Python.
- **spaCy**: An open-source library for advanced NLP in Python.
- **Gensim**: A library for topic modeling and document similarity analysis.
- **Scikit-learn**: Provides utilities for TF-IDF, BoW, and other feature extraction techniques.

This section focuses on feature extraction from text data by leveraging techniques like tokenization, TF-IDF, and word embeddings. Just be aware that capturing the underlying patterns and semantics in the text will help enhance the performance and interpretability of NLP models.

Identifying and extracting features from speech data

Feature extraction from speech data is a crucial step in speech processing and recognition. Speech data is a complex, high-dimensional signal that needs to be converted into a more manageable form. This involves extracting relevant features that capture the essential characteristics of the speech signal. Common features extracted from speech data include **Mel-Frequency Cepstral Coefficients (MFCCs)**, spectrograms, and pitch.

Techniques for feature extraction

There are several techniques involved in extracting features from speech or audio data, and the most important ones are listed in the following section.

Mel-frequency cepstral coefficients

MFCCs are used to capture the unique *fingerprint* of a sound in a way that computers can understand while also taking into account how we humans hear and perceive those sounds.

Imagine listening to different sounds, like music, speech, or even animal noises. Each sound has its unique pattern or fingerprint. Here is how it works:

1. **Breaking down sounds**: When we hear a sound, like someone speaking, it is made up of different frequencies or pitches. Think of it like different musical notes being played together.

2. **Mel-scale**: Humans do not perceive all frequencies equally. We are better at hearing some frequencies than others. The mel-scale is a tool to measure frequencies based on how we actually hear them. It is like a special ruler for sound.

3. **Filtering**: To get MFCCs, we first need to break down the sound into different frequency bands using filters. These filters are designed based on the mel-scale, so they match how we hear sounds.

4. **Cepstral coefficients**: After filtering the sound, we end up with a set of numbers that represent the different frequency bands. These numbers are called cepstral coefficients, and they capture the unique fingerprint of the sound.

5. **MFCCs**: These are the final set of numbers that represent the sound. They combine the cepstral coefficients with the mel-scale, which makes them more accurate for how we perceive sounds.

MFCCs are widely used in speech recognition systems, like virtual assistants or voice-controlled devices. By converting sounds into MFCCs, these systems can more easily recognize and understand different words and sounds. MFCCs are also used in other areas, like music classification or identifying different animal species based on their calls or sounds.

Spectrogram

A spectrogram is like a colorful, visual map that shows how the different frequencies within a sound change over time, allowing us to see and understand the different components that make up that sound.

Imagine we are at a music concert, and the band plays a great song. We can hear different instruments like the guitar, drums, and vocals, but they all blend into one big sound. A spectrogram is like a special picture that helps us see and understand all the different parts of that sound. Here is how it works:

1. **Sound waves**: When someone sings or plays an instrument, they create sound waves. These waves travel through the air and reach our ears, allowing us to hear the sound.

2. **Frequencies**: Every sound is made up of different frequencies. Frequencies are like different musical notes. Some sounds have low frequencies (like a bass guitar), while others have high frequencies (like a whistle).

3. **Time and frequency**: A spectrogram is a two-dimensional image that shows how the frequencies of a sound change over time. The horizontal axis represents time, and the vertical axis represents frequency.

4. **Colors and patterns**: In a spectrogram, different colors and patterns represent the strength or intensity of different frequencies at different points in time. Brighter colors or darker patterns usually indicate stronger frequencies.

5. **How it is made**: Spectrograms are typically generated using the **Short-Time Fourier Transform (STFT)**, which analyzes the audio signal over small, overlapping time windows. This technique captures how the frequency content of the signal evolves, making it ideal for visualizing complex sounds like speech or music.

So, when we look at a spectrogram, we can see a visual representation of the sound. We can see how different frequencies come and go, how they overlap, and how they change over time. This can help us identify different instruments or sounds within a complex audio signal. For example, in the spectrogram of a song, we might see bright patterns at low frequencies representing the bass guitar, and bright patterns at higher frequencies representing the vocals or cymbals. We can even see how the frequencies change as the song progresses from verse to chorus. Spectrograms are useful in many fields, such as music analysis, speech recognition, and even studying animal calls or environmental sounds. They help us understand and analyze the complex patterns within sounds, which would be difficult to do just by listening.

Pitch and fundamental frequency

Pitch makes a sound high or low, and the **fundamental frequency (F0)** is the lowest frequency in a sound wave that determines the basic pitch we hear. It is the foundation on which all the other frequencies are built and what our ears and brains use to identify the pitch of a sound.

Pitch is what makes a sound high or low. For example, when we sing a high note, that's a high pitch, and when we sing a low note, that is a low pitch. Pitch makes a violin sound different from a bass guitar, even if they are playing the same note. F0 is the lowest frequency in a sound wave. It is the main frequency that determines the pitch we hear. Think of it like the foundation of a building, it is the base that everything else is built on.

Let us discuss an example to help understand F0.

Imagine we have a guitar string. When we pluck it, the string vibrates back and forth. The faster it vibrates, the higher the pitch. The slower it vibrates, the lower the pitch. The F0 is the rate at which the entire string vibrates back and forth. It is the lowest frequency of that vibration, which gives the note its basic pitch but the string does not just vibrate at one frequency. It also vibrates at higher frequencies called overtones or harmonics. These higher frequencies add richness and complexity to the sound, but the F0 is still the main frequency that determines the pitch we hear. For example, if the guitar string vibrates at **440 times per second** (**440 Hz**), that is the fundamental frequency we hear as note A. However, the string also vibrates at higher frequencies, like 880 Hz, 1320 Hz, and so on, which are overtones that add character to the sound. In speech and music, the F0 is what our ears and brains use to identify the pitch of a sound. It's like the foundation that everything else is built on.

Extracting features from speech data is essential for speech recognition, speaker identification, and emotion detection. By converting raw audio signals into meaningful features, such as MFCCs, spectrograms, and pitch, we can improve the accuracy and efficiency of ML models in processing speech data.

Identifying and extracting features from an image

Feature extraction from image data is essential in computer vision and image processing. This process involves identifying and extracting significant characteristics or patterns from images that can be utilized for tasks such as object recognition, classification, and segmentation. Features include edges, textures, shapes, and colors, among others.

Techniques for feature extraction are as follows:

- **Color histogram**:
  - **What it does**: Counts how often each color appears in an image.
  - **Why use it**: Helps in comparing and matching images based on color.

- **Edge detection**:
  - **What it does**: Finds the outlines of objects in an image.
  - **Why use it**: Useful for identifying shapes and objects.

- **Scale-Invariant Feature Transform (SIFT)**:
  - **What it does**: Detects and describes key points in an image.
  - **Why use it**: Helps in recognizing objects even if the image is scaled or rotated.

- **Speeded-Up Robust Features (SURF)**:
  - **What it does**: Similar to SIFT but faster.
  - **Why use it**: Good for real-time applications where speed is crucial.

- **Histogram of oriented gradients (HOG)**:
    - o **What it does**: Looks at the direction of light and dark transitions (gradients) in small parts of an image.
    - o **Why use it**: Often used for detecting objects like pedestrians.

- **Local binary patterns (LBP)**:
    - o **What it does**: Compares each pixel to its neighbors to create a pattern.
    - o **Why use it**: Effective for texture analysis and face recognition.

- **Gabor filters**:
    - o **What it does**: Uses specific frequencies and orientations to detect texture.
    - o **Why use it**: Good for texture segmentation and identifying edges.

- **Convolutional neural networks (CNNs)**:
    - o **What it does**: Automatically extracts features from images using layers of filters, learning a hierarchy of patterns, from edges and textures in early layers to shapes and complete objects in deeper layers.
    - o **Why use it**: Very powerful for image classification and object detection.

- **PCA**:
    - o **What it does**: Reduces the number of features while keeping important information
    - o **Why use it**: Simplifies the data, making it easier to process.

- **Wavelet transform**:
    - o **What it does**: Breaks down an image into different frequency components.
    - o **Why use it**: Useful for image compression and noise reduction.

Extracting features from image data is a foundational step in computer vision tasks. By employing techniques such as edge detection, HOG, SIFT, and CNNs, we can transform raw image data into meaningful representations that enhance the performance of ML models. Effective feature extraction not only improves model accuracy but also enables a deeper understanding of the visual content in images.

In our real-world use cases, we deal with lots of numeric data. It is important to understand how to identify those and extract key features. The following section will cover that topic in detail.

Identifying and extracting features from numerical data

Feature engineering from numerical data involves using domain knowledge and various techniques to transform raw numerical data into features that better represent the underlying patterns to ML algorithms. This step is crucial for improving model performance and interpretability.

The following techniques range from scaling numerical values to encoding data to extract meaningful information:

- **Scaling (Normalization):** Scaling involves adjusting the range of numerical features to a standard scale. This is important for algorithms sensitive to the magnitude of data, such as gradient descent-based algorithms.

  Example:

  o **Min-Max scaling**: Transforming features to lie within a fixed range, usually [0, 1].

  Example: A feature with values ranging from 0 to 100 can be scaled to 0 to 1.

  o **Standardization (Z-score normalization)**: Transforming features to have a mean of 0 and a standard deviation of 1.

  Example: A feature with a mean of 50 and standard deviation 10 would be standardized such that it follows a standard normal distribution (mean 0, standard deviation 1),

- **Binning**: Binning converts continuous variables into discrete bins. This technique can simplify the model and help handle non-linearity.

  Example:

  o **Equal-width binning**: Dividing the range of the variable into equal-sized bins.

  Example: Ages 0-20, 21-40, 41-60, and 61-80.

  o **Equal-frequency binning**: Dividing the variable into bins with an equal number of observations.

  Example: Income data split such that each bin contains the same number of individuals.

- **Creating interaction terms:** Interaction terms involve creating new features that are the product of two or more features. This can capture interactions between variables that may not be evident individually.

  Example:

  o **Multiplicative interaction**: Creating a feature by multiplying two features.

Example: If we have features X1 (price) and X2 (quantity), we could create an interaction term X1*X2 (total cost).

- o **Additive interaction**: Creating a feature by adding two features.

Example: If we have features A (height) and B (width), we could create an interaction term A+B.

- **Polynomial features:** Polynomial features involve creating new features by raising existing features to a power and/or creating interaction terms.

Examples:

- o **Quadratic features**: Creating squared terms of the features.

Example: If we have a feature X, we can create a new feature X^2.

- o **Cubic features**: Creating cubed terms of the features.

Example: If we have a feature X, we can create a new feature X^3.

- o **Combination of features**: Creating interaction terms with polynomial degrees.

Example: If we have features X1 and X2, we can create features like X1*X2, $X1^2$, and $X2^2$.

- **Log transformation**: Log transformation applies a logarithmic function to skewed data to reduce skewness and handle a wide range of values. If the dataset contains zero or negative values, a constant offset can be added before applying the log transformation (i.e., if some of the numbers are 0 or negative, which do not work with logs, we just add a small number (called an offset) to make everything positive before using the log.

Example:

- o **Log transformation**: Applying a natural logarithm to features with a skewed distribution

Example: If we have a feature X with values ranging from 1 to 1000, we can transform it to log(X)

- **Feature imputation**: Feature imputation involves filling in missing values in the dataset, ensuring that the data can be used effectively in ML models.

Example:

- o **Mean imputation**: Filling missing values with the mean of the feature.

Example: If the mean of a feature X is 50, missing values in X can be replaced with 50.

- o **Median imputation**: Filling missing values with the median of the feature.

Example: If the median of a feature X is 50, missing values in X can be replaced with 50.

      o **Mode imputation**: Filling missing values with the mode of the feature.

Example: If the most frequent value of a feature X is 10, missing values in X can be replaced with 10.

- **Encoding temporal data**: Temporal data can be used to extract meaningful features such as day, month, year, hour, day of the week, and so on.

Example:

      o **Day of the week**: Extracting the day of the week from a date feature.

Example: From the date 2024-05-18, extract Saturday.

      o **Month and year**: Extracting the month and year from a date feature.

Example: From the date 2024-05-18, extract May and 2024.

Feature engineering from numerical data is a pivotal step in the data preprocessing pipeline. It involves transforming raw numerical inputs into features that can significantly enhance the performance of ML models. By applying techniques such as normalization, polynomial features, and log transformations, data scientists can uncover the hidden patterns in the data, leading to more accurate prediction results and insights.

The following section shows a comparison table that helps explain each of the above techniques and the advantages and disadvantages of using each of those, along with appropriate application scenarios.

Comparing feature engineering techniques

Here is a comparison of some common feature engineering techniques in a table format:

Technique	Description	Advantages	Disadvantages	Applications
Scaling (Normalization)	Adjusting the range of features to a standard scale (e.g., 0-1 or z-score).	Improves convergence of gradient descent algorithms.	It can distort the original data distribution.	ML algorithms requiring distance measures (e.g., **k-nearest neighbor (KNN)**, **support vector machines (SVM)**.

Binning	Converting continuous variables into discrete bins.	Simplifies the model, handles non-linearity.	May lose information; the choice of bins can be arbitrary.	Decision trees, logistic regression
One-hot encoding	Converting categorical variables into binary vectors.	Removes the ordinal nature from categorical data.	Increases dimensionality, can lead to sparse matrices.	Linear models, tree-based models.
Polynomial features	Creating interaction terms and higher-degree features.	Captures non-linear relationships.	It can lead to overfitting and increase dimensionality.	Linear regression, polynomial regression.
Feature selection	Selecting a subset of relevant features.	Reduces overfitting, improves model interpretability.	It can miss important features, depending on the selection method used.	Any model, especially high-dimensional data.
PCA	Reducing dimensionality by transforming to a new set of orthogonal features.	Reduces overfitting, improves computational efficiency.	Loss of interpretability can discard useful information.	Any model, especially when dealing with high-dimensional data.
Feature imputation	Filling missing values in the dataset.	Utilizes more data, can improve model performance.	It can introduce bias; the choice of the imputation method can affect results.	Any model
Log transformation	Applying a logarithmic transformation to skewed data.	Reduces skewness, handles a wide range of values.	Only applicable to positive values, it can be sensitive to outliers.	Linear models, regression analysis.
Encoding temporal data	Extracting features like day, month, and year from temporal data.	Captures seasonality, trends in data.	It can lead to high dimensionality if not managed properly.	Time series analysis, forecasting models.

Text vectorization	Converting text data into numerical features (e.g., TF-IDF, Word2Vec, and so on).	Allows the use of text data in models.	It can lead to high-dimensional sparse matrices and may require significant preprocessing.	NLP models, text classification

Table 5.1: Comparison of feature engineering techniques

Conclusion

In this chapter, we explored the essential role of feature engineering in the ML pipeline. This chapter provided insights into various techniques for identifying, extracting, and transforming features from diverse data sources, including text, speech, images, and numerical data. By understanding methods such as tokenization, TF-IDF, MFCCs, and PCA, and applying strategies like scaling, binning, and polynomial feature creation, readers gained the tools to improve model performance and interpretability. Feature engineering was emphasized as a critical step in building effective ML solutions.

In the next chapter, we will discuss the techniques for understanding and visualizing data. Readers will learn how to uncover patterns, trends, and insights within datasets using various visualization tools and analysis methods. This knowledge will form a strong foundation for informed decision-making and effective communication of data-driven results.

Multiple choice questions

1. **What is the primary goal of feature engineering?**

   a. To create new features from raw data

   b. To improve model performance and interpretability

   c. To clean and preprocess data

   d. To select the best ML algorithm

2. **Which technique is commonly used for handling categorical variables in ML models?**

   a. Normalization

   b. Binning

   c. One-hot encoding

   d. PCA

3. **What is the purpose of applying a log transformation to a feature?**

   a. To reduce skewness in the data distribution

   b. To handle missing values

   c. To reduce dimensionality

   d. To create interaction terms

4. **Which feature engineering technique is useful for capturing non-linear relationships in the data?**

   a. Scaling

   b. Polynomial features

   c. One-hot encoding

   d. Imputation

5. **What is the advantage of using PCA for feature engineering?**

   a. It reduces overfitting

   b. It increases model interpretability

   c. It handles missing values

   d. It reduces dimensionality while preserving important information

6. **Which technique is commonly used for extracting features from text data?**

   a. Edge detection

   b. SIFT

   c. TF-IDF

   d. MFCCs

7. **What is the purpose of feature imputation?**

   a. To create interaction terms

   b. To reduce dimensionality

   c. To fill the missing values in the dataset

   d. To handle categorical variables

8. **Which feature engineering technique is useful for capturing image textures?**

   a. Color histogram

   b. Gabor filters

   c. BoW

   d. Tokenization

9. **What is the purpose of binning in feature engineering?**

   a. To convert continuous variables into discrete bins

   b. To reduce dimensionality

   c. To handle missing values

   d. To create interaction terms

10. **Which feature engineering technique is commonly used for speech recognition?**

    a. MFCCs

    b. HOG

    c. Word2Vec

    d. PCA

Answer key

1. b
2. c
3. a
4. b
5. d
6. c
7. c
8. b
9. a
10. a

Join our Discord space

Join our Discord workspace for latest updates, offers, tech happenings around the world, new releases, and sessions with the authors:

https://discord.bpbonline.com

CHAPTER 6

Data Analysis and Visualization

Introduction

Data analysis and visualization are critical components of any ML workflow. They enable data scientists and **machine learning** (**ML**) engineers to understand the underlying patterns, trends, and relationships within their data. This understanding is crucial for building effective ML models that can accurately predict outcomes and provide valuable insights.

AWS provides a suite of services that facilitate data analysis and visualization at scale. For example, Amazon SageMaker offers integrated Jupyter notebooks for data exploration and visualization, AWS Glue supports scalable data preprocessing and transformation, and Amazon QuickSight enables the creation of interactive dashboards and visual analytics.

In this chapter, we will discuss the various techniques and tools used to create informative graphs, interpret descriptive statistics, and perform cluster analysis. These skills are essential for anyone aiming to pass the AWS Certified ML - Specialty (MLS-C01) exam.

Structure

This chapter covers the following topics:

- Creating graphs
- Interpreting descriptive statistics
- Performing cluster analysis

Objectives

By the end of this chapter, you will develop skills to visualize data effectively using various types of plots, including scatter plots, time series plots, histograms, and box plots. These visualization techniques will

help you communicate data insights and trends clearly. You will also learn to interpret key descriptive statistics, such as correlation, summary statistics, and p-values, equipping you with the ability to make informed decisions based on statistical data. Additionally, the chapter will provide hands-on experience with cluster analysis techniques, such as hierarchical clustering and the elbow plot method. You will learn to diagnose and determine the optimal number of clusters, a critical step for segmenting data and uncovering hidden patterns.

By mastering these skills, you will be well-prepared to tackle the data analysis and visualization questions on the AWS Certified ML - Specialty (MLS-C01) exam. You will be able to design, build, deploy, optimize, train, tune, and maintain ML solutions for various business problems using the AWS Cloud, enhancing your expertise and career prospects in AI/ML.

Creating graphs

Graphs are essential tools for data visualization. They help in simplifying complex data and making it more comprehensible. In this section, we will explore how to create different types of graphs, including scatter plots, time series plots, histograms, and box plots. We will explain each type of graph, provide practical examples, and illustrate key concepts to ensure you grasp the fundamentals.

Scatter plots

A scatter plot is a type of graph used to display the relationship between two numerical variables. Each point on the plot represents an observation from the dataset. Scatter plots help identify correlations, patterns, and potential outliers within the data.

The following are the steps to create a scatter plot:

1. **Collect data**: Ensure you have two numerical variables to plot.

   Tip: **Consider using Amazon S3 to store and manage your datasets.**

2. **Plot points**: On a Cartesian coordinate system, plot each observation as a point based on its values for the two variables.

3. **Analyze**: Look for patterns, clusters, or any form of correlation.

> **Note: SageMaker provides built-in visualization tools to analyze these patterns directly within the SageMaker Studio environment.**

Imagine you have a dataset of students' study hours and their corresponding exam scores. A scatter plot can help visualize the relationship between study hours and exam performance, as shown in the following code block:

```python
import matplotlib.pyplot as plt


# Sample data
study_hours = [1, 2, 3, 4, 5, 6, 7, 8, 9, 10]
exam_scores = [50, 55, 60, 65, 70, 75, 80, 85, 90, 95]


# Creating the scatter plot
plt.scatter(study_hours, exam_scores)
plt.title("Study Hours vs Exam Scores")
plt.xlabel("Study Hours")
plt.ylabel("Exam Scores")
plt.show()
```

The following illustration shows the relationship between study hours and exam performance as a scatter plot:

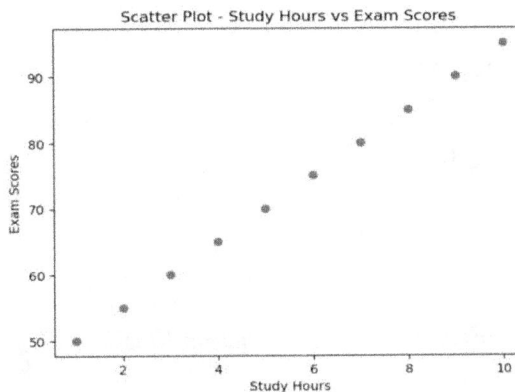

Figure 6.1: Scatter plot

In this example, the scatter plot shows a positive correlation between study hours and exam scores.

Time series plots

A time series plot displays data points at successive time intervals. It is used to observe how a variable changes over time.

Time series plots are essential for identifying trends, seasonal patterns, and potential anomalies over time.

Follow these steps to create a time series plot:

1. **Collect data**: Ensure you have data points indexed by time.
2. **Plot points**: On a graph, the x-axis represents time, and the y-axis represents the variable of interest.
3. **Analyze**: Look for trends, cycles, or irregular patterns.

Consider a dataset of daily temperatures recorded over a month. A time series plot can visualize the temperature changes over the days, as shown in the following code block:

```python
import pandas as pd

# Sample data
dates = pd.date_range(start='2023-01-01', periods=30)
temperatures = [30, 32, 31, 29, 35, 36, 37, 34, 32, 31, 30, 29, 28, 27, 26, 25, 24, 23, 22, 21, 20, 19, 18, 17, 16, 15, 14, 13, 12, 11]

# Creating the time series plot
plt.plot(dates, temperatures)
plt.title("Daily Temperatures Over a Month")
plt.xlabel("Date")
plt.ylabel("Temperature (°C)")
plt.xticks(rotation=45)
plt.show()
```

For time series data collection, consider using *Amazon Kinesis Data Streams* or *AWS IoT Core* to ingest real-time data.

The following illustration shows a time series plot that captures the temperature trend over a period of time:

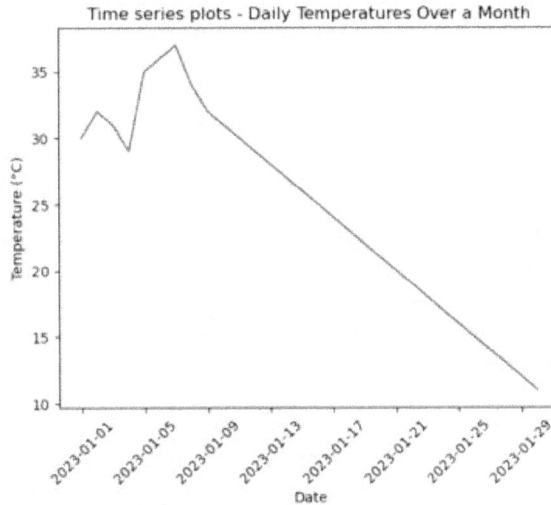

Figure 6.2: *Time series plot*

The time series plot clearly shows the temperature trend over the month.

For time series analysis, Amazon Forecast can be used to analyze time series data and make predictions.

Histograms

A histogram is a graphical representation of the distribution of a dataset. It displays the frequency of data points within specified intervals (bins).

Histograms help understand the distribution, central tendency, and variability of data.

The steps to create a Histogram are as follows:

1. **Collect data**: Ensure you have a numerical dataset.
2. **Create bins**: Divide the range of data into intervals.
3. **Plot frequency**: Plot the frequency of data points within each bin.

Consider a data set of students' scores on a test. A histogram can show the distribution of scores, as you can see in the next code block:

```python
# Sample data
scores = [50, 55, 60, 65, 70, 75, 80, 85, 90, 95, 100, 45, 67, 88, 77, 92, 84,
74, 63, 56]
```

```
# Creating the histogram
plt.hist(scores, bins=5, edgecolor='black')
plt.title("Distribution of Test Scores")
plt.xlabel("Scores")
plt.ylabel("Frequency")
plt.show()
```

The following illustration shows a histogram that captures the relationship between student stores and the frequency of occurrence:

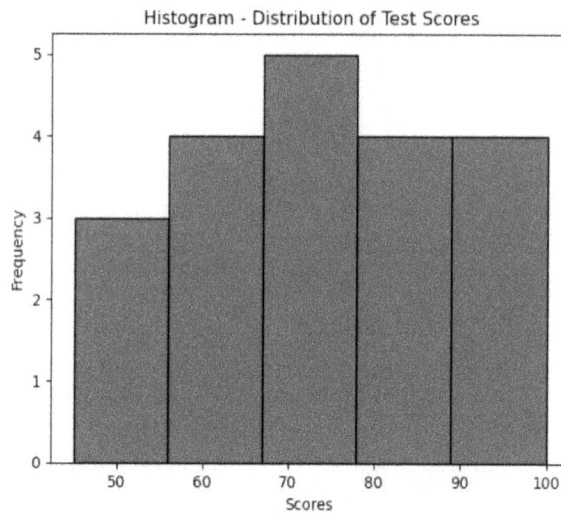

Figure 6.3: Histogram

The histogram shows the frequency distribution of the test scores.

Box plots

A box plot (or whisker plot) is a standardized way of displaying the distribution of data based on a five-number summary: minimum, **first quartile (Q1)**, median, **third quartile (Q3)**, and maximum.

Box plots are useful for identifying outliers and understanding the spread and skewness of data.

Follow these steps to create a box plot:

1. **Collect data**: Ensure you have a numerical dataset.

2. **Calculate a five-number summary**: Determine the minimum, Q1, median, Q3, and maximum.

3. **Plot summary**: Draw a box from Q1 to Q3 with a line at the median. Extend whiskers from the box to the minimum and maximum values.

Consider a dataset of monthly salaries of employees. A box plot can show the distribution and identify any outliers, as shown in the following code:

```python
# Sample data
salaries = [3000, 3200, 3400, 3600, 3800, 4000, 4200, 4400, 4600, 4800, 5000,
5200, 5400, 5600, 5800]

# Creating the box plot
plt.boxplot(salaries)
plt.title("Distribution of Monthly Salaries")
plt.ylabel("Salary ($)")
plt.show()
```

The following illustration shows box plots that capture information about salary distribution and outliers involved in that distribution:

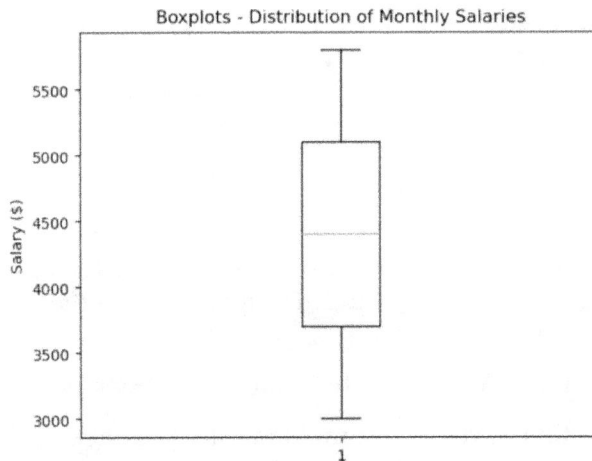

Figure 6.4: Box plots

The box plot reveals the salary distribution and highlights any outliers.

Here is a table for a quick comparison of all graphs:

Graph type	Purpose	Example use case
Scatter plot	Identify correlations and patterns.	Relationship between study hours and exam scores.
Time series plot	Observe changes over time.	Daily temperatures over a month.
Histogram	Understand distribution and frequency.	Distribution of test scores.
Box plot	Display distribution, identify outliers.	Monthly salaries of employees.

Table 6.1: Graph comparison table

In this section, we have explored the types of graphs essential for data visualization. Understanding how to create and interpret these graphs is crucial for effective data analysis. Scatter plots help identify relationships between variables, time series plots reveal trends over time, histograms show data distributions, and box plots highlight spread and outliers. By mastering these visualization techniques, you will be well-prepared to tackle data analysis tasks and excel in the AWS Certified ML - Specialty (MLS-C01) exam. Now, we will read about interpreting values associated with statistical concepts that are relevant to ML.

Interpreting descriptive statistics

Descriptive statistics summarize and provide information about your data. They help in understanding the basic features of the data, giving a simple summary about the sample and the measures. In this section, we will cover correlation, summary statistics, and p-values. Each concept will be explained in detail with practical examples and illustrations to ensure clarity.

Correlation

Correlation measures the strength and direction of a linear relationship between two variables. The correlation coefficient ranges from -1 to 1. The following are the types of correlations that we need to be familiar with:

- **Positive correlation**: A Value close to 1 indicates a strong positive linear relationship.

- **Negative correlation**: A Value close to -1 indicates a strong negative linear relationship.

- **No correlation**: A Value around 0 indicates no linear relationship.

Here is how you can calculate correlation:

1. **Collect data**: Ensure you have paired numerical data for the two variables.

2. **Calculate the covariance**: Measure how much the two variables change together.

3. **Normalize**: Divide the covariance by the product of the standard deviations of the two variables to get the correlation coefficient.

Consider a dataset of students' study hours and their corresponding exam scores. The following code shows how to load the data and then find the correlation coefficient associated with those data patterns:

```python
import numpy as np

# Sample data
study_hours = np.array([1, 2, 3, 4, 5, 6, 7, 8, 9, 10])
exam_scores = np.array([50, 55, 60, 65, 70, 75, 80, 85, 90, 95])

# Calculating correlation
correlation_coefficient = np.corrcoef(study_hours, exam_scores)[0, 1]
correlation_coefficient
```

The following are code illustrations showing how to determine the types of correlation involved in a data pattern or distribution:

```python
#Demostration of Positive Correlation
import numpy as np

# Sample data
study_hours = np.array([1, 2, 3, 4, 5, 6, 7, 8, 9, 10])
exam_scores = np.array([50, 55, 60, 65, 70, 75, 80, 85, 90, 95])

# Calculating correlation
correlation_coefficient = np.corrcoef(study_hours, exam_scores)[0, 1]
correlation_coefficient

1.0

#Demostration of Negative Correlation
import numpy as np

# Sample data
study_hours = np.array([1, 2, 3, 4, 5, 6, 7, 8, 9, 10])
exam_scores = np.array([95, 90, 85, 80, 75, 70, 65, 60, 55, 50])

# Calculating correlation
correlation_coefficient = np.corrcoef(study_hours, exam_scores)[0, 1]
correlation_coefficient

-1.0

#Demostration of No Correlation
import numpy as np

# Sample data
study_hours = np.array([1, 2, 3, 4, 5, 6, 7, 8, 9, 10])
exam_scores = np.array([50, 33, 10, 80, 66, 88, 44, 33, 10, 5])

# Calculating correlation
correlation_coefficient = np.corrcoef(study_hours, exam_scores)[0, 1]
correlation_coefficient

-0.3350785215615115
```

Figure 6.5: Positive, negative, and no correlation

The preceding figure shows how to calculate the correlation coefficient and demonstrates positive, negative, and no correlation coefficient scenarios. In the case of positive correlation, the value is 1, for negative correlation it is -1, followed by -0.33 (close to zero) for no correlation.

Summary statistics

Summary statistics are numerical values that describe and summarize the key features of a dataset. Common summary statistics include mean, median, mode, standard deviation, and range:

- **Mean**: Average of the data.
- **Median**: Middle value when the data is sorted.
- **Mode**: Most frequently occurring value.
- **Standard deviation**: Measures the dispersion or spread of the data.
- **Range**: Difference between the maximum and minimum values.

Here is how you can calculate these summary statistics:

- **Mean**: Add all the values and divide by the number of values.
- **Median**: Sort the data and find the middle value.
- **Mode**: Identify the value that appears most frequently.
- **Standard deviation**: Calculate the square root of the average of the squared deviations from the mean.
- **Range**: Subtract the minimum value from the maximum value.

Tip: **For summary statistics, you can also use `pandas.describe()` as a quick and comprehensive way to calculate them.**

This code block calculates and displays summary statistics for a sample dataset of scores using Python's statistics module and the tabulate library. First, the sample data is defined as a list of numerical scores. The code then computes key statistical metrics: the mean (average), median (middle value), mode (most frequent value), standard deviation (measure of data spread), and range (difference between the maximum and minimum values). These calculated values are formatted into a table using the tabulate library for easy readability. The table includes two columns: one for the names of the summary statistics and another for their corresponding values, which are printed as the output.

Consider a dataset of test scores:

```python
import statistics as stats
from tabulate import tabulate
```

```
# Sample data
scores = [50, 55, 60, 65, 70, 75, 80, 85, 90, 95, 100, 45, 67, 88, 77, 92, 84,
74, 63, 56]

# Calculating summary statistics
mean = stats.mean(scores)
median = stats.median(scores)
mode = stats.mode(scores)
std_dev = stats.stdev(scores)
range_value = max(scores) - min(scores)
print(tabulate([['Mean', mean], ['Median', median], ['Mode', mode],
            ['Standard Deviation', std_dev], ['Range Value', range_
value]],
            headers=['Summary Statistics', 'Value']))```
```

To understand the distribution and central tendencies of the dataset, the following figure summarizes the key statistical measures calculated from the sample test scores:

Summary Statistics	Value
Mean	73.55
Median	74.5
Mode	50
Standard Deviation	15.763
Range Value	55

Figure 6.6: Summary statistics of sample test scores

Calculating the correlation coefficient

The correlation coefficient is a statistical measure that quantifies the strength and direction of the relationship between two numerical variables. It ranges from:

- **+1**: Perfect positive correlation (as one variable increases, the other increases)
- **0**: No correlation
- **-1**: Perfect negative correlation (as one variable increases, the other decreases)

In Python, you can calculate the correlation coefficient using NumPy's **corrcoef()** function. Here is a breakdown of how it works:

```
import numpy as np
#Example data
```

```
study_hours = [1, 2, 3, 4, 5, 6, 7, 8] exam_scores = [50, 55, 60, 65, 70, 75, 80, 85]
#Calculate correlation matrix
correlation_matrix = np.corrcoef(study_hours, exam_scores)
#Extract the correlation coefficient
correlation_coefficient = correlation_matrix[0, 1]
print("Correlation Coefficient:", correlation_coefficient)
```

np.corrcoef() returns a 2×2 matrix:

[0, 0] and [1, 1] are the self-correlations (always 1)

[0, 1] and [1, 0] are the actual correlation coefficients between the two arrays

You extract the value at [0, 1] to get the final correlation coefficient

A correlation close to +1 or -1 indicates a strong relationship, while a value near 0 suggests a weak or no linear relationship.

P-value

A p-value is a measure of the strength of evidence against the null hypothesis in a statistical test. It quantifies the probability of obtaining results at least as extreme as the observed results, assuming the null hypothesis is true.

Let us discuss the null hypothesis. Imagine you have a friend who loves cookies, and she says she can eat ten cookies in one minute. You do not believe her, so you want to test her claim. The null hypothesis is the idea that your friend is not telling the truth, and she cannot really eat ten cookies in one minute. It is like saying, *I do not think she can do it*. To test the null hypothesis, you decide to give her ten cookies and a timer. If she can eat all the cookies within one minute, it means the null hypothesis was wrong, and she was telling the truth, but if she cannot eat all the cookies in one minute, it means the null hypothesis was right, and she was not able to do what she claimed. The null hypothesis is like a starting point or a default assumption that we make before we do an experiment or a test. If the results of the experiment show that the null hypothesis is wrong, then we can say that the claim or idea we were testing is true, but if the results support the null hypothesis, it means the claim or idea was not true. In science and research, scientists often start with a null hypothesis and then conduct experiments or collect data to see if they can reject or disprove the null hypothesis. If they cannot reject it, it means there is not enough evidence to support the idea they were testing.

The significance of the low and high p-values is mentioned, as follows:

- **Low p-value (≤ 0.05)**: Indicates strong evidence against the null hypothesis, so you reject the null hypothesis.

- **High p-value (> 0.05):** Indicates weak evidence against the null hypothesis, so you accept the null hypothesis.

The following is the process to interpret the p-value:

1. **Choose a significance level:** Commonly 0.05

2. **Calculate the p-value:** Using a statistical test

3. **Compare p-value with the significance level:** Decide whether to reject the null hypothesis

Consider a hypothesis test to determine if a new teaching method significantly improves test scores compared to the traditional method. This code checks if two groups of scores are different or if the difference is just random. It uses a t-test, which is like a math test that compares the average scores of the two groups: **traditional_scores** and **new_method_scores**. It gives two results: a t-score (which measures how big the difference is) and a p-value (which tells us if the difference is important or just happened by chance). If the p-value is very small (usually less than 0.05), it means the two groups are likely different for real.

```python
from scipy import stats


# Sample data
traditional_scores = [50, 55, 60, 65, 70, 75, 80, 85, 90, 95]
new_method_scores = [60, 65, 70, 75, 80, 85, 90, 95, 100, 105]


# Performing a t-test
t_stat, p_value = stats.ttest_ind(traditional_scores, new_method_scores)
p_value
```

The following is an illustration of the execution that shows the p-value as the output:

```
#Demostration of t-test
from scipy import stats

# Sample data
traditional_scores = [50, 55, 60, 65, 70, 75, 80, 85, 90, 95]
new_method_scores = [60, 65, 70, 75, 80, 85, 90, 95, 100, 105]

# Performing a t-test
t_stat, p_value = stats.ttest_ind(traditional_scores, new_method_scores)
p_value

0.15693219584685508
```

Figure 6.7: Calculation of p-value

In this example, if the p-value is less than 0.05, we reject the null hypothesis, indicating that the new teaching method significantly improves test scores.

Let us take a look at this table comparing the descriptive statistics:

Statistic	Definition	Example use case
Correlation	Measures the strength and direction of a linear relationship.	Relationship between study hours and exam scores.
Mean	The average of the data.	Average test scores.
Median	The middle value of the data.	Central tendency of salaries.
Mode	The most frequently occurring value.	Most common test score.
Standard Deviation	Measures the spread of the data.	Variation in employee performance.
Range	Difference between maximum and minimum values.	Spread of ages in a group.
P-value	Measures evidence against the null hypothesis.	Significance of a new drug's effect.

Table 6.2: Descriptive statistics terminology comparisons

In this section, we have explored various descriptive statistics crucial for summarizing and interpreting data. Understanding correlation helps identify relationships between variables, while summary statistics provide a snapshot of the dataset's key features. P-values aid in making decisions based on statistical tests. By mastering these concepts, you will be well-equipped to analyze data effectively and excel in the AWS Certified ML - Specialty (MLS-C01) exam. The following section talks about performing an analysis of clusters.

Performing cluster analysis

Cluster analysis, or clustering, is a technique used to group similar data points based on their characteristics. It is an essential tool for identifying patterns and segmenting data into meaningful groups. In this section, we will cover:

- Hierarchical clustering
- Diagnosis of clusters
- Elbow plot method
- Determining cluster size

Cluster analysis is important in real life because it helps organize large amounts of information into meaningful groups based on shared characteristics, making data easier to understand and use. For example, in marketing, businesses can use clustering to group customers with similar preferences and create personalized campaigns. In healthcare, clustering helps identify groups of patients with similar symptoms, enabling more accurate diagnoses and treatment plans. In education, it can group students by learning styles or performance levels to tailor teaching methods effectively. Additionally, researchers in environmental studies use clustering to analyze areas with similar climate patterns or pollution levels. Techniques such as hierarchical clustering, cluster diagnosis, and the elbow plot method ensure that the groups formed are meaningful and applicable to solving real-world problems.

Hierarchical clustering

Hierarchical clustering is a method of cluster analysis that seeks to build a hierarchy of clusters. It can be divided into two types:

- **Agglomerative clustering**: Starts with each data point as a single cluster and merges them step-by-step based on similarity.

- **Divisive clustering**: Starts with all data points in one cluster and splits them step-by-step based on dissimilarity.

You can follow this process to perform hierarchical clustering:

1. **Calculate distance matrix**: Compute the distance between every pair of data points.

2. **Linkage criteria**: Choose a method to calculate the distance between clusters (e.g., single, complete, or average).

3. **Merge clusters**: Merge the closest clusters iteratively until only one cluster remains.

4. **Dendrogram**: Create a tree-like diagram to visualize the merging process.

Consider a dataset of customers based on their annual income and spending score.

The following code is like organizing a group of people into smaller teams based on how similar they are. Each person has two pieces of information, like, their age and how much money they earn. The program starts by looking at how close each person is to others and groups the closest ones together. Then, it combines the groups step by step until everyone is in one big group.

To show this process, it creates a dendrogram, which is like a family tree but for groups. The bottom of the tree has all the people (or data points), and as you move up, you see how they are grouped together. The higher the branch, the further apart the groups are. This helps us see which people (or data points) are similar and how the groups are formed step by step.

```python
import matplotlib.pyplot as plt
import numpy as np
from scipy.cluster.hierarchy import dendrogram, linkage
```

```
# Sample data
data = np.array([[40, 20000], [20, 15000], [30, 18000], [25, 17000], [35,
22000], [50, 25000]])


# Perform hierarchical clustering
linked = linkage(data, 'single')

# Create a dendrogram
plt.figure(figsize=(10, 7))
dendrogram(linked, orientation='top', labels=range(1, 7), distance_
sort='descending', show_leaf_counts=True)
plt.title('Dendrogram')
plt.xlabel('Data Points')
plt.ylabel('Distance')
plt.show()
```

The following figure illustrates the formation of dendrogram:

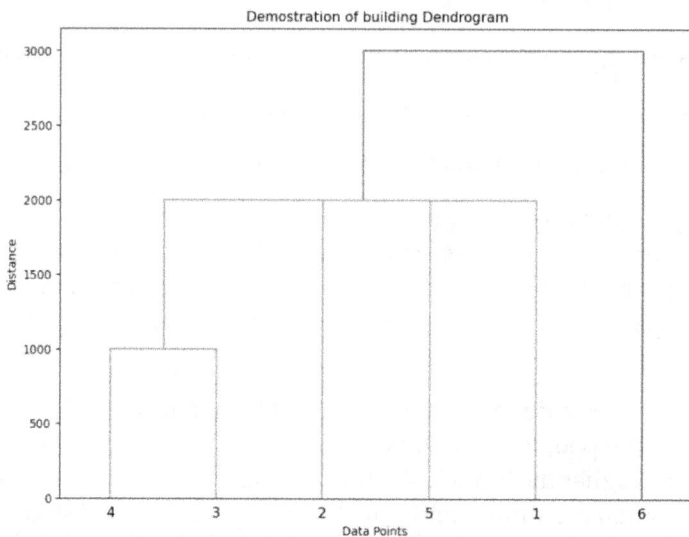

Figure 6.8: Demonstration of building dendrogram

The dendrogram helps visualize the process of hierarchical clustering, showing how data points are merged into clusters.

The screenshot displays a dendrogram, a tree-like diagram commonly used to visualize the arrangement of clusters produced by hierarchical clustering algorithms. In this specific dendrogram, there are 6 data points represented on the x-axis, labeled from 1 to 6.

The y-axis represents the distance or dissimilarity metric used in the clustering process. The higher the vertical line connecting two clusters or data points, the more dissimilar they are from each other.

The graph in *Figure 6.8* shows a building dendrogram, which is a hierarchical clustering visualization. The data consists of six data points, labeled 1 through 6 on the x-axis.

The dendrogram shows how these data points are progressively grouped together into clusters based on their similarity or distance from each other. The y-axis represents the distance at which clusters are merged.

At the lowest level, each data point starts out as its own cluster. As you move up the dendrogram, the most similar data points or clusters are merged together at various distance thresholds.

For example, data points 4 and 3 are merged into a cluster first, at a relatively low height, indicating they are very similar to each other. Then, the data points 2, 5 and 1 join them at a slightly higher level to form a cluster of 5 points.

The two main clusters remain separate until near the very top, where they finally merge into a single cluster containing all 6 data points. This suggests there are two quite distinct groups in this data set.

Diagnosis of clusters

Diagnosing clusters involves evaluating the quality and characteristics of the clusters formed. This helps understand the significance and validity of the clusters.

These are the key metrics that you can look for:

- **Silhouette score**: Measures how similar a data point is to its own cluster compared to other clusters. It ranges from -1 to 1, where a higher value indicates better clustering.

- **Cluster centroids**: The mean position of all the points in a cluster. It helps understand the central tendency of clusters.

Follow these steps to diagnose clusters:

1. **Calculate silhouette score**: Compute the silhouette score for each data point.

2. **Analyze cluster centroids**: Determine the centroid for each cluster to understand their characteristics.

3. **Visualize clusters**: Use scatter plots and other visual tools to assess the separation and cohesion of clusters.

Continuing with the customer dataset, let us diagnose the clusters formed by hierarchical clustering.

This following code helps evaluate how good a grouping (or clustering) is after dividing data into clusters. It starts by using k-means clustering, a method that splits data into groups based on their similarities. In this case, the data is divided into two groups (**n_clusters=2**), where the goal is to ensure that data points within the same group are similar to each other and different from those in other groups. Once the groups are formed, the code calculates the silhouette score, which acts like a report card for the clustering. This score checks whether the data points within a group are close to each other and whether the groups are well-separated. The final output is a numerical score, where a higher value (closer to 1) indicates well-defined and meaningful groups, while a lower score suggests that the groups may not be a good fit. This process helps determine if the clustering makes sense or needs adjustments.

```python
from sklearn.metrics import silhouette_score
from sklearn.cluster import KMeans


# Sample data
data = np.array([[40, 20000], [20, 15000], [30, 18000], [25, 17000], [35, 22000], [50, 25000]])


# Perform k-means clustering for comparison
kmeans = KMeans(n_clusters=2)
kmeans.fit(data)
labels = kmeans.labels_


# Calculate silhouette score
silhouette_avg = silhouette_score(data, labels)
silhouette_avg
```

The following is an illustration of how to calculate the silhouette average value:

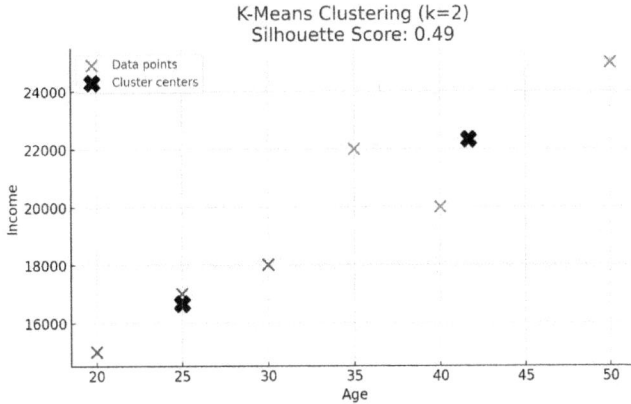

Figure 6.9: *Calculation of the silhouette average value*

The preceding figure is a visualization of the k-means clustering applied to the dataset. The data points are color-coded based on their cluster assignments (red and blue), with the black **X** markers indicating the cluster centers. The **silhouette score** shown in the title quantifies how well-separated and compact the clusters are a higher score indicates better-defined clusters.

Elbow plot

The elbow plot method is used to determine the optimal number of clusters by plotting the sum of squared distances (inertia) from each point to its assigned cluster centroid.

Here is the process to create an elbow plot:

1. **Perform clustering**: Run k-means clustering for a range of cluster numbers.

2. **Calculate inertia**: Compute the sum of squared distances for each cluster number.

3. **Plot inertia**: Plot the inertia values against the number of clusters.

4. **Identify elbow point**: Look for the *elbow* point where the inertia starts to decrease more slowly, indicating the optimal number of clusters.

Let us create an elbow plot for the customer dataset, as shown in the following code block:

```python
from sklearn.cluster import KMeans
import matplotlib.pyplot as plt


# Sample data
data = np.array([[40, 20000], [20, 15000], [30, 18000], [25, 17000], [35,
22000], [50, 25000]])
```

```
inertia = []

# Calculate inertia for different numbers of clusters
for i in range(1, 11):
    kmeans = KMeans(n_clusters=i)
    kmeans.fit(data)
    inertia.append(kmeans.inertia_)

# Plot the elbow plot
plt.figure(figsize=(10, 7))
plt.plot(range(1, 11), inertia, marker='o')
plt.title('Elbow Plot')
plt.xlabel('Number of Clusters')
plt.ylabel('Inertia')
plt.show()
```

The following is an illustration of elbow plot:

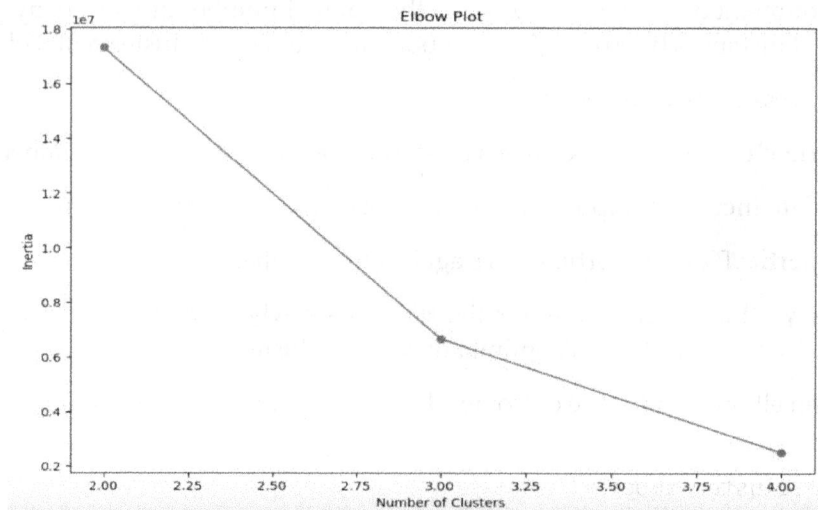

Figure 6.10: Elbow plot

The elbow plot helps determine the optimal number of clusters by identifying the point where adding more clusters does not significantly reduce inertia.

Determining cluster size

Determining cluster size involves selecting the appropriate number of clusters for a dataset, which is crucial for meaningful clustering. Let us look at the methods to determine cluster size:

- **Elbow method**: Elbow plot is used to identify the optimal number of clusters. Imagine you have a bunch of different colored balls, and you want to group them into different baskets based on their colors. The elbow method is a way to help you decide how many baskets you need. You start by putting all the balls in one big basket. Then, you start creating new baskets by separating the balls based on their colors. As you create more baskets, the balls become more organized and sorted by color. However, after a certain number of baskets, adding more baskets doesn't really make the balls much more organized. The elbow method helps you find the point where adding more baskets doesn't really help much in organizing the balls better. It is like looking for the *elbow* or bend in a graph that shows how organized the balls become as you add more baskets. At the elbow point, adding more baskets does not improve the organization significantly.

  As shown in *Figure 6.10*, the elbow point is where the inertia (within-cluster sum of squares) stops decreasing significantly. This visual **elbow** marks the optimal number of clusters. In the above example it is at 3 clusters.

  Tip: Amazon SageMaker's hyperparameter tuning capabilities can be used to explore different values of K (number of clusters) efficiently. By leveraging built-in tuning jobs, you can automate the selection of optimal cluster numbers based on metrics like inertia or silhouette score.

- **Silhouette method**: Uses silhouette scores to evaluate the quality of clusters for different numbers of clusters. This method is about checking how well the balls are grouped into their baskets. It looks at how similar each ball is to the other balls in its basket and how different it is from the balls in other baskets. For each ball, the silhouette method calculates a score based on these similarities and differences. A high score means the ball is similar to the other balls in its basket and really different from the balls in other baskets. A low score means the ball might be in the wrong basket. The silhouette method helps you choose the right number of baskets by looking at the overall score for different numbers of baskets. The number of baskets with the highest overall score is considered the best choice.

- **Gap statistic**: Compares the total (Total refers to the sum of all the within-cluster variation for a given number of clusters) within intra-cluster variation for different numbers of clusters with their expected values under null reference distribution. Imagine you have a bunch of balls, and you want to group them into baskets based on their colors. but this time, you also have a special way to measure how spread out the balls are in each basket. The gap statistic looks at how spread out the balls are in each basket and compares it to how spread out they would be if you randomly threw them into baskets without considering their colors. If the balls are more spread out in the baskets than they would be if you just randomly threw them in, it means that grouping them based on their colors is meaningful and useful. The gap statistic helps you choose the right number of baskets by looking at how much better the balls are grouped compared to just randomly throwing them into baskets. The number of baskets with the biggest gap (difference) between the actual spread and the random spread is considered the best choice.

Here is a quick comparison of all these methods:

Method	Description	Advantages	Disadvantages
Elbow method	Uses inertia to find the optimal number of clusters	Simple and intuitive	Subjective identification of elbow point
Silhouette method	Uses silhouette scores to evaluate cluster quality	Provides a clear metric for cluster validity	Computationally intensive for large datasets
Gap statistic	Compares cluster variation with null distribution	Robust and statistically sound	Complex and requires more computation

Table 6.3: Comparison of clustering methods

In this section, we have explored various aspects of cluster analysis, including hierarchical clustering, diagnosis of clusters, elbow plot method, and determining cluster size. Understanding these concepts is crucial for effectively grouping data and identifying meaningful patterns.

Conclusion

In this chapter, we explored the vital concepts of data analysis and visualization, focusing on their role in understanding patterns, trends, and relationships within datasets. This chapter provided practical guidance on creating various types of graphs, such as scatter plots, time series plots, histograms, and box plots, enabling clear and effective communication of data insights. We also discussed interpreting descriptive statistics, including correlation, summary statistics, and p-values, which are essential tools for summarizing and analyzing data effectively.

Additionally, the chapter introduced cluster analysis as a powerful technique for grouping data points based on shared characteristics. Methods such as hierarchical clustering, cluster diagnosis, and the elbow plot were discussed in detail, equipping you with the knowledge to identify meaningful patterns and determine the optimal number of clusters. Through practical examples and step-by-step guides, you gained hands-on experience with these concepts, ensuring a solid understanding of their applications in real-world scenarios.

By mastering the skills and techniques covered in this chapter, you are well-prepared to analyze data effectively, visualize insights, and approach data-driven problems with confidence. These abilities are critical for excelling in the AWS Certified ML - Specialty (MLS-C01) exam and advancing your career in ML and data science. In the next chapter, we will transition into understanding how to frame a business problem as a ML problem.

Multiple choice questions

1. **What type of graph is used to display the relationship between two numerical variables?**

    a. Time series plot

    b. Histogram

    c. Scatter plot

    d. Box plot

2. **Which of the following is true about the correlation coefficient?**

    a. It ranges from 0 to 1

    b. It measures the strength and direction of a linear relationship

    c. A value close to 0 indicates a strong positive linear relationship

    d. A value close to -1 indicates no linear relationship

3. **What does a p-value measure in a statistical test?**

    a. Strength of evidence against the null hypothesis

    b. Average of the data

    c. Spread of the data

    d. Difference between the maximum and minimum values

4. **Which clustering method starts with each data point as a single cluster and merges them step-by-step based on similarity?**

    a. Divisive clustering

    b. K-means clustering

    c. Agglomerative clustering

    d. Gaussian mixture modeling

5. **What is the purpose of an elbow plot in cluster analysis?**
   a. To visualize the merging process of hierarchical clustering
   b. To determine the optimal number of clusters
   c. To measure the similarity of data points to their own cluster
   d. To compare cluster variation with null distribution

6. **Which of the following is not a common summary statistic?**
   a. Mean
   b. Median
   c. P-value
   d. Standard deviation

7. **What does a silhouette score close to 1 indicate?**
   a. The data point is similar to its own cluster and different from other clusters
   b. The data point is dissimilar to its own cluster and similar to other clusters
   c. The data point is equally similar to all clusters
   d. The data point is an outlier

8. **Which type of plot is used to observe how a variable changes over time?**
   a. Scatter plot
   b. Histogram
   c. Box plot
   d. Time series plot

9. **What is the purpose of hierarchical clustering?**
   a. To build a hierarchy of clusters based on similarity or dissimilarity
   b. To partition data into a predetermined number of clusters
   c. To identify outliers in the dataset
   d. To visualize the distribution of a single variable

10. **Which method compares the total ("total" refers to the sum of all the within-cluster variation for a given number of clusters) within intra-cluster variation for different numbers of clusters with their expected values under null reference distribution?**
    a. Elbow method
    b. Silhouette method
    c. Gap statistic
    d. Dendrogram

Answer key

1. c
2. b
3. a
4. c
5. b
6. c
7. a
8. d
9. a
10. c

Join our Discord space

Join our Discord workspace for latest updates, offers, tech happenings around the world, new releases, and sessions with the authors:

https://discord.bpbonline.com

CHAPTER 7

Framing Business Problems as ML Problems

Introduction

In today's data-driven world, businesses are constantly seeking innovative ways to leverage data to gain a competitive edge. ML has emerged as a powerful tool that can transform raw data into actionable insights, drive strategic decisions, and automate processes. However, the journey to unlocking the potential of ML begins with a crucial step, correctly framing business problems as ML problems.

Imagine you are an entrepreneur facing declining customer retention rates. Alternatively, you are a supply chain manager grappling with unpredictable demand fluctuations. In both scenarios, the ability to frame these challenges as ML problems can be the difference between guesswork and data-driven solutions.

This chapter is designed to guide you through this pivotal process. We will start by exploring the essential criteria for determining when ML is the appropriate tool for your business challenges and when it might not be the best fit.

Structure

This chapter covers the following topics:

- Identifying ML applicability in business scenarios

- Supervised vs. unsupervised learning

- Hybrid learning

- Comparison of supervised and unsupervised learning

Objectives

This focuses on framing business problems as ML problems, providing a comprehensive guide for readers to navigate this crucial process. The chapter begins by introducing the importance of correctly identifying when ML is an appropriate solution and when it is not. It then delves into the fundamental distinction between supervised and unsupervised learning, explaining their characteristics and use cases. In this chapter, various types of ML models are explored, including classification, regression, clustering, dimensionality reduction, recommendation systems, and foundation models. Throughout the chapter, practical examples and real-world scenarios are used to illustrate key concepts, helping readers understand how to match their business objectives with the right ML approach. The chapter's structure and objectives are designed to equip readers with the knowledge to identify ML opportunities within their organizations, select the appropriate model type, and ultimately leverage ML to drive business success.

By the end of the chapter, readers should have a solid foundation in framing business problems as ML problems, enabling them to make informed decisions about implementing ML solutions in their business contexts.

Identifying ML applicability in business scenarios

ML is a powerful tool, but it is not a one-size-fits-all solution. Understanding when to apply ML and when to rely on other methods is crucial for effective problem-solving. In this chapter, the readers will explore the characteristics of problems suitable for ML and scenarios where ML might not be the best approach.

Here is a list of the characteristics of problems that can be considered suitable for an ML solution:

- **Availability of data**: Suppose a retail company wants to predict future sales. They have historical sales data from the past five years, including factors like marketing spend, seasonal trends, and economic indicators. This rich dataset is ideal for training an ML model to forecast sales accurately.

  ML algorithms thrive on data. The more high-quality data available, the better the model can learn and make accurate predictions. If the data is sparse or of poor quality, its performance will be compromised.

- **Clear objectives and metrics**: A healthcare provider wants to reduce patient readmission rates. They have a clear objective: to decrease readmissions by 20% within a year. Metrics such as readmission rates and patient health scores will measure success.

  ML projects need well-defined goals and measurable outcomes. Clear objectives help in choosing the right algorithm and evaluating its performance effectively.

- **Patterns in data that can be learned**: An e-commerce platform wants to recommend products to users. By analyzing past purchase behaviours and browsing history, patterns that can predict future purchases emerge.

  ML models excel in identifying patterns and relationships within data. If such patterns exist and can be learned, ML can provide significant value through accurate predictions or classifications.

To understand these concepts better, let us consider some practical examples of when the use of ML would be appropriate:

- **Customer sentiment analysis**: A company wants to analyze customer feedback from social media and online reviews to understand sentiment towards their products. They have thousands of reviews and social media posts. Using **natural language processing (NLP)** models, they can classify sentiments as positive, negative, or neutral, providing valuable insights into customer opinions.

- **Predictive maintenance**: An industrial plant wants to predict equipment failures before they happen to minimize downtime. They have extensive historical data on equipment performance, maintenance logs, and failure incidents. By applying ML models to this data, they can predict when a machine is likely to fail and schedule maintenance proactively.

Conversely, there are scenarios where ML is not appropriate, such as:

- **Lack of sufficient data:** A startup wants to predict customer churn but only has three months of customer interaction data. This limited data is insufficient to train a reliable ML model.

  ML models need a substantial amount of data to learn effectively. Without enough data, the model cannot generalize well, leading to poor performance and unreliable predictions.

- **Problems requiring deterministic solutions**: A financial institution needs to calculate monthly loan repayments. This problem requires precise and deterministic output that involves straightforward mathematical calculations, which provide probabilistic outputs but might introduce unnecessary complexity without any added benefit.

- **Simpler statistical methods are sufficient:** A company wants to understand the average spending habits of its customers. Basic statistical analysis, such as mean and median calculations, can provide these insights without the need for complex ML models.

Not all data-driven problems require ML. Simple statistical methods can often provide the necessary insights more efficiently and with less computational overhead.

Understanding when to use and when not to use ML is essential for leveraging its power effectively. By recognizing the characteristics of suitable problems and being aware of scenarios where simpler methods are more appropriate, you can make informed decisions that lead to successful ML implementations.

Supervised vs. unsupervised learning

Understanding the difference between supervised and unsupervised learning is fundamental to framing business problems as ML problems. These two approaches are like two sides of the same coin, each with its unique characteristics and use cases. In this section, we will dive into the definitions, key differences, and practical examples to illustrate when to choose supervised versus unsupervised learning.

Supervised learning

Supervised learning is a type of ML where a model is trained using labeled data. This means that the dataset used for training includes both input features and corresponding correct outputs. The goal of supervised learning is to learn a mapping function from inputs to outputs so that the model can make accurate predictions on new, unseen data.

Working of supervised learning

The following steps outline how supervised learning works:

1. **Training with labeled data**: The algorithm is provided with a dataset containing input-output pairs. For example, in a spam email detection model, the input would be an email's text, and the output would be a label indicating whether it is spam or not.

2. **Learning the pattern**: The model analyzes the relationships between inputs and outputs by minimizing errors. It adjusts itself using optimization techniques such as gradient descent.

3. **Making predictions**: Once trained, the model can predict outputs for new data. For instance, a trained housing price predictor can estimate the price of a house based on features like square footage, location, and number of bedrooms.

4. **Evaluation and improvement**: The model is tested using a separate dataset to evaluate its accuracy. If needed, adjustments such as tuning hyperparameters or providing more data can improve performance.

Types of supervised learning models

There are two types of supervised learning models, that is, Regression models and Classification models:

Regression models

Regression is a fundamental technique in ML used to predict continuous numerical values based on input data. It is a type of supervised learning, meaning that the model learns from labeled training data to make future predictions.

Regression works by identifying relationships between independent variables (input features) and a dependent variable (the target outcome). Imagine you want to predict the price of a house based on factors like size, location, and number of bedrooms. Regression helps establish a mathematical relationship between these factors and the house price, allowing accurate predictions for new houses.

The process of regression typically involves selecting a suitable regression model such as linear regression, polynomial regression, or logistic regression (used for classification). The model then learns by analyzing historical data, identifying patterns, and creating a mathematical function that best fits the data. It minimizes errors using techniques like the least squares method, adjusting the model iteratively to improve accuracy.

Businesses use regression for financial forecasting, predicting stock prices based on historical market trends. In healthcare, regression helps in predicting patient outcomes based on medical history and lifestyle factors. In marketing, companies analyze customer spending patterns to estimate future sales and optimize advertising budgets. Weather forecasting relies on regression to predict temperature, rainfall, and other meteorological conditions.

Regression is an essential tool in ML, providing valuable insights for decision-making by modeling numerical relationships between variables. Whether predicting prices, trends, or risks, regression enables businesses and researchers to make data-driven decisions with greater confidence.

The following shows a sample pseudocode followed by a Python snippet demonstrating the usage of regression models:

Pseudocode:

```
Input: Features X (e.g., size, location, bedrooms), Target y (e.g., price)
        Step 1: Initialize a regression model
        Step 2: Fit model on (X, y)
        Step 3: Use model to predict the price for a new house
```

Output: `Predicted price`

Python code:

```
from sklearn.linear_model import LinearRegression
X = [[1200], [1400], [1600]]  # Square footage
y = [200000, 220000, 250000]  # House prices
model = LinearRegression()
model.fit(X, y)
print("Predicted price for 1500 sq.ft:", model.predict([[1500]])[0])
```

Classification models

Classification is an ML technique used to categorize data into predefined groups or labels based on input features. It is a type of supervised learning, meaning the model is trained using labeled data to recognize patterns and make accurate predictions on new, unseen data.

Classification works by learning the relationships between input features and their corresponding categories. Imagine an email filtering system that classifies incoming messages as either spam or not spam based on keywords, sender details, and past user interactions. The classification model analyzes these features and assigns each email to one of the two categories.

The process typically involves selecting an appropriate classification algorithm, such as decision trees, **support vector machines** (**SVM**), Naïve Bayes, or neural networks. The model is trained on historical data, learning patterns that define different categories. Once trained, it can predict the category of new data points with a certain level of confidence.

Classification is widely used across industries. In healthcare, it helps diagnose diseases by classifying patient data into different medical conditions. In finance, banks use it to detect fraudulent transactions by categorizing them as normal or suspicious. In image recognition, it enables the identification of objects, faces, and handwritten digits. In customer service, chatbots use classification to understand user queries and provide relevant responses.

Classification is a fundamental tool in ML that enables intelligent decision-making by assigning data points to meaningful categories. Whether improving security, enhancing automation, or streamlining processes, classification plays a crucial role in various applications, making data more structured and actionable.

Supervised learning is widely used in various industries because of its ability to provide accurate and reliable predictions when trained with high-quality labeled data.

The following shows a sample pseudocode followed by a Python snippet demonstrating the usage of classification models:

Pseudocode:

Input: `Email text and labels (spam or not spam)`

      `Step 1: Convert text to numerical features`

      `Step 2: Train a classifier (e.g., Naive Bayes)`

      `Step 3: Predict whether a new email is spam`

Output: `"Spam" or "Not Spam"`

Python code:

```
from sklearn.feature_extraction.text import CountVectorizer
from sklearn.naive_bayes import MultinomialNB
emails = ["Win a free prize", "Meeting tomorrow", "Buy now", "Project update"]
labels = [1, 0, 1, 0]  # 1 = spam, 0 = not spam
vectorizer = CountVectorizer()
X = vectorizer.fit_transform(emails)
model = MultinomialNB()
model.fit(X, labels)
test_email = ["Free money now"]
X_test = vectorizer.transform(test_email)
print("Prediction:", model.predict(X_test)[0])  # Output: 1 = spam
```

Unsupervised learning

Unsupervised learning is a type of ML where a model is trained on data that does not have labeled outputs. Unlike supervised learning, where the model learns from input-output pairs, unsupervised learning finds hidden patterns, relationships, or structures within the data without predefined labels.

Working of unsupervised learning

The following steps outline how unsupervised learning works:

1. **Providing unlabeled data**: The algorithm is fed a dataset containing only input features with no corresponding output labels. For example, in customer segmentation, the data might include customer purchase history, age, and location, but without predefined groupings.

2. **Discovering patterns**: The model analyzes the data and groups similar data points based on their characteristics. It identifies relationships or clusters using statistical techniques without prior knowledge of expected outputs.

3. **Grouping or structuring the data**: The algorithm organizes data points into meaningful clusters or representations, revealing underlying structures.

Techniques used in unsupervised learning

Several popular techniques are used in unsupervised learning, including clustering, dimensionality reduction, anomaly detection, and topic modeling:

*   **Clustering**: Clustering is a type of ML technique used to group similar data points based on certain characteristics. It is an unsupervised learning method, meaning that the model learns patterns and structures in the data without predefined labels.

    Clustering works by organizing data points into groups that share common traits. Imagine you have a basket of mixed fruits, and you want to organize them based on their similarities, such as shape, color, or size. Clustering works in a similar way; it groups data points that share common traits into clusters, helping us find patterns in complex datasets.

    The process of clustering typically involves choosing a clustering algorithm such as k-means, hierarchical clustering, or DBSCAN. It then defines similarity using distance measures like Euclidean distance to determine how close or far data points are from each other. The algorithm assigns data points to clusters based on these similarities and iteratively refines the clusters to improve accuracy.

    Businesses use clustering for customer segmentation, grouping customers based on purchasing behavior to personalize promotions and product recommendations. In computer vision, clustering is used for image segmentation to detect different objects in medical imaging or facial recognition. In cybersecurity, banks and security firms use clustering to identify unusual transactions that might indicate fraud. News websites use clustering to automatically categorize articles on similar topics, making it easier for users to find relevant content.

    Clustering is a powerful tool in ML that helps discover hidden patterns in data. Whether it is used for business, healthcare, or security, clustering simplifies large datasets and makes them more meaningful. Understanding clustering allows us to harness data effectively and make informed decisions based on structured insights.

    The following shows a sample pseudocode followed by a Python snippet demonstrating the usage of the clustering technique.

    Pseudocode:

```
Input: Customer features (e.g., age, spending)
        Step 1: Choose number of clusters (k)
        Step 2: Assign each customer to the nearest cluster center
        Step 3: Recalculate centers and repeat
```

Output: `Customer segments`

Python code:

```
from sklearn.cluster import KMeans
X = [[25, 400], [30, 500], [45, 1500], [50, 1600]]  # Age, Spending
model = KMeans(n_clusters=2)
model.fit(X)
print("Cluster labels:", model.labels_)
```

- **Dimensionality reduction**: Dimensionality reduction is a technique in ML used to simplify complex datasets by reducing the number of input variables while preserving the most important information. It is an essential method when working with high-dimensional data, as it helps improve efficiency, visualization, and model performance.

  Dimensionality reduction works by transforming data into a lower-dimensional space while retaining meaningful patterns. Imagine a dataset with hundreds of variables, such as a collection of images with thousands of pixels. Processing such data can be computationally expensive and difficult to interpret. Dimensionality reduction techniques help by filtering out redundant or less significant features, making the data more manageable without losing critical insights.

  The process typically involves selecting a suitable technique, such as **Principal Component Analysis (PCA)**, **t-Distributed Stochastic Neighbor Embedding (t-SNE)**, or Autoencoders. The algorithm then analyzes correlations between features and projects the data into a new space with fewer dimensions while maintaining essential characteristics. This transformation reduces noise and redundancy while improving computational efficiency.

  Businesses use dimensionality reduction in various applications. In image processing, it helps compress images while maintaining quality. In genetics, researchers use it to analyze high-dimensional biological data to identify key genetic markers. Financial analysts apply it to reduce risk factors in stock market predictions. In natural language processing, dimensionality reduction improves topic modeling and document classification by distilling essential word relationships.

  Dimensionality reduction is a crucial tool in ML, enabling better data interpretation, faster processing, and more efficient modeling. Reducing complexity without sacrificing important information helps unlock meaningful insights from large datasets while optimizing ML performance.

  The following shows a sample pseudocode followed by a Python snippet demonstrating the usage of the dimensionality reduction technique:

Pseudocode:

Input: `High-dimensional dataset X with many features`

> `Step 1: Standardize the data (mean = 0, variance = 1)`
>
> `Step 2: Compute the covariance matrix of X`
>
> `Step 3: Calculate eigenvectors and eigenvalues of the covariance matrix`
>
> `Step 4: Sort eigenvectors by descending eigenvalues`
>
> `Step 5: Select the top k eigenvectors to form a projection matrix`
>
> `Step 6: Transform the data into the lower-dimensional space using the projection matrix`

Output: `Reduced-dimension dataset X_reduced`

Python code:

```python
from sklearn.decomposition import PCA
import numpy as np
X = np.random.rand(10, 5)   # 10 samples with 5 features
pca = PCA(n_components=2)
X_reduced = pca.fit_transform(X)
print("Reduced data shape:", X_reduced.shape)
```

- **Anomaly detection:** Anomaly detection is an ML technique used to identify rare or unusual patterns in data that do not conform to expected behavior. It is particularly useful for detecting fraud, network intrusions, manufacturing defects, and other irregularities that may indicate potential risks or errors.

Anomaly detection works by analyzing data and learning what constitutes normal behavior. Once a pattern of normalcy is established, the algorithm can identify instances that deviate significantly from the expected range. Imagine monitoring credit card transactions; most follow a common spending pattern, but a sudden large transaction in a foreign country might be flagged as an anomaly.

The process typically involves choosing an appropriate anomaly detection method, such as statistical methods, clustering-based techniques, or ML models like isolation forests, autoencoders, and one-class SVMs. The model then evaluates new data points and assigns an anomaly score based on their deviation from normal patterns. The higher the score, the more likely it is that an anomaly has been detected.

Anomaly detection is widely applied across industries. In cybersecurity, it helps detect potential data breaches by identifying unusual access patterns. In finance, it is used for fraud detection by recognizing irregular banking transactions. Manufacturers use it to identify defects in production lines before faulty products reach customers. Healthcare professionals apply anomaly detection to monitor patient vitals and detect early signs of medical conditions.

Anomaly detection is a critical tool in ML that enables businesses and organizations to proactively identify risks, prevent losses, and improve decision-making. Uncovering hidden irregularities in data enhances security, quality control, and operational efficiency in various domains.

The following shows a sample pseudocode followed by a Python snippet demonstrating the usage of anomaly detection:

Pseudocode:

Input: Dataset X containing regular and possibly anomalous data points

    Step 1: Select an anomaly detection algorithm (e.g., Isolation Forest)

    Step 2: Train the model using data X (assumed mostly normal)

    Step 3: For each new data point x:

        - Compute an anomaly score based on its deviation from the training data

    Step 4: Compare score to a predefined threshold:

        - If score exceeds threshold → mark as anomaly

        - Else → mark as normal

Output: Labels or scores indicating anomalous vs. normal data

Python code:

```python
from sklearn.ensemble import IsolationForest
import numpy as np
# Sample dataset: rows are daily transaction amounts (normal + outliers)
X = [[100], [110], [120], [115], [105], [5000], [95], [108], [102], [4900]]
# Initialize the Isolation Forest model
model = IsolationForest(contamination=0.2)  # 20% expected anomalies
model.fit(X)
# Predict anomalies (-1 = anomaly, 1 = normal)
predictions = model.predict(X)
# Display results
for i, value in enumerate(X):
    label = "Anomaly" if predictions[i] == -1 else "Normal"
    print(f"Transaction: {value[0]} → {label}")
```

- **Topic modeling**: It is ML technique used to automatically discover hidden themes or topics in large collections of text data. It is particularly useful for organizing, summarizing, and understanding large volumes of unstructured text, such as news articles, research papers, and customer reviews.

Topic modeling works by analyzing patterns in word usage across documents and grouping similar words together to form topics. Imagine you have thousands of online reviews for a product, and you want to understand common themes without reading each review individually. Topic modeling helps by identifying recurring topics, such as customer satisfaction, product quality, or delivery issues, making it easier to analyze sentiment and trends.

The process typically involves selecting an appropriate algorithm, such as **Latent Dirichlet Allocation (LDA)** or **Non-negative Matrix Factorization (NMF)**. The algorithm scans the text data, learns word associations, and assigns probabilities to words belonging to different topics. Each document is then represented as a mixture of topics, allowing for a deeper understanding of textual data.

Topic modeling is widely applied across industries. In journalism, it helps categorize news articles into different topics, improving content recommendations. In academia, researchers use it to analyze large bodies of literature and identify emerging research trends. Businesses leverage topic modeling for customer feedback analysis, helping them understand key concerns and improve products. Social media analysis assists in identifying trending discussions and public sentiment.

Topic modeling is a powerful tool in ML that enables the automatic extraction of meaningful insights from text data. By uncovering hidden themes and structures, it enhances content organization, trend analysis, and decision-making across various domains.

The following shows a sample pseudocode followed by a Python snippet demonstrating the usage of Topic modeling:

Pseudocode:

Input: `Collection of text documents D`

```
Step 1: Preprocess documents (remove stopwords, tokenize, lowercase)
Step 2: Convert documents into a document-term matrix (DTM)
Step 3: Choose the number of topics (K)
Step 4: Initialize topic distributions randomly
Step 5: For each word in each document, assign it to a topic based
on word-topic and topic-document probabilities
Step 6: Repeat until topic distributions converge (e.g., via Gibbs
Sampling or Variational Inference)
```

Output: Topics (groupings of keywords) and topic distributions for each document

Python code:

```python
from sklearn.feature_extraction.text import CountVectorizer
from sklearn.decomposition import LatentDirichletAllocation
import nltk
import string
# Sample collection of documents
documents = [
    "The battery life of this phone is amazing.",
    "Excellent camera quality and photo resolution.",
    "The delivery was late and the packaging was poor.",
    "Customer service was very helpful and friendly.",
    "I love the screen quality and elegant design."
]
# Step 1: Preprocess documents
def preprocess(text):
    # Lowercase
    text = text.lower()
    # Remove punctuation
    text = text.translate(str.maketrans('', '', string.punctuation))
    # Tokenize and remove stopwords
    tokens = text.split()
    stopwords = set(nltk.corpus.stopwords.words('english'))
    tokens = [word for word in tokens if word not in stopwords]
    return " ".join(tokens)
# Download NLTK stopwords if not already available
nltk.download('stopwords')
# Apply preprocessing to all documents
processed_docs = [preprocess(doc) for doc in documents]
# Step 2: Convert to Document-Term Matrix (DTM)
vectorizer = CountVectorizer()
X = vectorizer.fit_transform(processed_docs)
# Step 3: Choose number of topics (K)
```

```
K = 2
# Step 4-6: Train LDA using Variational Inference
lda = LatentDirichletAllocation(n_components=K, random_state=42)
lda.fit(X)
# Output: Show top words per topic
feature_names = vectorizer.get_feature_names_out()
for idx, topic in enumerate(lda.components_):
    top_words = [feature_names[i] for i in topic.argsort()[-5:][::-1]]
    print(f"Topic #{idx + 1}: {', '.join(top_words)}")
# Optional: Topic distribution per document
doc_topics = lda.transform(X)
for i, topic_probs in enumerate(doc_topics):
    print(f"Document {i + 1} topic distribution: {topic_probs}")
```

Hybrid learning

ML techniques often fall into two primary categories: supervised and unsupervised learning. However, some advanced approaches blend elements of both, creating a powerful hybrid that leverages the strengths of each. These hybrid methods are particularly useful when dealing with complex data structures, where a combination of labeled and unlabeled data can yield more accurate and efficient results.

Imagine trying to sort a massive pile of books in a library without any predefined cataloging system. At first, you might start by grouping books with similar characteristics—perhaps those with similar cover designs, authors, or genres. This is akin to unsupervised learning, where the model identifies hidden patterns in data without explicit labels. Once an initial grouping is established, a librarian might step in to refine the categorization by labeling sections and organizing them more precisely. This step represents supervised learning, where a system is trained using labeled data to improve accuracy and decision-making.

One of the most common hybrid approaches is semi-supervised learning, where a model is trained on a small set of labeled data alongside a much larger volume of unlabeled data. This technique is widely used in areas such as medical imaging, where manually labeling thousands of scans is time-consuming and expensive. By first identifying patterns in the images and then applying supervised learning to refine the model, the system can accurately classify diseases with minimal human intervention.

Another form of hybrid learning is self-supervised learning, where a model generates its own labels by recognizing structures in the data. This is particularly useful in natural language processing, where models learn word relationships without human annotation. By training itself on massive text datasets, the model gradually builds an understanding of context, grammar, and meaning.

A more advanced application is found in reinforcement learning with unsupervised pretraining, where an AI agent first explores an environment in an unsupervised manner before receiving supervised signals through rewards. This method is widely used in autonomous systems, including robotics and self-driving cars, where an agent must learn from experience before being fine-tuned with labeled instructions.

Hybrid learning methods also play a crucial role in business applications. For example, companies can first use clustering techniques to segment customers based on their purchasing behavior and then apply supervised learning to classify these segments into predefined customer categories. This approach enables businesses to personalize marketing strategies and improve customer engagement.

Beyond these traditional hybrid approaches, some modern advancements have further demonstrated the power of combining supervised and unsupervised learning techniques. Two key examples of such advancements are recommendation systems and foundation models:

- **Recommendation systems** are another example of hybrid learning. These systems combine collaborative filtering, which is based on user interactions and preferences, with content-based filtering, which analyzes product characteristics and similarities. For instance, a streaming platform like Netflix first groups users with similar viewing habits (unsupervised clustering) and then refines recommendations using past user ratings and preferences (supervised learning). This hybrid approach enhances personalization, ensuring users receive highly relevant content suggestions.

- **Foundation models** are a recent advancement in hybrid learning, where a single large-scale model is pre-trained on massive amounts of data and then fine-tuned for specific tasks. These models, such as OpenAI's GPT and Google's BERT, initially learn through unsupervised learning by analyzing vast, unlabeled datasets, extracting general knowledge and representations of language, vision, or other domains. They are then adapted through supervised fine-tuning to solve specific downstream tasks such as sentiment analysis, translation, or image captioning.

  Unlike traditional models, which are typically trained from scratch on a narrow, task-specific dataset, foundation models benefit from broad, general pretraining and can transfer their knowledge across a wide range of applications. This not only reduces the need for large volumes of labeled data for every new task but also enables faster deployment and improved performance, especially in low-resource or few-shot learning scenarios. The hybrid learning approach underpinning foundation models allows them to generalize better, adapt more flexibly, and scale efficiently across diverse domains, demonstrating a significant leap forward from conventional ML pipelines.

- However, hybrid learning is not without limitations. One of the primary challenges is the complexity of implementation, integrating both supervised and unsupervised components often requires advanced model design, careful data handling, and increased computational resources. Additionally, the effectiveness of hybrid methods can heavily depend on the quality and balance of labeled and unlabeled data. If labeled data is scarce or noisy, or if the unsupervised component introduces incorrect assumptions, the overall model performance may suffer. Interpretability can also be a concern, as the layered learning process can obscure how decisions are made, making it harder to audit or debug the system. As such, while hybrid learning provides a powerful framework, it must be carefully managed to avoid overfitting, misclassification, or unintended bias.

By combining the exploratory nature of unsupervised learning with the precision of supervised learning, hybrid ML approaches provide a more scalable, efficient, and intelligent way to handle vast amounts of data. Whether detecting fraud, recommending personalized content, leveraging foundation models, or advancing medical diagnostics, these methods bridge the gap between raw data and meaningful insights, paving the way for more adaptive and capable AI systems.

Comparison of supervised and unsupervised learning

The following tables help illustrate the key differences between supervised and unsupervised learning:

Aspect	Supervised learning	Unsupervised learning
Definition	Trains on labeled data with known outputs.	Trains on unlabeled data to discover hidden patterns.
Goal	Learn a mapping from inputs to known outputs for accurate prediction.	Identify structure, groupings, or anomalies in data without predefined labels.
Input data	Labeled (input-output pairs).	Unlabeled (only input features).
Output type	Predicts specific categories (classification) or continuous values (regression).	Finds hidden patterns, clusters, anomalies, or topics.
Common algorithms	Linear/Polynomial regression, logistic regression, decision trees, SVM, Naïve Bayes, neural networks.	K-means, hierarchical clustering, DBSCAN, PCA, t-SNE, autoencoders, LDA.
Problem types	Regression (e.g., house price prediction), classification (e.g., spam detection).	Clustering (e.g., customer segmentation), dimensionality reduction (e.g., PCA), anomaly detection, and topic modeling.

Example use cases	Email spam filtering, housing price estimation, disease diagnosis, fraud detection, and image recognition.	Grouping customer types, market segmentation, fraud anomaly detection, document topic analysis, and social media trend analysis.
Evaluation metrics	Accuracy, precision, recall, F1 score, mean squared error, and root mean squared error (depending on task type).	Silhouette score, cluster purity, Davies-Bouldin index, reconstruction error (depending on technique).
Data labeling needs	Requires labeled datasets, often with human annotation.	No labeling required works with raw, unstructured data.
Human intervention	More manual effort is needed for data labeling and preparing the ground truth.	Less manual work for setup, but human interpretation is often needed after the results.
Interpretability	Easier to interpret and validate results due to known expected outputs.	Interpretation of output can be abstract (e.g., clusters or topics may need further labeling or exploration).
Scalability	Scales well if labels are available at a large scale.	Easily scales with large unlabeled datasets.
Overfitting risk	Prone to overfitting, especially with small or biased datasets; requires tuning.	Less prone to overfitting due to a lack of direct supervision, but may identify noise as a pattern.
Analogy	A student learning with a textbook and an answer key.	A student exploring ideas and grouping them without knowing the test questions.

Table 7.1: Comparison of supervised and unsupervised learning

Conclusion

Framing business problems as ML problems is a critical first step in leveraging the full potential of ML for data-driven decision-making. Throughout this chapter, we have explored the importance of correctly identifying problems suitable for ML, distinguishing between supervised and unsupervised learning, and selecting the right ML models based on business objectives.

By understanding the characteristics of problems that benefit from ML, businesses can determine when ML is the best approach and when traditional methods might be more appropriate. Supervised learning models, such as classification and regression, excel at making accurate predictions based on historical data, while unsupervised learning methods, such as clustering and anomaly detection, help uncover hidden patterns in complex datasets. Additionally, hybrid learning approaches, including recommendation systems and foundation models, highlight the evolving landscape of ML solutions that integrate both supervised and unsupervised techniques to optimize performance.

The practical examples provided in this chapter illustrate how ML can be effectively applied to real-world business scenarios, such as customer sentiment analysis, predictive maintenance, and fraud detection. By framing business challenges in a structured ML context, organizations can harness data more effectively, drive strategic decisions, and improve automation processes.

As ML continues to evolve, the ability to frame problems appropriately will remain a valuable skill for decision-makers, data scientists, and business leaders. By applying the principles outlined in this chapter, businesses can confidently implement ML solutions that align with their goals, maximize efficiency, and gain a competitive advantage in an increasingly data-driven world.

In the next chapter, you will learn how to navigate the wide range of ML models and select the best fit for your data and problem.

Multiple choice questions

1. **What is the main goal of framing business problems as ML problems?**

    a. To automate all business processes

    b. To transform raw data into actionable insights and drive strategic decisions

    c. To replace human decision-making with ML

    d. To increase computational complexity in business operations

2. **Which of the following is not a characteristic of problems suitable for ML?**

    a. Availability of sufficient high-quality data

    b. Clear objectives and metrics

    c. Problems requiring deterministic solutions

    d. Patterns in data that can be learned

3. **When is it appropriate to use simpler statistical methods instead of ML?**

    a. When dealing with large amounts of labeled data

    b. When the problem requires complex pattern recognition

    c. When basic statistical analysis can provide the necessary insights

    d. When the goal is to automate decision-making processes

4. **What is the key difference between supervised and unsupervised learning?**

    a. The presence or absence of labels in the training data

    b. The complexity of the algorithms used

    c. The size of the dataset required

    d. The computational resources needed

5. **Which of the following is an example of a supervised learning task?**

    a. Customer segmentation based on purchasing behavior

    b. Image compression using dimensionality reduction techniques

    c. Email spam detection using labeled examples

    d. Anomaly detection in network traffic data

6. **In which scenario would unsupervised learning be most appropriate?**

    a. Predicting customer churn based on historical data with labeled outcomes

    b. Forecasting stock prices using past stock prices and economic indicators

    c. Discovering new customer segments from unlabeled transaction data

    d. Calculating monthly loan repayments using deterministic formulas

7. **What are foundation models in the context of ML?**

    a. Simple statistical models used for basic data analysis

    b. Large-scale models pre-trained on vast amounts of data that can be fine-tuned for specific tasks

    c. Deterministic algorithms that provide exact solutions to problems

    d. Models that combine both supervised and unsupervised learning techniques

8. **Which of the following is not a common use case for unsupervised learning?**

    a. Clustering

    b. Dimensionality reduction

    c. Regression

    d. Recommendation systems

9. **When choosing between supervised and unsupervised learning, what is one of the key decision criteria for selecting supervised learning?**

    a. Absence of labeled data

    b. Interest in discovering hidden structures or patterns

    c. Need for precise predictions or classifications

    d. Need for data exploration or preprocessing

10. **In the practical example of market basket analysis, which unsupervised learning technique is used to identify groups of products frequently bought together?**

    a. Regression

    b. Classification

    c. Clustering

    d. Dimensionality reduction

Answer key

1. b

2. c

3. c

4. a

5. c

6. c

7. b

8. c

9. c

10. c

Join our Discord space

Join our Discord workspace for latest updates, offers, tech happenings around the world, new releases, and sessions with the authors:

https://discord.bpbonline.com

CHAPTER 8
Selecting Appropriate ML Models

Introduction

Selecting the right model for a given problem is a crucial step that can significantly impact the success of your project. With a plethora of models available, each with its strengths and weaknesses, making an informed choice is essential. This chapter will guide you through the diverse landscape of **machine learning** (**ML**) models, from traditional algorithms like logistic regression and decision trees to advanced techniques like neural networks and ensemble methods.

Imagine you are an architect tasked with designing a building. You have a variety of tools and materials at your disposal; each suited for different aspects of construction. Similarly, as a ML practitioner, you have an array of models, each designed to excel at specific types of problems and data. Your challenge is to select the model that will provide the most robust and accurate solution for your particular task.

In this chapter, we will explore some common ML models like **eXtreme Gradient Boosting** (**XGBoost**), logistic regression, and decision trees, as well as the power of neural networks, including RNNs and CNNs. We will also discuss ensemble methods and transfer learning techniques, along with model selection criteria based on data types and problem characteristics. Finally, we will introduce AWS tools and services that can help you efficiently implement your chosen models.

Structure

This chapter covers the following topics:

- Overview of common ML models
- Understanding neural networks
- Insights into ensemble and transfer learning techniques
- Model selection criteria based on data and problem type
- AWS tools and services for model implementation

Objectives

This chapter provides a concise overview of key ML models and their applications. You will learn core concepts behind models like XGBoost, logistic regression, decision trees, random forests, and neural networks (including **convolutional neural networks (CNNs)** and **recurrent neural networks (RNNs)**). The focus is on understanding each model's strengths, limitations, and suitability for different data types and tasks such as classification, regression, and time series prediction.

You will explore advanced techniques like ensemble learning and transfer learning, which enhance model performance and adaptability. The chapter also introduces essential AWS tools, SageMaker, deep learning AMIs, and Lambda, for deploying ML workflows efficiently. The key focus for AWS certification is this chapter, which emphasizes understanding when and why to use specific models rather than just how to implement them. Pay particular attention to the decision-making process for model selection, including trade-offs between model complexity, interpretability, performance, and operational requirements. AWS exams prioritize architectural thinking and appropriate service selection over low-level implementation details.

By the end, you will be equipped to choose the right model based on data characteristics, task requirements, and resource constraints. Real-world examples will help solidify your understanding and prepare you for both practical ML projects and the AWS Certified ML Specialty exam.

Overview of common ML models

This section discusses some popular ML models that the reader should be aware of for the certification.

XGBoost

XGBoost is an advanced implementation of gradient boosting machines. It is a powerful and versatile ML algorithm designed for speed and performance. Developed by *Tianqi*

Chen, XGBoost has gained widespread popularity in the data science community due to its effectiveness in a variety of ML tasks.

Working of XGBoost

XGBoost works on the principle of ensemble learning, specifically using a technique called gradient boosting. Here is a simplified explanation of how it operates:

1. **Initial prediction**: XGBoost begins by making a simple first guess before improving its predictions. For regression problems, this initial guess is usually the average value of the target variable. For classification problems, it starts with a basic probability estimate (log-odds) of each class before refining its predictions.

2. **Sequential tree building**: It then builds decision trees sequentially. Each new tree aims to correct the errors made by the combined ensemble of previous trees.

3. **Gradient boosting**: The algorithm uses the gradient of the loss function to identify the shortcomings of the current model's predictions.

4. **Feature importance**: While constructing the tree, XGBoost evaluates and scores the importance of each feature.

5. **Regularization**: XGBoost employs regularization techniques to prevent overfitting, allowing it to generate more generalizable models

6. **Optimization**: The algorithm optimizes both the model's structure and the weights of individual trees to minimize the overall loss function.

Let us now look at the key features and advantages of using XGBoost algorithm.

Key features and advantages

XGBoost is a powerful and efficient ML algorithm known for its speed, flexibility, and robust performance. The following are some of its key features that make it a popular choice for a wide range of ML tasks:

*   **Speed and performance**: XGBoost is designed for speed. It can automatically use parallel processing, making it significantly faster than traditional gradient boosting algorithms.

*   **Regularization**: Built-in L1 (Lasso) and L2 (Ridge) regularization help prevent overfitting, resulting in better-generalized models.

*   **Handling missing values**: XGBoost can automatically handle missing values, learning the best direction to take for missing data during the training process.

*   **Tree pruning**: The algorithm uses a 'max_depth' parameter to grow trees sideways, which can lead to better performance than growing very deep trees.

- **Built-in cross-validation**: XGBoost allows you to run a cross-validation at each iteration of the boosting process, making it easier to get the exact optimum number of boosting iterations.

- **Early stopping**: XGBoost includes early stopping functionality that automatically halts training when the model's performance on a validation set stops improving. This prevents overfitting and reduces unnecessary computational overhead, making it particularly valuable for large datasets or when computational resources are limited.

- **Flexibility**: It works well with a variety of ML tasks, including regression, classification, and ranking problems

- **Feature importance**: XGBoost provides a clear view of which features are most important in predicting the target variable.

These features collectively make XGBoost one of the most effective and widely used algorithms in ML, providing both speed and accuracy while handling complex datasets with ease.

Best use cases and practical examples

XGBoost shines in many areas of ML. Here are some prime use cases:

- **Structured/Tabular data**: XGBoost excels with structured data, making it ideal for many business and scientific applications. For example, predicting customer churn for a telecom company based on usage patterns, demographics, and service history.

- **Kaggle and other ML competitions**: XGBoost has been the algorithm of choice for many winning solutions in data science competitions. For example, predicting house prices based on various features like location, size, age, etc.

- **Fraud detection**: XGBoost's ability to handle imbalanced datasets makes it suitable for fraud detection scenarios. For example, identifying fraudulent credit card transactions based on transaction history and user behavior.

- **Ad click prediction**: The algorithm's speed and accuracy make it excellent for real-time predictions. For example, predicting the likelihood of a user clicking on a specific advertisement.

- **Recommendation systems**: XGBoost can be used to predict user ratings or preferences. For example, recommending movies to users based on their viewing history and preferences.

- **Medicine and healthcare**: XGBoost's interpretability makes it valuable in healthcare applications. For example, predicting the likelihood of a patient being readmitted to a hospital based on their medical history and current condition.

Remember, while XGBoost is powerful, it is not always the best solution for every problem. It is particularly well-suited for structured data problems where interpretability is important, and computational resources are not a major constraint. For very large datasets or when dealing with unstructured data like images or text, other algorithms (like deep learning models) might be more appropriate.

Disadvantages of XGBoost

While XGBoost is powerful and widely used, it is not without its drawbacks:

- **Complexity**: XGBoost models can be complex and may require careful tuning of hyperparameters to achieve optimal performance.

- **Overfitting risk**: Despite built-in regularization, XGBoost can still overfit, especially on small datasets or with too many boosting rounds.

- **Computational resources**: XGBoost can be memory-intensive and computationally expensive, particularly for large datasets.

- **Less effective for unstructured data**: XGBoost is not inherently suited for unstructured data like images, audio, or text.

- **Black box nature**: While feature importance is provided, the decision-making process can still be hard to interpret, especially compared to simpler models.

- **Training time**: Although fast compared to other boosting algorithms, training time can still be significant for large datasets or complex problems.

While XGBoost is a powerful and versatile algorithm, it is not always the best choice for every ML problem. In certain scenarios, other models may provide better performance, efficiency, or interpretability. The following are some cases where alternative approaches might be more suitable:

- **Deep learning tasks**: For tasks typically handled by neural networks, such as image recognition or natural language processing, XGBoost is generally not the best choice. For example, classifying images of handwritten digits. A **convolutional neural network (CNN)** would likely perform better in this case.

- **Very large datasets**: When dealing with extremely large datasets that do not fit into memory, other algorithms or distributed versions of gradient boosting might be more suitable. For example, analyzing petabytes of satellite imagery data. A distributed system like Apache Spark with MLlib might be more appropriate here.

- **Real-time systems with strict latency requirements**: In systems where prediction speed is critical and must be in microseconds, simpler models might be preferred. For example, high-frequency trading systems require decision-making to be near-instantaneous.

- **Highly interpretable models required**: When model interpretability is crucial, simpler models like linear regression or decision trees might be more appropriate. For example, credit scoring in highly regulated industries where every decision must be clearly explainable.

- **Sparse high-dimensional data**: In some cases, with very high-dimensional sparse data, linear models might perform better. For example, text classification with a large vocabulary. A simple linear model like logistic regression might perform comparably or better.

- **Online learning scenarios**: XGBoost is not designed for online learning, where the model needs to adapt to new data in real-time. For example, adapting to user preferences on a streaming platform in real-time. Online learning algorithms would be more suitable for this scenario.

Understanding the limitations of XGBoost is just as important as recognizing its strengths. Choosing the right algorithm depends on the specific needs of your problem, including data size, interpretability, real-time requirements, and computational constraints. By considering these factors, you can ensure that you select the most effective model for your use case.

Logistic regression

Logistic regression is a fundamental statistical method used for binary classification problems. Despite its name, it is a classification algorithm rather than a regression algorithm. Logistic regression is widely used due to its simplicity, interpretability, and efficiency.

The primary goal of logistic regression is to estimate the probability that an instance belongs to a particular class. It is particularly useful when you need to understand the relationship between one dependent binary variable and one or more independent variables.

Logistic regression works by applying the logistic function (also known as the **sigmoid function**) to a linear combination of input features. Here is a step-by-step explanation:

1. **Linear combination**: First, it calculates a weighted sum of the input features:

$$z = b_0 + b_1 x_1 + b_2 x_2 + \ldots + b_n x_n$$

   Where b_0 is the bias term, and b_1, b_2, ..., b_n are the weights for the input features $x_1, x_2, \ldots, x_n$.

2. **Sigmoid function**: The result is then passed through the sigmoid function:

$$\sigma(z) = 1 / (1 + e^{(-z)})$$

   This transforms the output to a value between *0* and *1*, which can be interpreted as a probability.

3. **Decision boundary**: A threshold (typically 0.5) is used to classify the instance. If the probability is above the threshold, the instance is classified as the positive class; otherwise, it is classified as the negative class.

4. **Training**: The model is trained using an optimization algorithm (often gradient descent) to find the weights that minimize the difference between predicted probabilities and actual class labels.

Working of logistic regression

Imagine you are trying to decide whether to play outside or not based on the weather. You look at three things: temperature, cloudiness, and wind speed. Logistic regression is like a smart weather decision-maker. Here is how it works:

Gathering information: You collect information about the weather:

- Temperature (let us say 70°F)

- Cloudiness (30% cloudy)

- Wind speed (5 mph)

Weighing the importance: The smart decision-maker gives importance to each piece of information:

- Temperature is very important (weight: 3)

- Cloudiness is somewhat important (weight: 2)

- Wind speed is less important (weight: 1)

Doing the math: It multiplies each piece of information by its importance and adds them up:

$$(70 \times 3) + (30 \times 2) + (5 \times 1) = 210 + 60 + 5 = 275$$

Using a special calculator: This number (275) is put into a special calculator (that is, the sigmoid function). This calculator always gives a number between 0 and 1.

Make a decision:

- If the calculator gives a number bigger than 0.5, it says *Yes, play outside!*

- If it is smaller than 0.5, it says *No, stay inside.*

Learning and improving: The smart decision-maker checks if their decision was right. If it was wrong, it adjusts the importance it gives to temperature, cloudiness, and wind speed. It keeps doing this until it gets really good at making the right decision.

That is how logistic regression works! It takes information, weighs its importance, does some math, and makes a yes-or-no decision. And it keeps learning to make better decisions over time.

Advantages of logistic regression

Logistic regression remains a popular choice for many classification tasks due to its simplicity, efficiency, and reliability. The following are some key advantages that make it a strong candidate for various ML applications:

- **Simplicity and interpretability**: The model is easy to understand and interpret. The weights directly indicate the importance of each feature.

- **Efficiency**: It is computationally efficient and does not require high processing power, making it suitable for large datasets.

- **Probabilistic output**: It provides probability scores rather than just classifications, which can be useful in many applications.

- **Works well with linearly separable classes**: When classes are linearly separable, logistic regression can perform very well.

- **Less prone to overfitting**: Especially when L1 or L2 regularization is used, logistic regression is less likely to overfit compared to more complex models.

- **Handles multi-class problems**: It can be extended to handle multi-class classification problems using techniques like one vs. rest.

Now, let us look into the limitations of using the logistic regression algorithm.

Log odds interpretation

When logistic regression gives you results, the numbers (called coefficients) tell you how much each factor affects your prediction. Here is how to read them:

What the numbers mean:

- **Positive numbers** = this factor makes the *yes* outcome more likely

- **Negative numbers** = this factor makes the *yes* outcome less likely

- **Bigger numbers** = stronger effect

- **Temperature coefficient = +0.5**: Higher temperature increases log odds of rain

- **Cloudiness coefficient = -0.3**: More cloudiness decreases log odds of rain. This would indeed seem suspicious for rain prediction!

Tip: **The actual numbers are hard to interpret directly, but the positive/negative sign and relative size tell you what's important and in which direction each factor pushes your prediction.**

Limitations of logistic regression

While logistic regression is a powerful and widely used algorithm, it also has limitations that can impact its effectiveness in specific scenarios. Some key challenges to consider when using logistic regression are as follows:

- **Assumes linearity**: It assumes a linear relationship between the features and the log odds of the outcome, which may not always be the case in real-world scenarios.

- **Limited complexity**: It may underperform on complex datasets where the decision boundary is highly non-linear.

- **Requires more data**: For stable results, logistic regression typically requires larger sample sizes compared to some other techniques.

- **Sensitive to outliers**: The model can be significantly affected by outliers in the dataset

- **Assumes independence**: It assumes that the features are independent, which is often not true in real-world data.

- **Difficulty with imbalanced data**: Logistic regression can struggle with highly imbalanced datasets without proper adjustments.

Suitable applications and examples

Logistic regression is widely used across various industries for **binary classification problems**, where the goal is to predict an outcome with two possible values, such as **yes/no**, **success/ failure**, or **spam/not spam**. Its simplicity and interpretability make it popular for applications where clear decision-making is important. The following are some common real-world use cases where logistic regression is effectively applied:

- **Credit scoring**: Predicting whether a loan applicant will default based on their financial history, income, and other relevant factors.

- **Medical diagnosis**: Estimating the probability of a patient having a particular disease based on symptoms and test results.

- **Marketing**: Predicting whether a customer will respond to a marketing campaign based on demographic information and past behavior.

- **Spam detection**: Classifying emails as spam or not spam based on the content and metadata of the email.

- **Customer churn prediction**: Predicting whether a customer is likely to leave a service based on usage patterns and customer information.

- **Quality control**: In manufacturing, predicting whether a product will pass or fail quality checks based on various measurements.

- **Election forecasting**: Estimating the probability of a candidate winning an election based on polling data and demographic information.

Logistic regression is best suited for problems where you need a clear, interpretable model, and your data suggests a roughly linear relationship between the features and the log-odds of the outcome. It is often used as a baseline model in binary classification tasks due to its simplicity and interpretability. However, for more complex relationships or when dealing with high-dimensional data, more advanced techniques like decision trees, random forests, or neural networks might be more appropriate.

Use cases not suitable for logistic regression

While logistic regression is versatile, there are several scenarios where it may not be the best choice:

- **Complex non-linear relationships**: Predicting house prices based on multiple features like location, size, and amenities. The relationship between these features and price is often non-linear, making more complex models like random forests or neural networks more suitable.

- **Image classification**: Classifying images of different animal species. Logistic regression does not inherently handle the spatial relationships in image data, making CNNs a better choice.

- **Sequential data analysis**: Predicting the next word in a sentence or analyzing time-series data. Logistic regression does not account for the sequential nature of data, making models like **recurrent neural networks (RNNs)** more appropriate.

- **Multi-label classification**: Categorizing news articles into multiple, non-exclusive topics (e.g., an article could be about both *Technology* and *Business*). While logistic regression can be adapted for this, other methods like multi-label random forests often perform better.

- **High-dimensional data with complex interactions**: Analyzing genetic data to predict disease risk, where there are thousands of genetic markers with complex interactions. Techniques like support vector machines or ensemble methods might be more effective.

- **Recommendation systems**: Suggesting products to users based on their past behavior and similarities to other users. Collaborative filtering or matrix factorization techniques are typically more effective for this type of problem.

- **Anomaly detection in complex systems**: Detecting unusual patterns in network traffic that might indicate a security breach. The simplicity of logistic regression may miss subtle, complex patterns that methods like isolation forests or autoencoders could capture.

- **Hierarchical classification**: Classifying species of animals where there is a hierarchical structure (Kingdom | Phylum | Class | Order | Family | Genus | Species).

Hierarchical classification models or decision trees are more naturally suited to this type of problem.

- **Problems requiring feature learning**: In natural language processing tasks like sentiment analysis, where understanding context and nuance is crucial. Deep learning models that can learn features from raw text (like BERT or transformers) typically outperform logistic regression on raw word counts.

- **Very large-scale problems**: Click-through rate prediction in online advertising, where you have billions of data points and need real-time predictions. While logistic regression can work, more specialized algorithms like field-aware factorization machines might be more efficient at this scale.

While logistic regression is a simple and effective model for many classification problems, it has limitations, particularly when dealing with complex, non-linear relationships in data. In cases where the decision boundary is not linear, logistic regression may struggle to capture patterns effectively. Additionally, it assumes that input features are independent, which is often not the case in real-world datasets.

To address these challenges, more flexible models like decision trees can be used. Decision trees do not assume a linear relationship between features and the target variable, making them well-suited for datasets with intricate structures. Unlike logistic regression, which applies a mathematical function to determine probabilities, decision trees use a series of logical if-else conditions to split the data and make predictions. These properties make decision trees a powerful alternative, especially when interpretability and non-linearity are important considerations.

Let us now explore decision trees, how they work, and why they are a valuable tool in ML.

Decision trees

A decision tree is a popular and intuitive ML algorithm used for classification and regression tasks. It represents a model of decisions and their possible consequences in a tree-like structure. Each internal node represents a test on an attribute, each branch represents the outcome of the test, and each leaf node represents a class label (for classification) or a continuous value (for regression).

Working of decision trees

Here is a simplified explanation of how decision trees operate:

1. **Initial split**: The process begins with the entire dataset. The algorithm selects the best attribute and threshold to split the data into subsets. This split is based on criteria like Gini impurity or information gain for classification, and **mean squared error (MSE)** for regression.

2. **Recursive splitting**: Each subset is then split further using the same logic. The goal is to create nodes that increase the purity of the target variable within the subsets. This process continues recursively, creating a tree structure.

3. **Stopping criteria**: The recursive splitting stops when a stopping criterion is met. This could be a maximum tree depth, a minimum number of samples in a node, or when no further improvement can be made.

4. **Leaf nodes**: Once the stopping criteria are met, the leaf nodes are assigned a class label (in classification) or a continuous value (in regression). These leaf nodes represent the final predictions of the model.

Key features and advantages

Decision trees are widely used in ML due to their **simplicity, flexibility, and interpretability**. The following are some key features and advantages that make them a powerful tool for various tasks:

- **Simplicity and interpretability**: Decision trees are easy to understand and interpret. The tree structure can be visualized, making it simple to explain decisions to stakeholders.

- **Handling non-linear relationships**: Decision trees can capture non-linear relationships between features and the target variable.

- **Minimal data preparation**: They require little data preprocessing, such as scaling or normalization. They can handle both numerical and categorical data.

- **Feature importance**: Decision trees can provide a clear indication of which features are most important for prediction.

- **Robustness to outliers**: They are relatively robust to outliers compared to other algorithms.

- **Pruning techniques**: Decision trees use pruning methods to prevent overfitting and improve generalization. Pre-pruning stops tree growth early based on criteria like maximum depth or minimum samples per leaf, while post-pruning removes branches after the full tree is built. These techniques are fundamental to ensemble methods like random forest and XGBoost, where pruning helps create diverse, well-performing base learners that combine effectively in the ensemble.

Best use cases and practical examples

Decision trees are versatile and can be applied to various ML tasks. Here are some prime use cases:

- **Credit risk assessment**: Predicting whether a loan applicant is likely to default based on their financial history and demographic information.

- **Medical diagnosis**: Classifying patients as having a particular disease based on their symptoms and medical history.

- **Customer segmentation**: Grouping customers into different segments for targeted marketing based on their behavior and preferences.

- **Predicting sales**: Estimating future sales based on past sales data, advertising expenditure, and other relevant features.

- **Fraud detection**: Identifying fraudulent transactions based on transaction patterns and user behavior.

Disadvantages of decision trees

While decision trees are powerful and widely used, they have certain limitations:

1. **Overfitting**: Decision trees can easily overfit, especially when the tree is very deep. Pruning techniques and ensemble methods like random forests can help mitigate this.

2. **Instability**: Small changes in the data can result in large changes in the structure of the tree, making it less stable.

3. **Bias in splits**: They can be biased towards features with more levels (categories). This can be addressed by using ensemble methods.

4. **Complex trees**: As the complexity of the problem increases, the tree can become very complex and less interpretable.

There are several use cases where decision trees may not be appropriate.

While decision trees are a powerful and versatile tool for many ML applications, there are certain scenarios where they may not be the best choice. In cases involving high-dimensional data, real-time predictions, or unstructured datasets, other algorithms may offer better performance, efficiency, or accuracy. The following are some situations where decision trees might not be the most suitable option:

- **High-dimensional data**: For datasets with a large number of features, decision trees might not perform as well as other algorithms like support vector machines or neural networks.

- **Small datasets**: On very small datasets, decision trees can overfit easily. Simpler models might be more appropriate.

- **Real-time predictions**: For real-time predictions where speed is critical, simpler models might be preferred due to the overhead of traversing the tree structure.

- **Unstructured data**: Decision trees are not well-suited for unstructured data like text, images, or audio. Other algorithms like CNNs (for images) or RNNs (for text) might be more suitable.

Random forests

Random forest is a versatile and powerful ML algorithm that leverages the power of multiple decision trees to make more accurate and robust predictions. Developed by *Leo Breiman* and *Adele Cutler*, random forests can be used for both classification and regression tasks. The core idea behind random forests is to build a *forest* of decision trees, each trained on different parts of the same training set and then combine their predictions.

Working of random forests

Here is a simplified explanation of how random forests operate:

1. **Bootstrap sampling**: The algorithm starts by creating multiple subsets of the original dataset using a technique called bootstrap sampling. Each subset is created by randomly selecting samples from the original dataset with replacement.

2. **Decision tree training**: For each subset, a decision tree is trained independently. However, unlike traditional decision trees, random forests introduce additional randomness. At each split in the tree, a random subset of features is chosen, and the best feature from this subset is used for splitting.

3. **Ensemble prediction**: Once all the trees are trained, the predictions of all trees are combined. For classification tasks, the final prediction is the majority vote of all trees. For regression tasks, the final prediction is the average of the predictions of all trees.

Key features and advantages

Building on the strengths of decision trees, **random forests** offer a more robust and reliable approach by combining multiple trees to improve accuracy and reduce overfitting. This ensemble method enhances model performance while maintaining interpretability. The following are some key features and advantages of random forests:

- **Improved accuracy**: By averaging multiple decision trees, random forests reduce the risk of overfitting and generally provide better performance compared to individual decision trees.

- **Robustness to overfitting**: The randomness introduced in the tree-building process helps in reducing overfitting, especially for high-dimensional data.

- **Handling missing values**: Random forests can handle missing values naturally by using surrogate splits, making them robust in the presence of incomplete data.

- **Feature importance**: Like decision trees, random forests can provide insights into feature importance, helping in feature selection and understanding the data better.

- **Scalability**: Random forests are easily parallelizable and can handle large datasets efficiently.

- **Out-of-bag (OOB) error estimation**: Random forests provide a built-in validation method called **OOB error**. Since each tree is trained on a bootstrap sample (about 63% of the data), the remaining 37% of samples (called **OOB samples**) can be used to test that tree's performance. This gives an unbiased estimate of the model's generalization error without needing a separate validation set, making it particularly useful for model evaluation and hyperparameter tuning.

Best use cases and practical examples

Random forests are highly versatile and can be applied to a wide range of ML tasks. Here are some prime use cases:

- **Customer churn prediction**: Predicting whether a customer is likely to stop using a service based on their usage patterns and demographic information.

- **Credit scoring**: Assessing the creditworthiness of loan applicants based on their financial history and other relevant factors.

- **Medical diagnosis**: Classifying patients as having a particular disease based on their symptoms and medical history.

- **Stock market prediction**: Predicting stock prices or market trends based on historical data and other financial indicators.

- **Fraud detection**: Identifying fraudulent transactions by analyzing patterns in transaction data.

Disadvantages of random forests

While random forests are powerful and widely used, they have certain limitations:

- **Complexity**: The model can become complex and less interpretable as the number of trees increases.

- **Computational resources**: Training a large number of trees can be computationally expensive and memory intensive.

- **Long training time**: Compared to simpler models, random forests can take longer to train, especially on large datasets.

Use cases where random forests may not be appropriate:

- **Real-time predictions**: For applications requiring extremely fast predictions, random forests might not be the best choice due to the overhead of combining multiple trees.

- **Highly interpretable models required**: When model interpretability is crucial, simpler models like linear regression or decision trees might be more appropriate.

- **Very large datasets**: For extremely large datasets that do not fit into memory, other algorithms or distributed versions of random forests might be more suitable.

Understanding neural networks

Neural networks are at the heart of many modern ML systems, enabling models to recognize complex patterns and make intelligent decisions. In this section, you will gain a foundational understanding of two important types of neural networks: RNNs and CNNs. You will learn how these architectures function, when to use each, and their respective strengths and limitations. By the end, you will be equipped to choose the right neural network for various real-world tasks, from sequence modeling to image recognition.

Recurrent neural networks

RNN is a type of artificial neural network designed to recognize patterns in sequences of data, such as time series, natural language, or any other data that involves sequential relationships. Unlike traditional neural networks, RNNs have connections that form directed cycles, allowing them to maintain a memory of previous inputs. This makes RNNs particularly powerful for tasks where the order of the data is crucial.

Here is a simplified explanation of how RNNs operate:

1. **Sequential data processing**: RNNs process input data one element at a time while maintaining an internal state (memory) that captures information about previous elements.

2. **Hidden state update**: At each time step, the hidden state is updated based on the current input and the previous hidden state. This allows the network to retain information over long sequences.

3. **Output generation**: The output at each time step is generated based on the current hidden state. For tasks like sequence prediction, the output can be fed back into the network as the next input.

4. **Backpropagation through time (BPTT)**: RNNs are trained using this variant of backpropagation, which adjusts the weights of the network by considering the entire sequence of inputs and outputs.

Key features and advantages

Unlike traditional neural networks that treat inputs independently, RNNs are specifically designed to process **sequential data**, where the order of inputs matters. By retaining information from previous steps, RNNs excel at capturing temporal patterns and dependencies.

The following are some key features and advantages of RNNs:

- **Sequence learning**: RNNs are designed to handle sequential data, making them ideal for tasks where the order of inputs is significant.

- **Memory retention**: The hidden state in RNNs allows them to retain information about previous inputs, enabling them to capture temporal dependencies.

- **Versatility**: RNNs can be applied to a wide range of problems, including time series prediction, natural language processing, and speech recognition.

- **Handling variable-length inputs**: RNNs can process input sequences of varying lengths, making them flexible for different types of sequential data.

Best use cases and practical examples

RNNs are well-suited for various ML tasks involving sequential data. Here are some prime use cases:

- **Natural language processing**: RNNs are commonly used in NLP tasks such as language modeling, text generation, and machine translation. For example, translating text from one language to another.

- **Speech recognition**: RNNs can be used to transcribe spoken language into text by processing audio sequences. For example, converting a speech recording into written text.

- **Time series prediction**: RNNs are effective for forecasting future values in time series data. For example, predicting stock prices based on historical data.

- **Video analysis**: RNNs can analyze video sequences for tasks like activity recognition and video captioning. For example, automatically generating captions for video content.

- **Anomaly detection**: RNNs can detect anomalies in sequential data, such as identifying unusual patterns in sensor data or financial transactions. For example, detecting fraudulent transactions in a sequence of credit card purchases.

Disadvantages of RNNs

While RNNs are powerful and widely used, they have certain limitations:

- **Vanishing and exploding gradients**: RNNs can suffer from vanishing or exploding gradients during training, which can make it difficult to learn long-term dependencies.

- **Training complexity**: Training RNNs can be computationally intensive and time-consuming, especially for long sequences.

- **Limited memory**: Standard RNNs have a limited ability to retain information over long sequences, although variants like **long short-term memory (LSTM)** and **gated recurrent units (GRU)** address this issue.

- **Difficulty in parallelization**: Due to their sequential nature, RNNs are less amenable to parallelization compared to other neural network architectures.

Use cases where recurrent neural networks may not be appropriate:

- **Non-sequential data**: For tasks that do not involve sequential data, other neural network architectures like CNNs or feedforward neural networks might be more suitable.

- **Long-term dependencies**: While LSTMs and GRUs can handle longer sequences, tasks requiring extremely long-term dependencies might still pose challenges.

- **Real-time processing with low latency**: For real-time applications requiring very low latency, the sequential processing nature of RNNs might be a limitation.

- **Memory-intensive applications**: When dealing with very large datasets or sequences, the memory requirements for training RNNs can be prohibitive.

Convolutional neural networks

CNN is a specialized type of artificial neural network designed to process and analyze visual data. It is particularly well-suited for tasks such as image recognition, object detection, and video analysis. CNNs use a mathematical operation called convolution, which allows them to capture spatial hierarchies in images by applying filters to the input data. This architecture is inspired by the human visual system and has proven highly effective for computer vision tasks.

Unlike traditional neural networks, CNNs can automatically detect and learn patterns such as edges, textures, and shapes, reducing the need for manual feature extraction. The following is an overview of how CNNs work:

1. **Convolutional layers**: The core building block of a CNN is the convolutional layer. This layer applies a set of filters (or kernels) to the input image to create feature maps. Each filter detects specific features such as edges, textures, or patterns.

2. **Activation function**: After convolution, an activation function like **rectified linear unit (ReLU)** is applied to introduce non-linearity, allowing the network to learn more complex patterns.

3. **Pooling layers**: Pooling layers are used to reduce the spatial dimensions of the feature maps, which helps in reducing the computational load and controlling overfitting. Common pooling operations include max pooling and average pooling.

4. **Fully connected layers**: After several convolutional and pooling layers, the high-level reasoning in the neural network is done via fully connected layers. These layers take the flattened feature maps and output the final predictions.

5. **Output layer**: The final layer of the CNN produces the output. For classification tasks, this is typically a softmax layer that outputs class probabilities.

Key features and advantages

CNNs are widely used in computer vision tasks due to their ability to efficiently process and analyze image data. Their architecture is designed to automatically detect important patterns and features, making them highly effective for recognizing objects, textures, and spatial relationships. The following are some key features and advantages that make CNNs a powerful tool for image-related tasks:

- **Automatic feature extraction**: CNNs automatically learn to extract relevant features from raw input data, reducing the need for manual feature engineering.

- **Spatial invariance**: Through convolution and pooling, CNNs can recognize patterns regardless of their position in the input image.

- **Parameter sharing**: Filters are shared across different parts of the input image, leading to fewer parameters and improved computational efficiency.

- **Hierarchical feature learning**: CNNs build a hierarchy of features, where lower layers capture basic features (e.g., edges) and higher layers capture more complex patterns (e.g., objects).

Best use cases and practical examples

CNNs are particularly effective for a variety of computer vision tasks. Here are some prime use cases:

- **Image classification**: Identifying the class of objects in an image. For example, classifying images of animals into categories like cats, dogs, and birds.

- **Object detection**: Detecting and localizing objects within an image. For example, identifying and drawing bounding boxes around cars in a traffic scene.

- **Image segmentation**: Partitioning an image into segments where each segment corresponds to a different object or region. For example, segmenting medical images to identify different tissues or organs.

- **Face recognition**: Identifying or verifying individuals based on facial features. For example, unlocking a smartphone using facial recognition.

- **Medical imaging**: Analyzing medical images for diagnosis and treatment planning. For example, detecting tumors in MRI scans.

- **Autonomous vehicles**: Enabling self-driving cars to perceive and navigate their environment. For example, recognizing road signs and pedestrians.

Disadvantages of CNNs

While CNNs are powerful and widely used, they have certain limitations:

- **Computationally intensive**: Training CNNs can require significant computational resources, especially for large and complex models.

- **Data-intensive**: CNNs typically require large amounts of labeled training data to achieve high performance.

- **Lack of interpretability**: Understanding the decision-making process of CNNs can be challenging, as they function as black-box models.

- **Vulnerability to adversarial attacks:** CNNs can be susceptible to small perturbations in input data, leading to incorrect predictions.

Some use cases where convolutional neural networks may not be appropriate are as follows:

- **Non-visual data**: For tasks involving non-visual data, such as text or time series, other architectures like RNNs or transformers might be more suitable.

- **Small datasets**: When labeled data is scarce, simpler models or techniques like transfer learning might be more effective.

- **Real-time systems with low latency requirements**: In applications where extremely fast inference is crucial, the computational overhead of CNNs might be a limitation.

- **Highly interpretable models required**: When model interpretability is critical, simpler models like linear regression or decision trees might be more appropriate.

Neural networks are powerful tools in ML that enable models to recognize complex patterns in data. RNNs are particularly well-suited for tasks involving sequential data, such as time series prediction, speech recognition, and natural language processing. Unlike traditional neural networks, RNNs retain memory of previous inputs, allowing them to capture temporal dependencies and make informed predictions based on prior context. However, despite their strengths, RNNs face challenges such as vanishing gradients, high computational complexity, and difficulty in handling extremely long sequences.

Similarly, CNNs are designed specifically for visual data and have revolutionized fields like image classification, object detection, and facial recognition. CNNs automatically learn hierarchical patterns in images, enabling them to detect edges, textures, and complex objects without manual feature extraction. Their ability to recognize spatial relationships within an image makes them highly effective for tasks requiring detailed visual analysis. However, CNNs have limitations, including high computational requirements, the need for large datasets, and reduced interpretability compared to simpler models.

While RNNs and CNNs offer impressive capabilities in their respective domains, real-world ML applications often demand more robust and adaptable approaches. No single model is perfect for every problem, and this is where ensemble learning and transfer learning become invaluable. Ensemble learning improves predictive accuracy by combining multiple models, reducing the risk of errors, and enhancing overall performance. Meanwhile, transfer learning leverages pre-trained models, allowing new ML applications to benefit from existing knowledge, significantly reducing training time and data requirements. By understanding these advanced techniques, ML practitioners can build more efficient, accurate, and scalable models for a wide range of applications.

Insights into ensemble and transfer learning techniques

ML models often benefit from techniques that enhance their performance, accuracy, and efficiency. Two such techniques, ensemble learning and transfer learning, play a significant role in improving model effectiveness. Ensemble learning enhances predictive power by combining multiple models, reducing errors, and improving generalization. It is widely used in competitive ML applications where accuracy is critical. Meanwhile, transfer learning allows models to leverage knowledge from previously trained networks, significantly reducing training time and improving performance, especially in scenarios where labeled data is scarce. Understanding how these techniques work and when to apply them can help ML practitioners build more efficient, scalable, and high-performing models.

Ensemble methods

Ensemble methods are a class of ML techniques that combine the predictions of multiple base models to improve overall performance. The main idea behind ensemble methods is that a group of weak learners can come together to form a strong learner, resulting in better accuracy and robustness. These methods can be applied to both classification and regression tasks, and they have become a cornerstone in achieving top performance in many ML competitions.

Ensemble methods enhance model performance by combining multiple models to make more accurate and reliable predictions. Instead of relying on a single model, they leverage the collective power of multiple base models, each contributing to the final outcome. The way these models work together plays a crucial role in improving accuracy and reducing errors. The following is an overview of how ensemble methods function:

1. **Diverse base models**: Ensemble methods involve training multiple base models (also known as weak learners). These models can be of the same type (homogeneous) or different types (heterogeneous).

2. **Combination strategy**: The predictions of the base models are combined using various strategies such as averaging, voting, or stacking. This combination is designed to leverage the strengths of each base model while mitigating their weaknesses.

3. **Final prediction**: The combined prediction is used as the final output of the ensemble method. This can involve taking the majority vote (for classification) or the average (for regression).

Some key types of ensemble methods are as follows:

1. **Bagging (Bootstrap aggregating)**: This method involves training multiple instances of the same model on different subsets of the training data, created by random sampling with replacement. The final prediction is the average (regression) or majority vote (classification) of the individual models. For example, random forests.

2. **Boosting**: Boosting trains models sequentially, each new model correcting the errors of the previous ones. The final model is a weighted sum of all the models. For example, **Gradient Boosting Machines (GBM)**, AdaBoost, and XGBoost.

3. **Stacking**: Stacking involves training multiple base models and then using another model (meta-model) to combine their predictions. This meta-model learns how to best combine the base models' predictions to improve performance.

4. **Voting**: In voting ensembles, multiple models are trained, and their predictions are combined by taking a majority vote (hard voting) or by averaging the probabilities (soft voting).

Key features and advantages

Ensemble methods are widely used in ML because they offer several advantages over individual models. By combining multiple models, they enhance predictive accuracy, improve generalization, and provide more reliable results. The following are some key features and benefits that make ensemble learning a powerful technique in ML:

- **Improved accuracy**: By combining multiple models, ensemble methods can achieve higher accuracy than individual models.

- **Robustness**: Ensembles reduce the risk of overfitting and improve generalization to new data.

- **Versatility**: Ensemble methods can be applied to various ML tasks, including classification, regression, and ranking.

- **Error reduction**: They help in reducing both bias and variance, leading to more reliable predictions.

Best use cases and practical examples

Ensemble methods are highly effective for a wide range of ML tasks. Here are some prime use cases:

- **Classification**: Improving the accuracy of models in tasks like spam detection, image recognition, and medical diagnosis. For example, detecting spam emails using a voting ensemble of different classifiers.

- **Regression**: Enhancing the precision of predictive models in financial forecasting, real estate price prediction, and weather forecasting. For example, predicting house prices using a stacked ensemble of various regression models.

- **Anomaly detection**: Identifying outliers in datasets for fraud detection, network security, and quality control. For example, detecting fraudulent transactions using a boosting ensemble.

- **Recommender systems**: Combining multiple recommendation algorithms to improve the accuracy of suggestions. For example, recommending movies to users by stacking collaborative filtering and content-based models.

Disadvantages of ensemble methods

While ensemble methods are powerful and widely used, they have certain limitations:

- **Complexity**: Ensembles can be more complex and harder to interpret than individual models, making them less transparent.

- **Computational resources**: Training multiple models and combining their predictions can be computationally expensive and time-consuming.

- **Overfitting**: Despite their robustness, ensembles can still overfit if not properly tuned, especially when combining very complex models.

- **Implementation difficulty**: Implementing and tuning ensemble methods can be more challenging compared to single models, requiring more expertise and careful consideration.

Use cases where ensemble methods may not be appropriate:

- **Real-time predictions**: For applications requiring extremely fast predictions, the overhead of combining multiple models might be a limitation. For example, high-frequency trading systems require decision-making to be near-instantaneous.

- **Highly interpretable models required**: When model interpretability is crucial, simpler models like linear regression or decision trees might be more appropriate. For example, credit scoring in highly regulated industries where every decision must be clearly explainable.

- **Small datasets**: On very small datasets, the benefit of ensemble methods might be limited, and simpler models might perform just as well. For example, predicting outcomes based on a small medical study.

- **Limited computational resources**: In environments with restricted computational power, the resource-intensive nature of ensemble methods can be a drawback. For example, running models on low-power edge devices.

Transfer learning

Transfer learning is ML technique where a pre-trained model, initially developed for a specific task, is reused and fine-tuned for a different but related task. Instead of training a model from scratch, transfer learning leverages the knowledge gained from a large, generic dataset and applies it to a specific problem, often leading to faster and more efficient learning. This approach is particularly useful when dealing with limited data or computational resources.

Here is a simplified explanation of how transfer learning functions:

1. **Pre-trained model**: Start with a model that has been pre-trained on a large and diverse dataset, such as ImageNet for image-related tasks or a large text corpus for NLP.

2. **Feature extraction**: Use the pre-trained model as a fixed feature extractor. The initial layers of the model, which have learned to detect generic features, are retained, and only the final layers are retrained on the new dataset.

3. **Layer freezing strategy**: When implementing transfer learning, deciding which layers to freeze versus fine-tune is crucial. Typically, freeze the early layers that contain general, low-level features like edges and textures, while fine-tuning the later layers that hold task-specific features. A common approach is gradual unfreezing: start by training only new classifier layers, then progressively unfreeze deeper layers with lower learning rates to preserve pre-trained knowledge. The amount of freezing depends on your dataset size: smaller datasets require more frozen layers to prevent overfitting, while larger datasets can safely fine-tune more layers.

4. **Fine-tuning**: Optionally, fine-tune the entire model or a subset of layers using the new dataset. This step allows the model to adapt more specifically to the new task, while still benefiting from the knowledge encoded in the pre-trained weights.

5. **Transfer and adapt**: Apply the adapted model to the new task, leveraging the pre-trained features and any fine-tuning to make accurate predictions.

Key features and advantages

Transfer learning has gained popularity in ML due to its ability to leverage knowledge from pre-trained models, making training faster and more efficient. Instead of starting from scratch, models can build upon previously learned patterns, leading to improved performance with less data and computational resources. The following are some key features and advantages that make transfer learning a valuable approach in ML:

- **Reduced training time**: By leveraging pre-trained models, transfer learning significantly reduces the time required to train a model from scratch.

- **Improved performance**: Pre-trained models often achieve better performance, especially when the target dataset is small, by starting with features that have already been learned.

- **Resource efficiency**: Transfer learning can be more computationally efficient, as it reduces the need for extensive training on large datasets.

- **Versatility**: It can be applied across various domains and tasks, including image classification, NLP, and more.

Best use cases and practical examples

Transfer learning is particularly effective for tasks where labeled data is scarce or where computational resources are limited. Here are some prime use cases:

- **Image classification**: Utilizing a pre-trained model like ResNet or VGG on ImageNet and fine-tuning it for specific image classification tasks. For example, classifying medical images to identify diseases.

- **Object detection**: Adapting models pre-trained on large object detection datasets for specific applications. For example, detecting specific types of vehicles in traffic surveillance footage.

- **NLP**: Using pre-trained language models like BERT or GPT-3 and fine-tuning them for specific NLP tasks such as sentiment analysis, text classification, or named entity recognition. For example, analyzing customer reviews to determine sentiment.

- **Speech recognition**: Applying models pre-trained on large speech datasets to recognize speech in specific accents or languages. For example, transcribing spoken language in regional dialects.

- **Recommendation systems**: Leveraging pre-trained recommendation models and adapting them to new domains or specific user data. For example, recommending products on an e-commerce site based on a pre-trained model from a different retail domain.

Disadvantages of transfer learning

While transfer learning offers many benefits, it also has certain limitations:

- **Mismatch in data distribution**: If the source and target datasets are too different, the pre-trained model might not perform well without significant fine-tuning.

- **Model size and complexity**: Pre-trained models can be large and complex, requiring substantial computational resources for fine-tuning and inference.

- **Limited flexibility**: Transfer learning is less effective for tasks that are significantly different from the original training task of the pre-trained model.

- **Dependency on pre-trained models:** The quality and applicability of transfer learning depend on the availability and performance of suitable pre-trained models.

Use cases where transfer learning may not be appropriate:

- **Highly domain-specific tasks**: For tasks that are highly specific and lack relevant pre-trained models, transfer learning might not provide significant benefits. For example, predicting geological phenomena using very specialized scientific data.

- **Small-scale models**: For lightweight applications where model size and inference speed are critical, large pre-trained models might be impractical. For example, running models on edge devices with limited computational power.

- **Highly dynamic environments**: In environments where data distribution changes rapidly, continuously training a model from scratch might be more effective. For example, real-time fraud detection systems need to adapt quickly to new patterns.

- **Simple tasks**: For straightforward tasks where a simple model can achieve high accuracy, the complexity of transfer learning might be unnecessary. For example, basic linear regression on well-defined, low-dimensional data.

Ensemble learning and transfer learning have transformed the way ML models are built, enabling higher accuracy, robustness, and efficiency. Ensemble methods leverage multiple models to make stronger predictions, making them particularly useful in complex classification and regression tasks. However, their increased computational cost and complexity can make them unsuitable for real-time applications or cases requiring interpretability. On the other hand, transfer learning accelerates training by using pre-trained models, allowing organizations to apply deep learning techniques even with limited data. Despite its advantages, transfer learning is not ideal for highly domain-specific tasks where pre-trained models may not be relevant.

While understanding how models can be optimized through ensemble and transfer learning is important, selecting the right model based on the type of data and problem is equally critical. Different ML tasks, such as classification, regression, and clustering, require different approaches, and factors like dataset size, feature types, interpretability needs, and computational constraints play a role in model selection. Next, we will explore model selection criteria, examining how to choose the most suitable ML model based on data characteristics and problem type.

Model selection criteria based on data and problem type

Choosing the right ML model is essential for achieving optimal performance, as different models are designed to handle specific types of data and problem domains. Logistic regression is ideal for simple classification tasks, while decision trees provide interpretability for structured data. More advanced models like XGBoost excel in high-performance scenarios, whereas deep learning models such as RNNs and CNNs are specialized for sequential and visual data, respectively. Ensemble methods enhance accuracy and robustness by combining multiple models, and transfer learning allows for leveraging pre-trained models, making it particularly useful when data is limited. Understanding the strengths and limitations of each model ensures that ML practitioners can make informed decisions based on data characteristics and problem requirements.

Refer to the following table:

Model	Problem type	Best suited for	Key strengths	Key limitations
Logistic regression	Classification	Binary and multiclass classification tasks	Simplicity, interpretability, and low computational cost	Assumes linear decision boundary, not suitable for complex data
Decision trees	Classification, regression	Problems requiring interpretability, structured/tabular data	Easy to understand and interpret, handles both numerical and categorical data	Prone to overfitting, instability with small data changes
XGBoost	Classification, regression	High-performance tasks, structured/tabular data, ML competitions	Speed, performance, handles missing values, and regularization	Complexity, computational resources, risk of overfitting
RNN	Sequential data	Time series prediction, NLP, speech recognition	Sequence learning, memory retention	Vanishing/exploding gradients, training complexity

Model	Problem type	Best suited for	Key strengths	Key limitations
CNN	Image/Video analysis	Image classification, object detection, image segmentation, video analysis	Automatic feature extraction, spatial invariance, hierarchical learning	Computationally intensive, data-intensive, and less interpretable
Ensemble methods	Classification, regression	Tasks needing high accuracy and robustness, handling of bias/variance trade-offs	Improved accuracy, robustness, and versatility	Complexity, computational resources, implementation difficulty
Transfer learning	Various	Tasks with limited data, leveraging pre-trained models for related tasks	Reduced training time, improved performance, and resource efficiency	Mismatch in data distribution, model size, and complexity

Table 8.1: Comparison of ML models

To bridge the gap between model selection and real-world deployment, AWS offers a suite of tools and services designed to simplify ML implementation. From Amazon SageMaker for training and deployment to AWS Lambda for serverless execution, these services provide the computational power and scalability required to bring ML models to production efficiently. Next, we will explore AWS tools and services for model implementation, examining how they can streamline the entire ML workflow, from development to deployment.

AWS tools and services for model implementation

Building and deploying ML models effectively requires not only the right algorithms but also the right infrastructure. AWS provides a suite of powerful tools and services designed to streamline the entire ML lifecycle, from model development and training to deployment and monitoring. AWS SageMaker simplifies the end-to-end ML workflow with built-in algorithms, scalable training, and one-click deployment. For deep learning applications, AWS Deep Learning AMIs offer pre-configured environments with popular frameworks like TensorFlow and PyTorch, optimized for high-performance computing. Additionally, AWS Lambda and other cloud-based services enable serverless execution, scalable compute power, and seamless integration for deploying ML models efficiently. Understanding these AWS tools allows ML practitioners to develop, train, and deploy models more effectively, optimizing both performance and cost.

AWS SageMaker

AWS SageMaker is a fully managed service that provides every developer and data scientist with the ability to build, train, and deploy ML models quickly. It simplifies the end-to-end ML workflow, making it easier to develop high-quality models and bring them into production.

Key features of AWS SageMaker

AWS SageMaker offers a comprehensive suite of features designed to simplify the end-to-end ML workflow, from model development to deployment and monitoring. By providing an integrated environment, built-in algorithms, and automated scaling, SageMaker enables ML practitioners to build, train, and deploy models efficiently. The following are some key features that make it a powerful tool for ML implementation:

- **Integrated development environment:** SageMaker includes Jupyter notebooks, which offer an interactive development environment for building and testing models.

- **Built-in algorithms**: It provides numerous built-in, high-performance ML algorithms ready to use.

- **Automatic model tuning**: Also known as hyperparameter optimization, this feature helps in automatically finding the best version of a model by tuning the parameters.

- **Training and inference at scale**: SageMaker can train models on large datasets and deploy them across multiple availability zones.

- **One-click deployment**: After training, models can be deployed to production with a single click, and SageMaker handles all the infrastructure.

- **Model monitoring and management**: It includes tools for monitoring models in production to ensure they are operating as expected.

Best use cases

WS SageMaker is designed to support a wide range of ML tasks, making it a versatile solution for both beginners and advanced practitioners. Whether it is preparing large datasets, training scalable models, deploying them into production, or ensuring their ongoing performance, SageMaker provides the necessary tools to streamline each step of the ML pipeline. The following are some of the best use cases where SageMaker excels:

- **Data preparation**: Processing and preparing large datasets for ML.

- **Model training**: Training models using built-in algorithms or custom ones with the ability to scale.

- **Model deployment**: Deploying models into production environments with ease.

- **Model management**: Monitoring and managing models' post-deployment for consistent performance.

AWS Deep Learning AMIs

AWS Deep Learning **Amazon Machine Images** (**AMIs**) provide ML practitioners and researchers with the infrastructure and tools to accelerate deep learning in the cloud at any scale. These AMIs come pre-installed with popular deep learning frameworks and tools.

Key features of AWS Deep Learning AMIs

AWS Deep Learning AMIs provide a **pre-configured and optimized environment** for developing and deploying deep learning models in the cloud. These AMIs come with popular ML frameworks, GPU acceleration, and flexible computing options, making them a powerful tool for researchers and practitioners working on complex deep learning tasks. The following are some key features that make AWS Deep Learning AMIs a valuable resource for ML development:

- **Pre-installed frameworks**: Includes popular frameworks such as TensorFlow, PyTorch, Apache MXNet, and Keras.

- **Optimized performance**: Configured for high performance with NVIDIA CUDA, cuDNN, and NCCL libraries to leverage GPU acceleration.

- **Flexible environments:** Available on various Amazon EC2 instance types, including GPU instances for intensive deep learning tasks.

- **Customizable**: Users can customize the AMIs according to their specific requirements.

- **Cost-effective**: Pay only for the compute time you use, making it a cost-effective solution for running deep learning models.

Best use cases

AWS Deep Learning AMIs are designed to support a variety of deep learning workflows, providing the computational power and flexibility needed for efficient model development. Whether you are training large-scale models, experimenting with different architectures, or scaling infrastructure for intensive tasks, these AMIs offer a seamless and cost-effective solution. The following are some of the best use cases where AWS Deep Learning AMIs are particularly beneficial:

- **Model training**: Leveraging GPU acceleration to train deep learning models faster.

- **Experimentation**: Rapidly prototyping and experimenting with different deep learning frameworks.

- **Scalable infrastructure**: Scaling compute resources as needed for extensive model training sessions.

In the following section, we will understand the role of AWS Lambda which is a serverless computing product from AWS, and a few other services that would help us build scalable ML solutions.

AWS Lambda and other services

AWS Lambda is a serverless compute service that allows you to run code without provisioning or managing servers. You can execute your code based on triggers such as changes in data, shifts in system state, or actions by users.

Key features of AWS Lambda

AWS Lambda is a serverless compute service that enables developers to run code without managing servers, making it ideal for event-driven applications and scalable workloads. With its ability to automatically scale, integrate with various AWS services, and provide a cost-effective execution model, AWS Lambda is a powerful tool for deploying ML models and other cloud-based applications.

The following are some of its key features that make it a valuable component of the AWS ecosystem:

- **Automatic scaling**: Scales automatically in response to incoming traffic, handling from a few requests per day to thousands per second.

- **Event-driven**: Can be triggered by events from other AWS services like S3, DynamoDB, Kinesis, SNS, and more.

- **Cost efficiency**: Pay only for the compute time you consume, making it a cost-effective option for running sporadic code.

- **Flexible environment**: Supports various programming languages such as Python, Node.js, Java, and C#.

- **Easy integration**: Easily integrates with other AWS services, creating a seamless workflow for serverless applications.

Other AWS services for model implementation

In addition to AWS SageMaker, Deep Learning AMIs, and Lambda, AWS offers a variety of other services that support scalable, flexible, and efficient model implementation. These services provide essential infrastructure for computing, containerization, orchestration, and data storage, enabling seamless deployment and management of ML models. The following are some key AWS services that play a crucial role in ML workflows:

1. **Amazon EC2**: Provides scalable computing capacity in the cloud. It is used to run applications and models on virtual servers.

2. **Amazon ECS**: A fully managed container orchestration service that helps in deploying, managing, and scaling containerized applications.

3. **Amazon EKS**: A managed service that makes it easy to run Kubernetes on AWS without needing to install and operate your own Kubernetes control plane.

4. **AWS Fargate**: A serverless compute engine for containers that works with Amazon ECS and EKS, removing the need to manage servers or clusters.

5. **AWS step functions**: A serverless orchestration service that makes it easy to coordinate the components of distributed applications and microservices using visual workflows.

6. **Amazon S3**: Object storage built to store and retrieve any amount of data from anywhere, making it essential for storing large datasets used in training ML models.

Best use cases

AWS provides a range of tools and services that cater to different ML deployment needs, from serverless execution to scalable computing and containerized applications. These services allow organizations to efficiently manage data processing, model deployment, and real-time inference while optimizing cost and performance.

The following are some of the best use cases where AWS services enhance ML implementation:

- **Serverless model deployment**: Using AWS Lambda to deploy ML models in a serverless environment, enabling automatic scaling and cost savings.

- **Data processing**: Employing AWS Lambda and step functions to preprocess and transform data before feeding it into a ML model.

- **Real-time predictions**: Implementing real-time prediction services using AWS Lambda triggered by data events from S3 or Kinesis.

- **Scalable compute**: Utilizing Amazon EC2, ECS, and EKS to provide scalable infrastructure for training and deploying ML models.

- **Containerized applications**: Running containerized ML applications using ECS, EKS, or Fargate for flexible and scalable model implementation.

AWS provides a comprehensive ecosystem for implementing ML models, ensuring scalability, efficiency, and cost-effectiveness. AWS SageMaker facilitates model training, deployment, and monitoring, making it ideal for businesses looking to operationalize ML workflows. Deep Learning AMIs accelerate the training process by offering pre-installed frameworks optimized for cloud computing, while AWS Lambda and other services provide serverless and containerized solutions for deploying models at scale. Whether working with structured data, deep learning models, or real-time prediction systems, AWS offers a flexible and scalable infrastructure to support various ML needs.

With the right AWS tools in place, ML practitioners can focus on model optimization and performance tuning, ensuring their models are efficient and reliable in production. As we conclude this chapter, it is essential to reflect on how these ML models, techniques, and tools come together to form a complete, end-to-end ML solution that drives impactful results in real-world applications.

Conclusion

In this chapter, we explored the fundamental principles of ML model selection, evaluating various algorithms and their applications based on data characteristics and problem types. From traditional models like logistic regression and decision trees to more advanced approaches such as neural networks, ensemble methods, and transfer learning, we examined their strengths, limitations, and best use cases. The chapter provided a structured framework for selecting models based on interpretability, complexity, scalability, and computational efficiency.

Additionally, we introduced AWS tools and services that streamline model implementation, including AWS SageMaker, AWS Deep Learning AMIs, and AWS Lambda, highlighting their capabilities in model training, deployment, and management. These cloud-based solutions empower practitioners to build scalable and efficient ML workflows.

As we conclude, it is essential to reinforce the knowledge gained through hands-on practice.

In the next chapter, you will learn essential best practices for training ML models efficiently and effectively. You will explore how to properly split data, optimize model performance through techniques like hyperparameter tuning, and choose the right compute resources for various workloads. The chapter also covers strategies for updating and retraining models as new data becomes available. Finally, you will gain hands-on knowledge of AWS tools like Amazon SageMaker and AWS Batch to streamline your training workflows.

Multiple choice questions

1. **Which of the following is not a key feature of XGBoost?**

    a. Speed and performance

    b. Regularization

    c. Handling missing values

    d. Image recognition

2. **What is the primary goal of logistic regression?**
   a. To predict continuous values
   b. To estimate the probability of an instance belonging to a particular class
   c. To cluster data points
   d. To reduce dimensionality

3. **Which of the following is a limitation of decision trees?**
   a. They cannot handle non-linear relationships
   b. They require extensive data preprocessing
   c. They can easily overfit, especially when the tree is very deep
   d. They cannot provide feature importance

4. **What is the main advantage of random forests over individual decision trees?**
   a. They are faster to train
   b. They require less memory
   c. They improve accuracy by reducing overfitting
   d. They are more interpretable

5. **RNNs are particularly well-suited for which of the following?**
   a. Image classification tasks
   b. Processing sequential data
   c. Handling tabular data
   d. Dimensionality reduction

6. **Which of the following is not a typical use case for CNNs?**
   a. Image classification
   b. Object detection
   c. Time series prediction
   d. Face recognition

7. **What is the primary goal of ensemble methods in ML?**
   a. To reduce training time
   b. To improve model interpretability
   c. To combine predictions of multiple models for better performance
   d. To handle missing data

8. **Transfer learning is most beneficial in which of the following cases?**

   a. You have a very large dataset

   b. You need a highly interpretable model

   c. You have limited labeled data for your specific task

   d. Your task is completely unrelated to any existing pre-trained models

9. **Which AWS service provides a fully managed environment for building, training, and deploying ML models?**

   a. AWS Lambda

   b. AWS SageMaker

   c. AWS Deep Learning AMIs

   d. Amazon EC2

10. **What is the main advantage of using AWS Lambda for model deployment?**

    a. It provides pre-installed deep learning frameworks

    b. It offers automatic scaling and pay-per-use pricing

    c. It allows for easy management of containerized applications

    d. It provides GPU acceleration for model training

Answer key

1. b
2. c
3. c
4. b
5. c
6. c
7. c
8. b
9. b
10. b

Join our Discord space

Join our Discord workspace for latest updates, offers, tech happenings around the world, new releases, and sessions with the authors:

https://discord.bpbonline.com

CHAPTER 9
Training ML Models

Introduction

Training ML models involves more than just feeding data into an algorithm; it requires a deep understanding of how to properly split data, optimize models, and select the appropriate computational resources. As datasets grow larger and models become more complex, the ability to make informed decisions about these factors becomes increasingly important. Whether you are training a simple linear regression model or a sophisticated deep learning network, choosing the right strategies and tools can make a significant difference in both the time it takes to train your model and the quality of its predictions.

This chapter will explore the best practices for splitting data into training and validation sets, a crucial step in ensuring that your model generalizes well to unseen data. We will delve into various optimization techniques that can be employed during the training phase to enhance model performance, including hyperparameter tuning and learning rate adjustments. Furthermore, we will guide you through selecting the right compute resources, whether it is GPUs for deep learning, CPUs for less intensive tasks, or distributed platforms like *Spark* for handling large datasets.

Additionally, this chapter will cover strategies for updating and retraining models to keep them relevant as new data becomes available, ensuring that your ML solutions remain accurate and effective over time. Finally, we will introduce you to AWS services that are specifically designed to facilitate efficient ML model training, such as Amazon SageMaker and AWS Batch.

Structure

The chapter covers the following topics:

- Data splitting
- Optimization techniques for ML training
- Selecting compute resources
- Strategies for updating and retraining a model
- Need for updating and retraining a model
- AWS services for efficient ML model training

Objectives

By the end of this chapter, readers will gain comprehensive knowledge about ML model maintenance and optimization strategies. They will understand how to update and retrain models effectively, implement techniques for maintaining model accuracy as new data becomes available, and recognize the critical role of model maintenance in the ML lifecycle. The chapter introduces essential AWS services, particularly Amazon SageMaker, demonstrating how these tools enable efficient and scalable model training. This knowledge will not only prepare readers for the AWS Certified ML - Specialty exam but also equip them with practical skills for training and optimizing ML models in real-world scenarios.

Data splitting

In the realm of ML, the process of splitting data into training and validation sets is a critical step that lays the foundation for building models that generalize well to new, unseen data. Properly partitioning your dataset is crucial for ensuring that the model you train is robust and capable of making accurate predictions when applied to real-world scenarios. This section will delve into the methodologies, best practices, and considerations for effectively splitting your data, as well as the implications of doing so incorrectly.

Importance of data splitting

Data splitting is essential because it allows you to assess how well your ML model will perform on unseen data. Without this step, you risk overfitting your model to the training data, meaning your model will perform exceptionally well on the data it was trained on but poorly on any new data. By dividing your data into distinct sets, you can train your model on one portion (the training set) and then validate its performance on another (the validation set). This approach gives you a better sense of how your model will perform in the real world.

Basic approach to training and validation sets

At its core, data splitting involves dividing your dataset into two primary subsets:

- **Training set**: This is the portion of your data that you use to train your ML model. The model learns patterns, relationships, and insights from this data. Typically, the training set comprises the majority of the data, often around 70% to 80%.

- **Validation set**: After training the model, you need a way to evaluate its performance before deploying it. The validation set, typically making up 20% to 30% of the data, serves this purpose. It allows you to fine-tune your model and make adjustments without biasing the model by continuously tweaking it on the training data.

Real-world scenario

Consider a scenario where you are building a predictive model to determine whether a customer will churn (leave) a subscription service. You have a dataset containing information about customers, such as their age, usage patterns, and interaction history with customer support.

You start by splitting the data: 80% for training and 20% for validation. You train your model on the 80% training set, where it learns patterns such as high customer support interaction being correlated with a higher likelihood of churn. Once the model is trained, you test its predictions on the 20% validation set. Here, you might discover that while your model performs well on the training data, it slightly underperforms on the validation set, indicating that some adjustments are needed to improve its generalizability.

Advanced considerations in cross-validation

While a simple training/validation split works well for many scenarios, more advanced techniques like cross-validation offer a more robust approach to model evaluation, especially when working with smaller datasets.

Cross-validation involves dividing your data into multiple subsets, or *folds*. For example, in k-fold cross-validation, the data is split into k equal-sized folds. The model is trained k times, each time using a different fold as the validation set and the remaining $k-1$ folds as the training set. The final performance is then averaged over all k iterations. This method provides a more comprehensive evaluation of the model's performance and reduces the likelihood that the model's success is due to a particular data split.

Implementing k-fold cross-validation

Imagine you have a relatively small dataset of 500 customer records. Splitting 20% for validation would leave only 100 records to test your model, which might not be enough to reliably gauge performance. Instead, you opt for 5-fold cross-validation. In this case, the data is split into 5 folds, each containing 100 records. The model is trained five times, each time using 400 records for training and 100 for validation. The final accuracy is the average of the five validation accuracies, providing a more stable estimate of your model's performance.

Pitfalls to avoid

Even with the best intentions, it is easy to make mistakes when splitting data, which can lead to misleading results. Here are some common pitfalls:

- **Data leakage**: This occurs when information from the validation set inadvertently influences the model during training, resulting in overly optimistic performance estimates. For example, if you accidentally include features in the training set that are derived from the validation set, your model might learn to *cheat* by picking up on these signals.

- **Imbalanced data**: If your data is not evenly distributed across classes (e.g., predicting a rare event like fraud), a simple random split might result in a validation set that does not represent the true distribution of data. In such cases, stratified sampling, ensuring that each set maintains the same class distribution, should be used.

- **Temporal data splits**: When dealing with time series data, it is important to respect the temporal order. Training on future data and validating on past data can lead to unrealistic performance estimates. Always ensure that your validation set comes from a later time period than your training set to simulate real-world conditions.

Best practices for data splitting

To avoid these pitfalls and ensure robust model evaluation, consider the following best practices:

- **Stratify by class**: If you are dealing with a classification problem, use stratified sampling to ensure that both training and validation sets have a similar distribution of classes.

- **Keep validation data separate**: Ensure that the validation set is only used for evaluation purposes, not for training or model selection. Once you have finalized your model, you can use a separate test set for the final evaluation.

- **Multiple splits or cross-validation**: When possible, use cross-validation to get a more accurate estimate of your model's performance, especially with smaller datasets.

This section emphasized the importance of effective data splitting for building ML models that generalize well to unseen data. You learned the basics of dividing datasets into training and validation sets, typically using an 80/20 or 70/30 split, to prevent overfitting and evaluate performance accurately. The section also introduced advanced techniques like k-fold cross-validation, which provided a more reliable estimate of model performance, especially with smaller datasets.

Additionally, you explored common pitfalls, such as data leakage, class imbalance, and improper handling of time series data, and reviewed best practices like stratified sampling and keeping validation data separate. These insights helped reinforce the importance of careful data preparation in developing robust and trustworthy ML models.

Now, we will discuss another important topic related to optimizing while training ML models.

Optimization techniques for ML training

Optimization is at the heart of ML training. It is the process through which we fine-tune our models to minimize errors and maximize performance. Effective optimization techniques are critical for ensuring that the models we build are both accurate and efficient. In this section, we will explore various optimization techniques, discuss their importance, and provide practical examples to help you understand how to apply these techniques to your ML workflows.

Role of optimization in ML training

Optimization in ML typically revolves around finding the best parameters (often called weights) for a model that minimizes a loss function. The loss function quantifies how far off a model's predictions are from the actual outcomes, and the optimization process seeks to reduce this loss as much as possible.

For example, in linear regression, the goal is to find the line that best fits the data points by minimizing the sum of squared differences between the observed values and the values predicted by the model. In more complex models, like neural networks, the optimization process involves adjusting the weights of the network to minimize a chosen loss function, which could be something like mean squared error for regression tasks or cross-entropy loss for classification tasks.

Understanding gradient descent as foundation of optimization

One of the most common optimization techniques is gradient descent. Gradient descent is an iterative method used to minimize the loss function by adjusting the model's parameters in the direction that reduces the error. The *gradient* refers to the slope of the loss function, and *descent* refers to the process of moving down this slope to reach the lowest possible error.

There are several variations of gradient descent, each with its advantages:

- **Batch gradient descent**: In this method, the entire dataset is used to compute the gradient and update the model's parameters. While this can be accurate, it can also be computationally expensive, especially with large datasets.

- **Stochastic gradient descent** (**SGD**): Instead of using the entire dataset, SGD updates the parameters for each training example individually. This makes the process faster and less memory-intensive but introduces more noise in the updates, leading to a less stable convergence.

- **Mini-batch gradient descent**: This technique strikes a balance between batch gradient descent and SGD by updating the model's parameters based on a small, randomly chosen subset of the data (a mini-batch). This approach is widely used because it provides a good trade-off between convergence speed and computational efficiency.

Imagine you are in a playground looking for treasure (refer to *Figure 9.1*). One kid (batch gradient descent) stops and looks at the whole playground before taking a step. Another kid (mini-batch gradient descent) looks at just a few parts of the playground, then takes a step. The third kid (stochastic gradient descent) quickly looks at just one part and takes a step right away. They all want to reach the treasure, but they each use a different strategy to get there; some are slower but more accurate, while others move fast but might zig-zag a bit.

Figure 9.1: Three kids use different strategies to find the treasure

Practical application of mini-batch gradient descent

Imagine you are training a deep learning model to classify images of handwritten digits (like the famous MNIST dataset). Using mini-batch gradient descent, you can break down the training process into smaller steps by feeding the model a batch of thirty-two images at a time. After each batch, the model's parameters are updated, and the next batch is processed. This approach allows you to train the model efficiently even on large datasets, reducing memory usage while still making meaningful progress toward minimizing the loss function.

Advanced optimization techniques

While gradient descent forms the foundation of optimization, there are several advanced techniques that build on it to enhance training efficiency and model performance. We will now look at a few such techniques.

Momentum

Momentum is like giving your model a bit of extra push during training to help it move faster towards the best solution. Imagine you are rolling a ball down a hill. If the hill has bumps (which represent difficult parts of the problem), the ball might get stuck. Momentum helps by allowing the ball to build up speed from previous movements so it can roll over those bumps more easily. In ML, this means momentum helps the training process avoid getting stuck in bad spots and reach the best solution more quickly. It does this by adding a portion of the previous adjustments to the current one, which speeds up the learning process.

Adaptive learning rate methods

Adaptive learning rate methods automatically adjust how fast the model learns during training. This adjustment is crucial because some parts of the model might need bigger changes, while others need smaller ones. These methods are particularly helpful when the data is complex or unevenly distributed. Here is how some of the most popular adaptive learning rate methods work:

- **AdaGrad**: This method changes the learning rate for each part of the model separately. If a part has already learned a lot, AdaGrad slows down its learning rate, and if it has not learned much, it speeds up the learning rate. This approach is especially useful when working with data where some features appear frequently and others rarely, as it ensures that all parts of the model learn at an appropriate pace. However, a limitation of AdaGrad is that it can stop learning too early due to aggressive decay of the learning rate over time.

- **RMSProp**: RMSProp improves on AdaGrad by preventing the learning rate from getting too small. It does this by keeping track of a moving average of the learning progress, which helps the model continue to learn effectively even after many updates. This method keeps the learning process balanced and ensures that the model does not stop learning too early.

- **Adam:** Adam combines the best parts of both momentum and RMSProp. It adjusts the learning rate dynamically for each part of the model and also adds the benefit of momentum to help the model move faster toward the best solution. Because of its flexibility and effectiveness, Adam is one of the most widely used optimization methods in ML. It works well across different types of problems and models, making it a go-to choice for many practitioners.

Cloud Platform Support

Modern cloud platforms provide built-in support for these advanced optimization techniques. For example, AWS SageMaker supports choosing optimizers like Adam through both built-in algorithms and custom containers. This allows practitioners to easily experiment with different optimization methods without having to implement them from scratch. SageMaker provides pre-configured environments with popular optimizers and allows custom implementations through Docker containers for specialized use cases.

Similarly, other cloud platforms like Google Cloud AI Platform and Azure ML offer comparable optimization support, making advanced techniques accessible to practitioners regardless of their infrastructure setup.

Choosing the right optimizer

Consider a scenario where you are training a neural network to predict stock prices based on historical data. Given the volatility and complexity of financial data, choosing an optimization algorithm that can adapt to changing patterns in the data is crucial. Adam would be an excellent choice here because it dynamically adjusts the learning rate, helping the model converge faster and more reliably in the face of noisy and complex data.

Hyperparameter tuning

Another critical aspect of optimization is hyperparameter tuning. Hyperparameters are settings that control the training process itself, such as the learning rate, batch size, and the number of hidden layers in a neural network. Unlike the model parameters, which are learned during training, hyperparameters need to be set before training begins.

Common strategies for hyperparameter tuning include:

- **Grid search**: Testing all possible combinations of a predefined set of hyperparameter values. While this brute-force approach is exhaustive, it can be computationally expensive.

- **Random search**: Instead of testing all combinations, random search selects hyperparameter values randomly from the predefined range. This method is often more efficient than grid search, as it explores the hyperparameter space more broadly.

- **Bayesian optimization**: A more sophisticated approach that builds a probabilistic model of the function mapping hyperparameters to the objective (e.g., model accuracy) and uses this model to select the next set of hyperparameters to evaluate. This method is more efficient and can yield better results with fewer evaluations.

Imagine you are building a regression model to predict housing prices based on features like the number of bedrooms, location, and square footage. To get the best performance from your model, you need to fine-tune its hyperparameters, such as the learning rate and batch size.

Training ML Models ■ 207

Instead of testing every possible combination (which can be time-consuming and resource-intensive), you decide to use Bayesian optimization. This method is smarter because it learns from each test and uses that information to make better guesses about what hyperparameters might work best next. You start by testing a few random combinations of hyperparameters. Bayesian optimization then builds a model that predicts which hyperparameter settings are likely to perform well based on the results of these initial tests. It does not just pick random settings anymore; it chooses the ones that are most likely to improve your model's performance. As you continue this process, Bayesian optimization zeroes in on the best set of hyperparameters much faster than a random search or grid search would.

For example, after a few rounds, Bayesian optimization might suggest trying a slightly lower learning rate paired with a smaller batch size. You test this combination, and it turns out to significantly reduce the error in your housing price predictions. By using Bayesian optimization, you have efficiently found the best hyperparameters, saving both time and computational resources while improving your model's accuracy.

Optimization techniques are essential for training ML models that are not only accurate but also efficient and scalable. By understanding and applying these techniques, whether it is choosing the right variation of gradient descent, leveraging advanced optimizers like Adam, or fine-tuning hyperparameters, you can significantly improve the performance of your models. As you prepare for the AWS Certified ML Specialty exam, mastering these optimization strategies will equip you with the skills needed to build and deploy high-performance ML models on AWS.

Selecting compute resources

Choosing the right compute resources for your ML tasks is crucial for optimizing both performance and cost. The decision largely depends on the complexity of the model, the size of the dataset, and the nature of the task you are trying to accomplish. In this section, we will explore the different types of compute resources available, like GPUs, CPUs, Spark, and non-Spark platforms, and discuss when and how to use them effectively.

CPU

The **central processing unit** (**CPU**) is the traditional workhorse of computing and is well-suited for a wide range of ML tasks, especially those involving simpler models or smaller datasets. CPUs are general-purpose processors that excel in handling tasks that require sequential processing. They are often the default choice for many ML workflows because of their versatility and wide availability.

Choosing the right time to use CPUs:

- **Smaller datasets**: When working with smaller datasets, the speed advantage of GPUs might not justify the additional cost, making CPUs a more cost-effective option.

- **Linear models and decision trees**: Algorithms like linear regression, logistic regression, and decision trees typically run efficiently on CPUs, as they do not require the parallel processing capabilities that GPUs offer.

- **Model evaluation and inference**: Once your model is trained, using a CPU for evaluation and inference is often sufficient, particularly for less complex models or when real-time performance is not critical.

Training a simple linear regression model

Consider you are training a simple linear regression model to predict house prices based on a small dataset of features like square footage, number of bedrooms, and location. In this case, a CPU would be more than capable of handling the computations efficiently. The dataset is small enough that a CPU can process it quickly, and the linear nature of the model does not demand the parallel processing power of a GPU.

GPU

Graphics processing units (**GPUs**) are specialized hardware designed for handling tasks that can be parallelized, making them ideal for training complex ML models, particularly deep learning models. GPUs can perform many operations simultaneously, which significantly speeds up the training process for models with large datasets or complex architectures.

Choosing the right time to use GPUs:

- **Deep learning models**: Models such as **convolutional neural networks** (**CNNs**) and **recurrent neural networks** (**RNNs**) are computationally intensive and benefit greatly from the parallel processing capabilities of GPUs.

- **Large datasets**: When dealing with large datasets, GPUs can drastically reduce training time by processing multiple data points simultaneously.

- **Real-time processing**: For applications that require real-time processing, such as video analysis or live image recognition, the speed provided by GPUs is often necessary.

Training CNN

Imagine you are building a CNN to classify images in a large dataset like *CIFAR-10*. The model consists of several layers, including convolutional and pooling layers, which require a large number of matrix operations. Training this model on a CPU could take days, while a GPU can handle these operations much faster, reducing the training time to hours. In this case, using a GPU would significantly improve the efficiency of your workflow.

Spark

Apache Spark is a distributed computing framework that is designed for processing large-scale data across a cluster of computers. Spark is particularly well-suited for big data applications where datasets are too large to fit into the memory of a single machine. It supports distributed data processing, allowing you to scale out your ML tasks across multiple nodes.

Choosing the right time to use Spark:

- **Large-scale data processing**: When working with massive datasets that require distributed processing, such as those encountered in big data environments, Spark is a powerful tool.

- **ETL pipelines**: Spark is often used in **extract, transform, load** (**ETL**) pipelines to preprocess large datasets before they are fed into ML models.

- **Data exploration and feature engineering**: The ability to process large datasets in parallel makes Spark ideal for data exploration and feature engineering tasks on big data.

Distributed training with Spark

Suppose you are working on a project where you need to preprocess terabytes of log data to train an ML model for fraud detection. Using Spark, you can distribute the data processing across a cluster, significantly speeding up the ETL process. Once the data is preprocessed, you can leverage Spark's MLlib library to train your model on the distributed data, making it possible to handle datasets that would be impractical to process on a single machine.

Non-Spark platforms

Non-Spark platforms refer to various other distributed computing environments that are not built on Spark but still offer powerful tools for processing and training ML models at scale. These include systems like TensorFlow's distributed training, AWS's SageMaker, and Kubernetes for orchestrating ML workloads.

Choosing the right time to use non-spark platforms:

- **Deep learning with distributed training**: Frameworks like *TensorFlow* and *PyTorch* support distributed training across multiple GPUs or machines, which can be more efficient than using Spark for certain deep learning tasks.

- **Managed ML services**: Cloud-based platforms like *AWS SageMaker* offer managed services for distributed training, making it easier to scale your ML workflows without the need for extensive infrastructure management.

- **Containerized workloads**: When deploying ML models in production, platforms like *Kubernetes* allow you to manage and scale your models in a containerized environment efficiently.

Distributed deep learning with TensorFlow

Imagine you are training a deep learning model with TensorFlow on a very large dataset that requires multiple GPUs across several machines. TensorFlow's distributed training capabilities allow you to parallelize the training process across these GPUs, significantly speeding up the training time. This setup is ideal when the complexity and size of your model and dataset exceed the capabilities of a single machine or even a single GPU.

Selecting the right compute resources is a critical decision in any ML project. CPUs offer a cost-effective solution for simpler tasks, while GPUs excel in handling complex models and large datasets. Spark is invaluable for big data processing, especially in distributed environments, while non-Spark platforms provide flexibility for specific use cases like distributed deep learning and managed ML services. By understanding the strengths and appropriate use cases for each type of compute resource, you can optimize your ML workflows for both performance and cost, ensuring that you choose the right tool for the job. Business changes, data patterns change, and models change as well, so in the next section, we will talk about different strategies to update and retrain the model.

Strategies for updating and retraining a model

In the rapidly evolving landscape of ML, keeping models up-to-date is crucial for maintaining their accuracy and relevance. As new data becomes available or as the environment in which your model operates changes, the performance of your model can degrade. This makes it essential to have strategies in place for updating and retraining your models. In this section, we will explore the key strategies for model updating and retraining, discuss when and how to apply them, and provide practical examples to illustrate these concepts.

Need for updating and retraining a model

ML models are typically trained on historical data to make predictions about future events. However, as time passes, the patterns in the data that the model was trained on might change, leading to a decline in the model's performance. This phenomenon, known as *concept drift*, occurs when the statistical properties of the target variable, which the model is trying to predict, change over time.

For example, a model predicting customer behavior might become less accurate if consumer preferences shift due to new market trends. Similarly, a model forecasting sale might need adjustments if new products or services are introduced. In such cases, regularly updating and retraining the model with new data ensures that it remains accurate and continues to deliver value.

Strategies for updating a model

As data evolves over time, keeping your ML models up to date is essential for maintaining accuracy and relevance. The following strategies highlight different approaches to model updating based on data freshness, system resources, and performance needs:

- **Periodic retraining**: One of the simplest strategies is to retrain your model at regular intervals, such as daily, weekly, or monthly, depending on how quickly the underlying data is expected to change. Periodic retraining involves using the most recent data to update the model, allowing it to adapt to new patterns.

  Practical example: Suppose you have a model that predicts daily sales for an online retail store. To ensure that your model stays accurate, you might retrain it every week using the latest sales data. This way, the model remains responsive to short-term trends, such as seasonal promotions or changes in consumer behavior.

- **Incremental learning**: Incremental learning, also known as online learning, involves continuously updating the model as new data arrives, rather than retraining it from scratch. This approach is particularly useful when dealing with large datasets or when real-time updates are required.

  Practical example: Imagine you are managing a recommendation system for a streaming service that suggests movies based on users' viewing habits. As users watch more movies, their preferences may change. With incremental learning, the model can be updated in real-time with each new interaction, ensuring that recommendations remain relevant and personalized.

- **Trigger-based retraining**: Another strategy involves retraining the model only when its performance drops below a certain threshold. This approach is useful when retraining is resource-intensive or when the model's performance is expected to be stable most of the time.

  Practical example: Consider a fraud detection model used by a financial institution. If the model's accuracy in detecting fraudulent transactions begins to decline, an automated trigger could initiate retraining using the latest transaction data. This ensures that the model adapts to new fraud patterns without unnecessary retraining when performance is stable.

- **Ensemble methods for updating a model**: Ensemble methods, such as stacking or boosting, can be used to combine predictions from multiple models, including both older and newly retrained models. This approach helps in gradually transitioning from an old model to a new one while mitigating the risks of abrupt changes.

  Practical example: Let us say you have a well-performing model for predicting stock prices, but market conditions have changed, and you have developed a new model. Instead of discarding the old model, you can use an ensemble approach to combine predictions from both models, ensuring that the transition to the new model is smooth and that the predictions are robust.

Strategies for retraining a model

Retraining a model is a critical step when existing predictions no longer reflect current data trends. Depending on the scope of changes and available resources, different retraining strategies can be applied to keep models accurate, efficient, and relevant.

The following are key approaches to consider:

- **Full retraining**: Full retraining involves retraining the model from scratch using a new dataset that includes both historical and recent data. This approach is useful when the underlying patterns in the data have changed significantly, and the model needs to learn from these new patterns comprehensively.

  Practical example: Suppose you have a demand forecasting model for a product that has undergone a major redesign. The new version of the product appeals to a different demographic, rendering the old model obsolete. Full retraining using the most recent sales data, along with historical data for context, ensures that the model accurately reflects the current market dynamics.

- **Partial retraining**: In some cases, it might be sufficient to update only part of the model rather than retraining the entire model from scratch. Partial retraining is particularly useful for models with modular architectures, where certain components can be updated independently.

  Practical example: Consider a **natural language processing (NLP)** model used for sentiment analysis. If the vocabulary in your training data changes significantly, you might choose to update only the word embeddings (the component responsible for understanding word meanings) while keeping the rest of the model intact. This approach saves time and computational resources while ensuring that the model stays up-to-date.

- **Transfer learning**: Transfer learning involves taking a pre-trained model (usually on a large, general dataset) and fine-tuning it on a smaller, specific dataset. This approach is particularly useful when you do not have enough data to train a model from scratch but need to adapt an existing model to a new task or domain.

  Practical example: Imagine you have developed a model for classifying images of vehicles. Now, you want to adapt this model to classify images of different types of machinery. By using transfer learning, you can take the existing vehicle classification model and fine-tune it with a smaller dataset of machinery images, significantly reducing the time and resources required for training.

Best practices for updating and retraining a model

To ensure your ML models remain accurate and reliable over time, it is important to follow proven best practices. These guidelines help maintain performance, manage resources efficiently, and reduce risk when making updates or retraining models. The following practices are key to building robust and adaptable ML systems:

- **Monitor model performance continuously**: Set up automated monitoring to track your model's performance metrics, such as accuracy, precision, recall, or any other relevant metric. This allows you to detect performance degradation early and decide when retraining is necessary.

- **Maintain version control**: Keep track of different versions of your model, including the data used for training and the hyperparameters. This practice ensures that you can roll back to a previous version if needed and understand how different changes impact model performance.

- **Balance between frequency and cost**: While frequent retraining can keep your model up-to-date, it can also be resource-intensive. Striking the right balance between the frequency of updates and the cost involved is crucial. Use strategies like trigger-based retraining to optimize this balance.

- **Evaluate retrained models before deployment**: Always evaluate the performance of a retrained model on a separate validation set before deploying it. This step ensures that the new model is indeed an improvement over the previous one and prevents any potential negative impacts on production systems.

Updating and retraining ML models is essential for maintaining their effectiveness in a changing environment. By employing strategies such as periodic retraining, incremental learning, and trigger-based retraining, you can ensure that your models continue to deliver accurate and relevant predictions. Additionally, techniques like full retraining, partial retraining, and transfer learning offer flexibility in how you approach model updates, depending on the specific needs of your project. As you advance in your ML journey, mastering these strategies will help you build models that are not only accurate but also resilient to change, ensuring long-term success in dynamic real-world applications.

AWS services for efficient ML model training

AWS offers a robust suite of tools and services designed to streamline the ML model training process. These services cater to different aspects of the ML lifecycle, from data preparation and model training to deployment and monitoring. Leveraging AWS's scalable infrastructure and integrated tools can significantly enhance the efficiency and effectiveness of your ML workflows. In this section, we will explore the key AWS services that facilitate efficient ML model training, discuss their use cases, and provide practical examples to illustrate how they can be utilized in real-world scenarios.

Amazon SageMaker

Amazon SageMaker is a fully managed service that provides every developer and data scientist with the ability to build, train, and deploy ML models at scale. SageMaker abstracts much of the complexity involved in the ML process, offering a range of features that simplify model training, reduce time to deployment, and lower overall costs.

These are some key features of Amazon SageMaker:

- **Integrated Jupyter notebooks**: SageMaker comes with integrated Jupyter notebooks, which allow you to perform data preprocessing, model training, and evaluation in an interactive environment. These notebooks are fully managed, meaning AWS handles the underlying infrastructure, so you can focus on building your models.

- **Built-in algorithms**: SageMaker offers a variety of built-in, optimized algorithms that cover common ML tasks such as classification, regression, clustering, and dimensionality reduction. These algorithms are designed to scale efficiently on large datasets and can be used out of the box with minimal setup.

- **Managed spot training**: One of the most cost-effective features of SageMaker is managed spot training. This feature allows you to leverage unused AWS compute capacity at a reduced cost. SageMaker automatically resumes training from the last checkpoint if an interruption occurs, making it an economical choice for training large models.

- **Automatic model tuning hyperparameter optimization** (HPO): SageMaker provides automatic model tuning, also known as HPO. This feature automatically searches for the best set of hyperparameters by running multiple training jobs with different configurations, saving time and improving model performance.

- **Distributed training**: For large-scale deep learning models, SageMaker supports distributed training across multiple GPUs or instances, allowing you to train models faster by parallelizing the workload.

Training sentiment analysis model with SageMaker

Imagine you are developing a sentiment analysis model to analyze customer reviews. Using SageMaker, you can start by loading your dataset into an integrated Jupyter Notebook, where you perform data preprocessing such as tokenization and feature extraction. Next, you can choose one of SageMaker's built-in algorithms, like BlazingText, which is optimized for text classification tasks. By leveraging SageMaker's managed spot training, you can significantly reduce costs, especially if you are working with a large dataset. Finally, you can use the automatic model tuning feature to find the optimal hyperparameters, ensuring that your model performs well on unseen data.

AWS Batch

AWS Batch is a fully managed service that enables you to run batch computing jobs at any scale. It is particularly useful for running large-scale ML training jobs that require substantial compute resources. AWS Batch automatically provisions the optimal quantity and type of compute resources based on the volume and specific requirements of the batch jobs submitted.

Here is when you can use AWS Batch for model training:

- **High-volume model training**: If you need to train a large number of models simultaneously or process extensive datasets that would overwhelm a single instance, AWS Batch is an ideal choice.

- **Resource-intensive workloads**: AWS Batch is well-suited for workloads that require a lot of computational power, such as training deep learning models or performing complex simulations.

Running multiple training jobs with AWS Batch

Suppose you are working on a project that requires training multiple ML models, each with different configurations and datasets. Using AWS Batch, you can submit all these training jobs at once. AWS Batch will then automatically provision the necessary compute resources and manage the execution of each job in parallel. This approach ensures that your training jobs are completed efficiently, without the need for manual resource management.

Amazon EC2 and EC2 spot instances

Amazon **Elastic Compute Cloud (EC2)** provides scalable compute capacity in the cloud, allowing you to launch virtual servers tailored to your specific needs. EC2 is highly customizable, offering a wide range of instance types optimized for various workloads, including compute-intensive ML tasks. EC2 spot instances allow you to take advantage of unused EC2 capacity at a significant discount, making it a cost-effective option for training ML models.

Let us see when you can use Amazon EC2 and EC2 spot instances:

- **Custom environments**: If you need complete control over the environment in which your ML models are trained, such as installing specific software or configuring unique dependencies, EC2 is the right choice.

- **Cost-effective training**: EC2 spot instances are ideal for reducing training costs, especially for jobs that are flexible in terms of when they can be executed.

Training a neural network on EC2 spot instances

Consider a scenario where you are training a deep learning model using TensorFlow. You require a specific version of TensorFlow and other custom libraries. By launching a

GPU-optimized EC2 instance, you can configure your environment exactly as needed. To save on costs, you choose EC2 spot instances, which offer the same compute power as regular instances but at a fraction of the cost. If your training job is interrupted due to spot instance availability, you can use checkpointing to resume training from where it left off, ensuring that progress is not lost.

AWS Glue

AWS Glue is a fully managed ETL service that makes it easy to prepare data for analytics and ML. While not specifically a training service, AWS Glue plays a crucial role in the ML lifecycle by automating the data preparation process, which is a critical step before training models.

These are a few instances when you can use AWS Glue:

- **Data preparation for ML**: If your ML project involves large datasets that require extensive cleaning, transformation, or merging, AWS Glue can automate these tasks efficiently.

- **Integration with SageMaker**: AWS Glue integrates seamlessly with SageMaker, allowing you to easily prepare data and feed it into your training workflows.

Preparing data for model training with AWS Glue

Imagine you are building a predictive maintenance model for an industrial application. Your raw data comes from various sources, including IoT sensors, maintenance logs, and operational records. Using AWS Glue, you can create ETL jobs that automatically clean, normalize, and join these datasets into a single, cohesive training dataset. Once prepared, this data can be directly loaded into SageMaker for model training, streamlining the entire process from data preparation to model deployment.

Amazon EMR

Amazon **Elastic MapReduce (EMR)** is a cloud-based big data platform that provides a scalable environment for processing large amounts of data using open-source frameworks like *Apache Hadoop, Apache Spark,* and *Apache Hive*. EMR is particularly useful for data-intensive ML tasks that require distributed processing across a cluster of machines.

For ML tasks that involve processing massive datasets or require distributed computing, Amazon EMR offers a powerful and scalable solution. Consider using EMR in the following scenarios:

- **Big data processing**: EMR is ideal for processing and analyzing large-scale datasets, such as those found in genomic research, financial modeling, or clickstream analysis.

- **Integration with Spark MLlib**: If your ML tasks involve large datasets and you prefer using Spark's MLlib for training models, EMR provides a scalable and cost-effective environment.

Training a model using Spark on Amazon EMR

Suppose you are working on a recommendation system for an e-commerce platform, and you have a massive dataset of user interactions. Using Amazon EMR, you can spin up a Spark cluster that processes this data in parallel across multiple nodes. You can then use Spark MLlib to train your recommendation model on this distributed data. EMR handles the complexities of cluster management, allowing you to focus on developing and refining your model.

Here is a table that summarizes the different AWS services for ML model training, along with guidance on when to choose or not to choose each of them:

AWS service	When to choose	When not to choose
Amazon SageMaker	You need an end-to-end, fully managed ML service. You want to automate model tuning (HPO). You prefer built-in algorithms and managed spot training to reduce costs. You require distributed training across multiple GPUs.	You need a custom environment with specific dependencies. You want more control over the underlying infrastructure. Your workload is highly specialized and not suited for SageMaker's built-in features.
AWS Batch	You need to run a large number of batch training jobs simultaneously. Your ML tasks are computationally intensive and require significant resources. You want AWS to manage resource provisioning and job scheduling automatically.	Your ML workload requires real-time processing or continuous training. The job requires a specific environment that is not well-supported by AWS Batch. You have simple, low-volume tasks that do not need batch processing.
Amazon EC2 and EC2 spot instances	You need complete control over the environment for your ML tasks. You require a custom setup with specific libraries or configurations. You want to reduce costs using spot instances. Your model training can tolerate potential interruptions.	You prefer a managed service that handles infrastructure complexities. Your project requires high availability with no interruptions (spot instances might not be suitable). You are working on a small-scale project where SageMaker's simplicity is preferred.
AWS Glue	You need to prepare large datasets for ML training. Your project involves extensive ETL operations. You want to automate data preparation and feed it into other AWS services like *SageMaker*.	You do not have significant data preparation needs. Your dataset is small or simple enough that manual preparation is more efficient. You are not integrating with other AWS services that require ETL.

AWS service	When to choose	When not to choose
Amazon EMR	You are dealing with big data that requires distributed processing. You need to process large datasets using Spark, Hadoop, or Hive. Your ML tasks involve scalable data analytics and training with Spark MLlib.	Your datasets are small and do not require distributed processing. You are not familiar with big data frameworks like Spark or Hadoop. You prefer managed services that abstract the complexities of cluster management.

Table 9.1: Choosing the right AWS service for ML model training

This table helps you quickly identify which AWS service is most appropriate for your ML project based on your specific needs and circumstances.

AWS offers a diverse set of services designed to make ML model training more efficient, scalable, and cost-effective. Whether you are using SageMaker for its fully managed ML capabilities, AWS Batch for handling large-scale training jobs, EC2 for customizable environments, AWS Glue for data preparation, or EMR for big data processing, AWS provides the tools you need to streamline your ML workflows. By selecting the right AWS services for your specific needs, you can accelerate the training process, reduce costs, and build models that are ready to meet the challenges of real-world applications.

The next chapter focuses on hyperparameter optimization, a critical component in ML that directly influences model performance. Readers will learn various techniques for fine-tuning ML models, including regularization and cross-validation methods, with specific attention to different model types such as neural networks and tree-based models. The next chapter will equip aspiring AWS Certified ML Specialists with essential knowledge about optimizing hyperparameters using AWS solutions, providing a practical understanding necessary for developing and maintaining effective ML solutions in the AWS Cloud.

Conclusion

This chapter provided essential strategies for training, optimizing, and maintaining ML models. You learned the importance of data splitting to prevent overfitting and explored methods like simple train/validation splits and k-fold cross-validation to assess model performance. Optimization techniques such as gradient descent, momentum, and adaptive learning rates (e.g., Adam and RMSProp) were explained to improve training efficiency and accuracy.

We also covered how to choose the right compute resources like CPUs, GPUs, and distributed platforms like Spark based on model complexity and dataset size. The chapter then outlined key strategies for model updating, including periodic retraining, incremental learning, and trigger-based approaches, along with techniques like transfer learning and ensemble methods to improve model adaptability. Finally, you explored core AWS tools like SageMaker, EMR,

EC2, Glue, and Batch, learning when to use each for efficient model training and deployment. Together, these insights equip you with a strong foundation for building and scaling ML solutions effectively within the AWS ecosystem.

In the next chapter, we will focus on hyperparameter optimization, an essential step for fine-tuning ML models. You will explore techniques like regularization, cross-validation, and model-specific tuning strategies, along with AWS tools that simplify and automate this process.

Multiple choice questions

1. **What is the primary purpose of data splitting in ML?**
    a. To reduce the size of the dataset
    b. To increase the complexity of the model
    c. To prevent overfitting and assess model performance
    d. To speed up the training process

2. **Which technique is most suitable for evaluating model performance on small datasets?**
    a. Simple train-test split
    b. k-fold cross-validation
    c. Leave-One-Out cross-validation
    d. Batch gradient descent

3. **What is momentum in the context of gradient descent optimization?**
    a. A method to adjust the learning rate dynamically
    b. A technique to use past gradients to accelerate convergence
    c. A way to randomly select data points for training
    d. A method for parallelizing computations

4. **Which of the following optimization algorithms combines both momentum and adaptive learning rates?**
    a. AdaGrad
    b. RMSProp
    c. Adam
    d. Stochastic gradient descent

5. **When should you choose to use GPUs over CPUs for training an ML model?**

    a. When training simple linear regression models

    b. When working with small datasets

    c. When training deep learning models with large datasets

    d. When performing real-time inference on a small scale

6. **Which AWS service is best suited for running a large number of batch training jobs simultaneously?**

    a. Amazon SageMaker

    b. AWS Batch

    c. Amazon EC2

    d. AWS Glue

7. **What is the key advantage of using EC2 spot instances for ML training?**

    a. Guaranteed high availability of instances

    b. Reduced costs for compute resources

    c. Automatic model tuning

    d. Built-in algorithms for ML

8. **Which strategy involves retraining a model only when its performance falls below a certain threshold?**

    a. Periodic retraining

    b. Incremental learning

    c. Trigger-based retraining

    d. Transfer learning

9. **What is the primary use of AWS Glue in the ML workflow?**

    a. Model training

    b. Data preparation and ETL operations

    c. Model deployment

    d. Real-time inference

10. **Which of the following is true about Amazon SageMaker's automatic model tuning feature?**

   a. It requires manual selection of hyperparameters

   b. It uses grid search to find the best model configuration

   c. It automatically searches for the best hyperparameters through multiple training jobs

   d. It only works with deep learning models

Answer key

1. c.
2. b.
3. b.
4. c.
5. c.
6. b.
7. b.
8. c.
9. b.
10. c.

Join our Discord space

Join our Discord workspace for latest updates, offers, tech happenings around the world, new releases, and sessions with the authors:

https://discord.bpbonline.com

CHAPTER 10
Hyperparameter Optimization

Introduction

Hyperparameter optimization is a crucial aspect of machine learning that can significantly impact model performance. In this chapter, we delve into the intricacies of fine-tuning **machine learning (ML)** models by adjusting their hyperparameters. As an aspiring AWS Certified Machine Learning Specialist, understanding these concepts is essential for designing, building, and maintaining effective ML solutions in the Amazon Web Services Cloud.

We will explore various techniques and methodologies for optimizing hyperparameters, from regularization techniques to cross-validation methods. We will also examine specific strategies for tuning different types of models, including neural networks and tree-based models. Finally, we will investigate how AWS solutions can streamline and enhance the hyperparameter optimization process.

Structure

The chapter covers the following topics:

- Regularization techniques
- Cross-validation methods
- Neural network architecture optimization

- Tuning-tree-based models
- AWS solutions for hyperparameter optimization

Objectives

By the end of this chapter, readers will be equipped with the knowledge and skills to effectively optimize machine learning models for improved performance and generalization. They will understand and apply regularization techniques such as Dropout, L1, and L2 regularization to prevent overfitting, and implement various cross-validation methods to accurately assess model performance. Readers will also learn how to optimize neural network architectures by adjusting layers, nodes, and learning rates, as well as apply targeted tuning strategies to enhance the predictive capabilities of tree-based models like decision trees and random forests, as well as linear models. Additionally, the chapter will explore how to leverage AWS solutions, particularly Amazon SageMaker, for scalable and efficient hyperparameter optimization in the cloud. Emphasis will be placed on analyzing the trade-offs between model complexity, performance, and computational resources. Ultimately, readers will be able to design and implement effective hyperparameter optimization strategies tailored to real-world machine learning projects on the AWS platform.

By mastering these objectives, you will be well-prepared to tackle the hyperparameter optimization section of the *AWS Certified Machine Learning - Specialty exam* and apply these skills in practical ML scenarios using AWS services.

Regularization techniques

Regularization is a fundamental concept in ML that helps prevent overfitting, ensuring that our models generalize well to unseen data. At its core, regularization adds a penalty term to the loss function, discouraging the model from fitting the training data too closely. This section will cover three important regularization techniques: Dropout, L1 regularization, and L2 regularization.

Dropout

Dropout is a regularization technique primarily used in neural networks. It works on a simple principle: during training, randomly *drop out* (i.e., set to zero) a proportion of neurons in a layer. This prevents the network from relying too heavily on any particular set of neurons, forcing it to learn more robust features.

Basic approach

You can follow this by carrying out the following during a training iteration:

1. Randomly select a subset of neurons to drop out

2. Set the output of these neurons to zero

3. Perform forward and backward propagation as usual

If we set a dropout rate of 50%, on average, only half of the neurons are active in each training iteration.

During inference (testing), all neurons are used, but their outputs are scaled so that the expected total activation flowing through the network matches what it experienced during training.

If we simply used all neurons without any adjustment, the network would be receiving roughly twice as much total activation as it did during training (since we are using 100% of neurons instead of 50%). To compensate for this, we scale the outputs of each neuron by the keep rate (1 - dropout rate). In our 50% dropout example, we multiply each neuron's output by 0.5 during inference.

This scaling ensures that the expected total activation flowing through the network during inference matches what the network experienced during training:

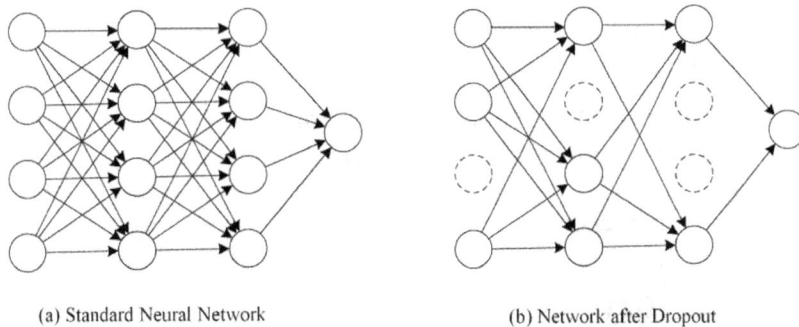

(a) Standard Neural Network   (b) Network after Dropout

Figure 10.1: Dropout regularization technique

The preceding figure shows two versions of a neural network layer. On the left, all neurons are active and connected. On the right, the same layer is shown with dropout applied some neurons are greyed out, indicating they have been temporarily removed from the network. Arrows connecting the layers are also selectively removed to show how information flow is affected.

L1 or LASSO regularization

L1 regularization, also known as **Least Absolute Shrinkage and Selection Operator (LASSO)**, is a technique used in ML to prevent overfitting and improve model generalization. It works by adding a penalty term to the model's loss function based on the absolute value of the model's weights. This penalty encourages the model to use fewer features by pushing some of the less important weights to exactly zero. As a result, L1 regularization effectively performs feature selection, creating a sparser model that is often more interpretable and can perform better on unseen data. This approach is particularly useful when dealing with high-dimensional datasets where many features may be irrelevant or redundant. By simplifying the model in this way, L1 regularization helps reduce complexity and can lead to more robust predictions, especially in scenarios where the number of features is large compared to the number of training examples.

Basic approach

L1 regularization is a technique that helps make machine learning models simpler and often more effective. It works by adding a special constraint to the training process that discourages the model from relying too heavily on too many features. In simple terms, it tells the model: Only use the features that really matter, and ignore the rest.

During training, the model not only tries to minimize prediction error but also keeps the overall magnitude of its weights as small as possible. It does this by adding the sum of the absolute values of all weights to its loss function:

$$Loss = Original\ Loss + \lambda * \Sigma i\,|wi\,|$$

Here, lambda is a regularization parameter that controls how much importance to place on minimizing weights, and w_i represents each individual weight in the model.

The clever part of L1 regularization is that it tends to drive less important weights exactly to zero. This effectively removes unhelpful features from the model, making it more interpretable and reducing the risk of overfitting. In the end, the model focuses on the features that truly matter, just like tuning out background noise to hear the main melody.

L2 regularization

L2 regularization, also known as **Ridge regularization**, improves model generalization by adding a penalty term to the loss function based on the squared values of the model's weights. This approach discourages large weight values, effectively reducing the model's sensitivity to individual features. As a result, L2 regularization typically produces more stable models that perform well on unseen data, without completely eliminating any features from the model.

Basic approach

It helps improve a model's generalization by discouraging it from assigning excessively large weights to any one feature. It does this by adding a penalty term to the loss function that is based on the **squared values** of the model's weights:

$$Loss = Original\ Loss + \lambda i \Sigma wi2$$

In this equation, lambda is the regularization parameter that controls how strongly the penalty is applied, and w_i represents each weight in the model.

Unlike L1 regularization, which can drive some weights to exactly zero and eliminate features entirely, **L2 regularization shrinks all weights smoothly** toward zero but rarely eliminates them completely. This results in models that are generally more stable and less sensitive to noise or fluctuations in individual features. The model learns to rely on all features more evenly, which helps prevent overfitting and improves performance on new, unseen data.

Cross-validation methods

Cross-validation is a fundamental technique in machine learning used to assess how well a model will generalize to an independent dataset. It helps us estimate the model's performance on unseen data and detect overfitting. Let us explore four key cross-validation methods: k-Fold cross-validation, Stratified k-Fold cross-validation, Leave-One-Out cross-validation, and Time Series cross-validation.

k-Fold cross-validation

k-Fold cross-validation is a technique that divides the dataset into k equally sized subsets or **folds**. The model is then trained k times, each time using *k-1* folds for training and the remaining fold for validation. This process ensures that each data point is used for validation exactly once.

Let us look at the step-wise working of this technique:

1. Divide the dataset into k equal-sized folds

2. For each iteration:

    a. Use k-1 folds for training

    b. Use the remaining fold for validation

    c. Calculate and store the performance metric

3. Average the k performance metrics to get overall model performance

Stratified k-Fold cross-validation

Stratified k-Fold cross-validation is a variation of k-Fold cross-validation that ensures each fold has approximately the same proportion of samples for each target class as in the complete dataset. This method is particularly useful for datasets with imbalanced classes.

Let us now see how this technique works:

1. Divide the dataset into k folds, ensuring that the proportion of samples for each class is roughly the same in each fold

2. Follow the same process as k-Fold cross-validation for training and validation

Leave-One-Out cross-validation

Leave-One-Out cross-validation is an extreme case of k-Fold cross-validation where k is equal to the number of samples in the dataset. In each iteration, the model is trained on all data points except one, which is used for validation.

This is how Leave-One-Out cross-validation works:

1. For each data point in the dataset:

    i. Train the model on all other data points

    ii. Validate the model on the single held-out data point

2. Calculate the average performance across all iterations

Time series cross-validation

Time series cross-validation is designed for datasets where the order of samples matters, such as in time series data. It ensures that we always train on past data and validate on future data, respecting the temporal nature of the dataset.

Here is how this cross-validation functions:

1. Start with a minimum number of samples for training

2. Use the next sample(s) for validation

3. Expand the training set to include the previous validation sample(s)

4. Repeat steps 2-3 until you reach the end of the dataset

When evaluating ML models, selecting the right cross-validation technique is critical to obtaining accurate and reliable performance estimates.

The following table compares common cross-validation methods, outlining their advantages, drawbacks, and ideal use cases:

Method	Pros	Cons	Best use case
k-Fold	Utilizes all data for both training and validation. Provides robust performance estimate	Can be computationally expensive for large datasets. May not preserve data distribution in each fold	General-purpose, when data order does not matter
Stratified k-Fold	Maintains class distribution in each fold. Provides more reliable performance estimate for imbalanced datasets	Slightly more complex to implement. May not be applicable for regression tasks	Classification tasks with imbalanced classes

Leave-One-Out	Uses maximum amount of training data. Provides unbiased performance estimate	Computationally very expensive. High variance in performance estimates	Small datasets where maximizing training data is crucial
Time series	Respects temporal order of data. Prevents data leakage from future to past	Uses less training data in initial folds. May not be suitable for non-temporal data	Time series data, sequential data

Table 10.1: Comparison of cross-validation methods

By understanding these cross-validation methods, you will be able to choose the most appropriate technique for your specific dataset and problem, ensuring reliable model evaluation and selection in your AWS ML projects. Remember, the choice of cross-validation method can significantly impact your model's performance assessment and, consequently, your hyperparameter optimization process.

Neural network architecture optimization

Neural network architecture optimization is a crucial aspect of developing effective deep learning models. It involves making decisions about the structure and parameters of a neural network to improve its performance on a given task. We will explore three key areas in this section, namely layers, nodes, and learning rates.

Layers

Layers are the building blocks of neural networks. Each layer transforms its input data and passes the result to the next layer. The depth of a network refers to the number of layers between the input and output.

The following list the type of layers that form the neural networks:

- **Input layer**: Receives the initial data
- **Hidden layers**: Processes the data. Common types include:
    o   Fully connected (dense) layers
    o   Convolutional layers
- **Recurrent layers, e.g., long short-term memory (LSTM)**: A type of **recurrent neural network (RNN)** designed to capture long-range dependencies in sequential data by using memory cells and gating mechanisms.

- **Gated recurrent unit (GRU)**: A simplified variant of LSTM that uses fewer gates to model dependencies in sequences, offering faster training with comparable performance in many tasks

- **Output layer**: Produces the final prediction

The depth is another important aspect while designing the Neural networks and following are some key considerations:

- Shallow networks (few layers) may underfit complex data

- Deep networks can learn more complex features, but may overfit or be difficult to train

Nodes

Nodes, or neurons, are the basic computational units in each layer. The width of a layer refers to the number of nodes it contains. Connectivity describes how nodes in adjacent layers are connected:

- **Width considerations**:
  - Narrow layers (few nodes) may not capture enough information
  - Wide layers can learn more features, but increase computational cost and risk of overfitting

- **Connectivity types**:
  - **Fully connected**: Each node connects to every node in the adjacent layers
  - **Convolutional**: Nodes connect to local regions in the input, effective for spatial data
  - **Recurrent**: Nodes have connections that span time steps, suitable for sequential data

Learning rates

The learning rate determines how much the model's weights are updated during training. It is crucial for the convergence and performance of the model. There are two types of approaches involved, as described in the following sub-sections.

Scheduling

Learning rate scheduling involves changing the learning rate during training.

The following are some common strategies that are followed:

- **Step decay**: Reduce the learning rate by a factor after a set number of epochs

- **Exponential decay**: Continuously decrease the learning rate exponentially

- **Cosine annealing**: Oscillate the learning rate between a maximum and minimum value

Adaptive methods

Adaptive optimization methods automatically adjust the learning rate. Popular techniques include the following:

- **Adam**: Adapts learning rates for each parameter

- **RMSprop**: Uses a moving average of squared gradients to normalize the gradient

- **Adagrad**: Adapts the learning rate to the parameters, performing smaller updates for frequent parameters

The following is a quick comparison of all neural network architecture optimization techniques discussed previously:

Technique	Pros	Cons	Best use case
Increasing depth	Can learn more complex features	Risk of overfitting, harder to train	Complex tasks with large datasets
Increasing width	Can capture more information per layer	Computationally expensive, risk of overfitting	When more feature extraction is needed at a particular level
Fully connected layers	Versatile, can learn global patterns	Many parameters, risk of overfitting	General-purpose tasks, final layers in many architectures
Convolutional layers	Efficient for spatial data, fewer parameters	Less effective for non-spatial data	Image-related tasks, spatial data
Recurrent layers	Can handle sequential data	Can be difficult to train, may have vanishing/exploding gradients	Time series, natural language processing
Learning rate scheduling	Can improve convergence and final performance	Requires tuning of schedule hyperparameters	When basic adaptive methods struggle
Adaptive learning rate methods	Automatically adjust learning rates, often work well out-of-the-box	May not always converge to the best solution	General-purpose, when you want a good baseline quickly

Table 10.2: Comparison of neural network architecture optimization techniques

By understanding these neural network architecture optimization techniques, you will be better equipped to design and fine-tune deep learning models for your specific tasks in AWS machine learning projects. Remember, the best architecture often depends on your specific dataset and problem, so experimentation and iterative improvement are key.

Tuning tree-based models

Tree-based models are powerful and interpretable ML algorithms widely used in various domains. In this section, we will explore the tuning of three popular tree-based models: decision trees, random forests, and gradient boosting machines.

Decision trees

A decision tree is a flowchart-like structure where each internal node represents a feature, each branch represents a decision rule, and each leaf node represents an outcome. The tree makes decisions by splitting the dataset based on feature values.

The following are the key hyperparameters:

- **Max depth**: The maximum depth of the tree

- **Min samples split**: The minimum number of samples required to split an internal node

- **Min samples leaf**: The minimum number of samples required to be at a leaf node

- **Max features**: The number of features to consider when looking for the best split

Let us look at the tuning process:

1. Start with a small tree and gradually increase complexity

2. Use cross-validation to evaluate performance

3. Monitor training and validation scores to avoid overfitting.

Random forests

A random forest is an ensemble of decision trees. It builds multiple trees on random subsets of the data and features, then aggregates their predictions to make a final prediction. This approach reduces overfitting and improves generalization.

Here are the key hyperparameters of random forests:

- **N_Estimators**: The number of trees in the forest

- **Max_Depth**: The maximum depth of each tree

- **Min_Samples_Split and Min_Samples_Leaf**: As in decision trees
- **Max_Features**: The number of features to consider for the best split

The following is the tuning process of a random forest:

1. Start with a moderate number of trees and increase if needed
2. Adjust tree-specific parameters to control individual tree complexity
3. Use cross-validation and monitor **out-of-bag (OOB)** error

Gradient boosting machines

A **gradient boosting machine (GBM)** builds trees sequentially, with each tree trying to correct the errors of the previous ones. It is a powerful technique that often achieves state-of-the-art results on many machine learning tasks.

The following are GBM's key hyperparameters:

- **N_Estimators**: The number of boosting stages (trees) to perform
- **Learning_Rate**: Shrinks the contribution of each tree
- **Max_Depth**: The maximum depth of each tree
- **Subsample**: The fraction of samples to be used for fitting the individual trees

The following is the tuning process:

1. Start with a small number of shallow trees and a low learning rate
2. Gradually increase the number of trees while monitoring validation performance
3. Adjust tree complexity and learning rate to find the optimal trade-off
4. Apply early stopping by tracking validation loss and halting training when performance stops improving.

In the following table, you can see a comparison of tree-based models:

Aspect	Decision trees	Random forests	Gradient boosting machines
Model complexity	Low	Medium	High
Training speed	Fast	Moderate	Slow
Prediction speed	Very fast	Fast	Moderate
Handling of overfitting	Prone to overfitting	Good resistance	Can overfit if not tuned properly

Feature importance	Provides	Provides (more robust)	Provides
Handling of imbalanced data	Poor	Good	Good
Interpretability	High	Medium	Low
Key advantage	Simple and interpretable	Robust and stable	Often highest accuracy
Key disadvantage	Can be unstable	Black-box model	Sensitive to noisy data

Table 10.3: Comparison of decision trees, random forests, and gradient boosting machines across key aspects

When tuning tree-based models, it is crucial to understand the trade-offs between model complexity, training time, and performance. Decision trees are simple and interpretable but can overfit easily. Random forests provide a good balance of performance and robustness. GBMs often achieve the highest accuracy but require careful tuning to prevent overfitting.

Remember that the best model and hyperparameters often depend on your specific dataset and problem. Always use cross-validation and consider the interpretability-performance trade-off when selecting and tuning your model for AWS ML projects.

Tuning linear models

Linear models are fundamental in ML, prized for their simplicity, interpretability, and effectiveness in many scenarios. In this section, we will explore the tuning of linear models for both regression and classification tasks.

Linear regression models

Linear regression models the relationship between a dependent variable and one or more independent variables by fitting a linear equation to observed data. The goal is to find the best-fitting line (or hyperplane in higher dimensions) that minimizes the difference between predicted and actual values.

The following are the key hyperparameters for these models:

- **Regularization type**: L1 (Lasso), L2 (Ridge), or Elastic Net (combination of L1 and L2)

- **Regularization strength (often denoted as α or lambda)**: Controls the amount of regularization

- **Fit intercept**: Whether to calculate the intercept for the model

The following is the step-wise tuning process:

1. Start with simple linear regression without regularization
2. Introduce regularization and tune its strength

3.   Use cross-validation to evaluate model performance

4.   Apply feature scaling (e.g., standardization) to ensure that all features contribute equally to the regularization penalty

Linear classification models

Linear classification models separate classes using a linear decision boundary. For binary classification, this boundary is a line (or hyperplane in higher dimensions) that best separates the two classes. For multi-class problems, techniques like one-vs-rest or one-vs-one are used to extend the binary case.

The following are the key hyperparameters:

- **Regularization type**: L1, L2, or Elastic Net

- **Regularization strength (C in scikit-learn)**: Inverse of regularization strength; smaller values specify stronger regularization

- **Multi-class strategy**: **One-vs-rest** (**ovr**) or **multinomial** (useful for logistic regression)

Let us now look at the steps in the tuning process:

1.   Start with a simple model (e.g., logistic regression with L2 regularization)

2.   Tune the regularization strength

3.   Experiment with different regularization types

4.   Use cross-validation to evaluate model performance

5.   Consider class balancing for imbalanced datasets

6.   Add non-linear terms (e.g., interaction features or polynomial expansions) to capture more complex relationships if needed

When tuning linear models, it is crucial to understand the trade-offs between model complexity and generalization. Regularization plays a key role in both regression and classification tasks, helping to prevent overfitting and improve model performance on unseen data.

Remember that while linear models are powerful and interpretable, they assume a linear relationship between features and the target variable. In cases where this assumption does not hold, consider using non-linear models or feature engineering techniques to capture more complex relationships.

For AWS ML projects, linear models can serve as excellent baselines and can be particularly useful when interpretability is a key requirement. Their quick training time and low computational requirements make them suitable for large-scale applications and real-time predictions in cloud environments.

AWS solutions for hyperparameter optimization

AWS provides powerful tools for hyperparameter optimization through Amazon SageMaker. These tools automate the process of finding the best hyperparameters for your machine learning models, saving time and improving model performance. Let us explore three key offerings: automatic model tuning, hyperparameter tuning jobs, and integration with SageMaker Pipelines.

Amazon SageMaker Automatic Model Tuning

Amazon SageMaker Automatic Model Tuning uses Bayesian optimization to intelligently search the hyperparameter space. It automatically launches multiple training jobs with different hyperparameter combinations, evaluates their performance, and focuses on the most promising areas of the hyperparameter space.

The following are the key features:

- **Intelligent search**: Uses Bayesian optimization and multi-armed bandit algorithms

- **Parallel execution**: Can run multiple training jobs in parallel

- **Early stopping**: Stops poorly performing jobs to save time and resources

- **Integration**: Works seamlessly with SageMaker's built-in algorithms and custom models.

The following are the steps to see how Amazon SageMaker Automatic Model Tuning works:

1. Define the hyperparameter ranges and the objective metric

2. SageMaker launches multiple training jobs with different hyperparameter settings

3. It evaluates the performance of each job based on the objective metric

4. The algorithm focuses on promising areas of the hyperparameter space in subsequent iterations

5. The process continues until the maximum number of training jobs is reached

Amazon SageMaker Hyperparameter Tuning Jobs

Hyperparameter Tuning Jobs in SageMaker provide a more granular control over the tuning process. While Automatic Model Tuning offers a high-level interface, Hyperparameter Tuning Jobs allow you to specify more detailed configurations and have finer control over the tuning process.

The following are the key features of this solution:

- **Custom search algorithms**: Choose between Bayesian optimization, random search, or grid search

- **Warm start**: Use information from previous tuning jobs to accelerate new ones

- **Resource management**: Specify instance types and limits for tuning jobs

- **Custom metrics**: Define and use custom evaluation metrics

Now, let us look at how this process works:

1. Define a training job that includes hyperparameters to tune

2. Specify the ranges or sets of values for each hyperparameter

3. Configure the tuning job settings (e.g., maximum number of jobs, parallel jobs, and so on)

4. Launch the tuning job and monitor its progress

5. Analyze results and select the best model

Integrating hyperparameter optimization in SageMaker Pipelines

SageMaker Pipelines allow you to create end-to-end ML workflows. By integrating hyperparameter optimization into these pipelines, you can automate the entire process from data preparation to model deployment, including finding the best hyperparameters.

The following are some of its key features:

- **Workflow automation**: Incorporate hyperparameter tuning as a step in your ML pipeline

- **Reproducibility**: Easily recreate and modify your tuning process

- **Scalability**: Leverage SageMaker's managed infrastructure for large-scale tuning

- **Monitoring and tracking**: Integrated with SageMaker Experiments for tracking and comparing runs

Let us look at how this works:

1. Define your pipeline steps (e.g., data processing, feature engineering, and so on)

2. Include a hyperparameter tuning step in your pipeline

3. Configure subsequent steps to use the best model from the tuning step

4. Execute the pipeline, which will automatically perform tuning and select the best model.

Here is a comparison of AWS hyperparameter optimization solutions:

Feature	Automatic model tuning	Hyperparameter tuning jobs	SageMaker Pipelines integration
Ease of use	High (abstracted interface)	Medium (more control, more complex)	Medium (requires pipeline knowledge)
Flexibility	Medium	High	Very high
Integration with SageMaker	Seamless	Direct	Complete workflow integration
Scalability	Managed by SageMaker	Configurable	Highly scalable
Best for	Quick, efficient tuning	Fine-grained control over tuning process	End-to-end ML workflows
Monitoring	Basic	Detailed	Comprehensive (with SageMaker Experiments)

Table 10.4: Comparison of AWS hyperparameter optimization solutions

By leveraging these AWS solutions for hyperparameter optimization, you can significantly improve the efficiency and effectiveness of your ML model development process. Automatic model tuning provides a user-friendly interface for quick results, hyperparameter tuning jobs offer more control for advanced users, and integration with SageMaker Pipelines allows for comprehensive, reproducible ML workflows. Choose the approach that best fits your project's needs and complexity.

Conclusion

In conclusion, hyperparameter optimization is a critical aspect of ML that can significantly impact model performance. This chapter has explored a range of techniques and methodologies for fine-tuning machine learning models. It covered regularization methods like L1, L2, and Dropout to prevent overfitting, along with cross-validation techniques for more accurate performance evaluation. Additionally, it introduced strategies for optimizing neural network architectures and tuning both tree-based and linear models to enhance predictive accuracy.

We have also examined how AWS solutions, particularly Amazon SageMaker, can streamline and enhance the hyperparameter optimization process through automatic model tuning, hyperparameter tuning jobs, and integration with SageMaker Pipelines. By mastering these concepts and leveraging the power of cloud computing, aspiring AWS Certified Machine Learning Specialists will be well-equipped to design, build, and maintain effective ML solutions that generalize well to unseen data and deliver optimal performance in real-world scenarios. Having covered techniques for fine-tuning ML models, such as regularization, cross-validation, and optimization strategies for neural networks, tree-based, and linear models, we now turn to the equally critical task of evaluation.

In the next chapter, you will learn how to assess model performance using key metrics, detect bias and variance, compare models effectively, and leverage AWS tools to ensure your models are both accurate and dependable.

Multiple choice questions

1. **Which regularization technique involves randomly setting a proportion of neurons to zero during training?**
   a. L1 regularization
   b. L2 regularization
   c. Dropout
   d. Learning rate

2. **In k-Fold cross-validation, what happens if k is equal to the number of samples in the dataset?**
   a. It becomes random sampling
   b. It becomes stratified sampling
   c. It becomes Leave-One-Out cross-validation
   d. It becomes bootstrapping

3. **Which of the following is not a key hyperparameter for tuning random forests?**
   a. N_Estimators
   b. Max_Depth
   c. Learning_Rate
   d. Min_Samples_Split

4. **What is the main advantage of GBMs over random forests?**
   a. Faster training time
   b. Higher interpretability
   c. Often achieves higher accuracy
   d. Requires less hyperparameter tuning

5. **Which AWS service uses Bayesian optimization for intelligent hyperparameter tuning?**

   a.   AWS Lambda

   b.   Amazon SageMaker Automatic Model Tuning

   c.   Amazon EC2

   d.   AWS Glue

6. **In neural network architecture optimization, what does increasing the depth of a network refer to?**

   a.   Adding more nodes to each layer

   b.   Adding more layers to the network

   c.   Increasing the learning rate

   d.   Increasing the batch size

7. **What is a characteristic of L1 (Lasso) regularization in linear models?**

   a.   It tends to produce dense solutions

   b.   It encourages exactly zero coefficients for some features

   c.   It is always preferred over L2 regularization

   d.   It is less computationally expensive than L2 regularization

8. **What is the purpose of learning rate scheduling in neural networks?**

   a.   To increase the number of neurons over time

   b.   To adjust the learning rate during training

   c.   To add more layers to the network automatically

   d.   To change the activation functions dynamically

9. **Which cross-validation method is most appropriate for imbalanced datasets?**

   a.   k-Fold cross-validation

   b.   Stratified k-Fold cross-validation

   c.   Leave-One-Out cross-validation

   d.   Time Series cross-validation

10. **What is a key advantage of using SageMaker Pipelines for hyperparameter optimization?**

   a. It is the only way to perform hyperparameter tuning in AWS

   b. It allows for end-to-end workflow automation including hyperparameter tuning

   c. It is always faster than other hyperparameter tuning methods

   d. It requires less computational resources than other methods

Answer key

1. c.

2. c.

3. c.

4. c.

5. b.

6. b.

7. b.

8. b.

9. b.

10. b.

Join our Discord space,

Join our Discord workspace for latest updates, offers, tech happenings around the world, new releases, and sessions with the authors:

https://discord.bpbonline.com

CHAPTER 11
Evaluating ML Models

Introduction

Evaluating **machine learning** (**ML**) models is a cornerstone of building reliable and high-performing AI/ML solutions. The AWS Certified Machine Learning – Specialty (MLS-C01) exam tests your understanding of key evaluation concepts and your ability to apply them effectively using AWS tools. Whether assessing the accuracy of a model, ensuring it generalizes well, or leveraging AWS services to streamline the process, a deep understanding of ML model evaluation is essential for certification success and real-world applications.

This chapter provides comprehensive guidance on evaluating ML models, addressing critical topics such as identifying bias and variance, understanding performance metrics, comparing models, and leveraging AWS tools for model evaluation. By mastering these areas, you will be equipped to confidently answer exam questions and apply these skills in practical scenarios.

Structure

The chapter covers the following topics:

- Detecting and handling bias and variance
- Interpreting key evaluation metrics

- Offline vs. online model evaluation techniques

- Model comparison using performance metrics

- Utilizing AWS tools for ML model evaluation

Objectives

This chapter covers essential concepts and techniques for evaluating ML models. You will learn how to detect and handle bias and variance, understand their impact on model performance, and apply strategies to mitigate them. The chapter also explains how to interpret key evaluation metrics such as AUC-ROC, precision, recall, and F1 score to assess model effectiveness. It differentiates between offline and online evaluation methods, guiding you on when and how to apply each. Additionally, you will explore how to compare models using performance metrics to select the most suitable one for your use case. Finally, the chapter provides hands-on insights into using AWS tools like *Amazon SageMaker Clarify, Model Monitor, and Experiments* to streamline and enhance the model evaluation process.

By mastering these objectives, you will be well-prepared to tackle the evaluate ML models section of the AWS Certified Machine Learning – Specialty (MLS-C01) exam and apply these skills in practical ML scenarios using AWS services.

Detecting and handling bias and variance

Bias and variance are two fundamental concepts that play a crucial role in the performance of ML models. They represent different sources of errors that can affect how well a model generalizes to unseen data. Understanding and addressing these concepts is essential for building reliable and effective ML solutions.

This section delves into the definitions of bias and variance, their impact on model performance, and techniques to detect and address them. We will use simple explanations, practical examples, and illustrations to clarify these ideas.

Bias

Bias refers to the error introduced by simplifying assumptions made by the model to learn the target function. High bias often results in underfitting, where the model fails to capture the underlying patterns in the data.

The following are a few characteristics of high bias:

- Low training accuracy indicates that the model is underfitting the data, meaning it is too simple to capture the underlying patterns even in the training set. This could result from inadequate model complexity, insufficient training time, or poor feature representation.

- Low test accuracy while having high training accuracy typically signals overfitting. The model has learned the training data too well—including noise—and fails to generalize to new, unseen data. This issue may require regularization, more data, or simplification of the model.

Example: Consider a linear regression model trying to predict house prices based on features like size, location, and age. If the relationship between features and prices is non-linear, but the model assumes linearity, it will have high bias and fail to capture the complexity of the data.

Variance

Variance refers to the error introduced by the model being overly complex and sensitive to the training data. High variance often results in **overfitting**, where the model memorizes the training data instead of generalizing to new data.

The following are the characteristics of high variance:

- **High training accuracy**: The model performs extremely well on the training data because it has effectively memorized it, including any noise or anomalies.

- **Low test accuracy**: The model performs poorly on new, unseen data because it fails to generalize; its predictions do not hold up outside the training environment.

Example: A decision tree with many branches might perfectly fit the training data but perform poorly on unseen data because it has learned the noise rather than the signal.

Bias-variance tradeoff

Bias and variance are inversely related; reducing one often increases the other. The goal is to find the right balance to minimize total error (bias + variance).

Detecting bias and variance

Performance metrics play a crucial role in diagnosing model issues such as underfitting and overfitting. By examining training and test accuracy, you can identify whether a model suffers from high bias or high variance.

- **High bias (underfitting)**:
  o Training and test accuracy are both low.
  o Model does not capture the underlying patterns of the data.

- **High variance (overfitting)**:
  o Training accuracy is high, but test accuracy is low.
  o The model is too sensitive to the training data.

The following figure illustrates the Bias-variance tradeoff:

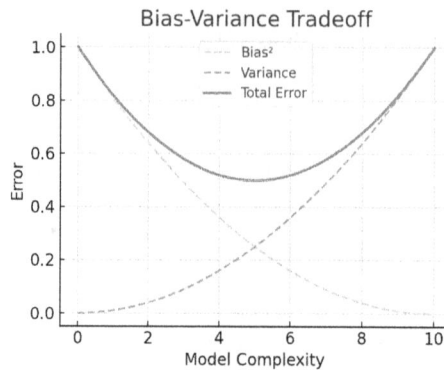

Figure 11.1: *Bias-variance tradeoff*

As model complexity increases, bias decreases while variance increases. The optimal model minimizes the total error by balancing bias and variance.

Learning curves

Learning curves are graphical tools that plot training and validation error against the number of training iterations or the size of the training data. By analyzing the shape and relationship of these curves, you can diagnose whether a model suffers from high bias or high variance. Details are as follows:

- **High bias**: Training and validation errors converge but remain high, indicating the model is too simple to capture the underlying patterns in the data.

- **High variance**: A large gap exists between training and validation errors, suggesting the model performs well on training data but fails to generalize to new data.

The following figure represents the learning curves:

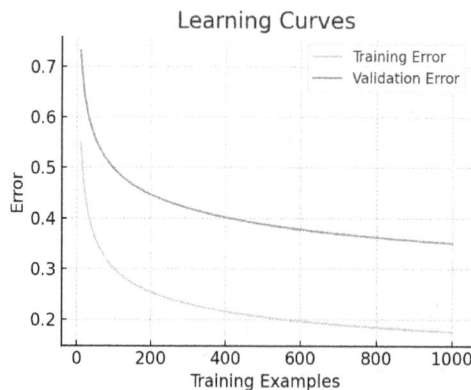

Figure 11.2: *Learning curves*

Learning curves illustrate training and validation error as the number of training examples increases. A gap between the curves suggests overfitting, while high error in both indicates underfitting.

Handling bias

When a model exhibits high bias, it underfits the data, failing to capture the underlying patterns and resulting in poor performance on both training and test sets. This typically occurs when the model is too simple, lacks informative features, or has not been trained sufficiently.

Common strategies to reduce bias include:

- **Increase model complexity**: Move from a simpler model (e.g., linear regression) to a more complex one (e.g., polynomial regression or neural networks) that can better capture non-linear relationships.

- **Feature engineering**: Add new relevant features or transform existing ones to more accurately represent the data and uncover hidden patterns.

- **Increase training time**: Allow the model to train longer so it has more opportunity to learn the data distribution.

- **Use ensemble methods**: Combine multiple weak models to create a stronger, more accurate predictive model.

Example: If a linear regression model underfits, switching to a polynomial regression model that includes quadratic and interaction terms can help capture more complex relationships.

Handling variance

High variance occurs when a model overfits the training data, capturing noise instead of general patterns. This leads to excellent performance on the training set but poor generalization to unseen data. The goal is to reduce the model's sensitivity to training data while maintaining predictive power.

Common techniques to reduce variance include:

- **Regularization**: Apply L1 (Lasso) or L2 (Ridge) regularization to penalize overly complex models. In neural networks, techniques like dropout help prevent overfitting by randomly deactivating neurons during training.

- **Simplify the model**: Reduce the complexity of the model, such as decreasing the depth of decision trees or the number of layers in a neural network.

- **Increase training data**: Providing more data helps the model learn broader patterns and reduces the risk of overfitting to a small sample.

- **Cross-validation**: Use methods like k-Fold cross-validation to validate model performance on multiple data subsets, helping ensure it generalizes well.

- **Early stopping**: Monitor the validation loss during training and halt the process when the loss starts to rise, preventing overfitting.

Example: For a decision tree model that overfits, reducing the tree depth or using random forests can mitigate high variance.

Practical example

In this section, you will explore a practical scenario that illustrates how bias and variance manifest in a real-world machine learning task. By examining the outcomes of different model choices, you will learn how to recognize and correct underfitting and overfitting in your own projects:

- **High bias**:

  o Using a simple linear regression model leads to poor predictions because it cannot capture non-linear relationships between study habits and grades.

  o **Solution**: Switch to a polynomial regression model or a neural network.

- **High variance**:

  o Using a deep neural network with many layers leads to perfect predictions on training data but poor performance on test data.

  o **Solution**: Apply dropout regularization and limit the number of layers.

Issue	Symptom	Solution
High bias	Low training/test accuracy	Use a more complex model
High variance	High training, low test accuracy	Simplify the model, add regularization

Table 11.1: Examples in a student performance prediction model

Cast studies

Let us discuss the case studies highlighing real-world scenarios that illustrate how bias and variance affect machine learning models. These case studies demonstrate how to identify underfitting and overfitting and the steps you can take to correct them.

The following are the case studies:

- **Case study 1: High bias in predicting student grades**:

- o **Problem**: A university is building a model to predict student grades based on study hours, attendance, and sleep quality. A simple linear regression model is initially used.

- o **Observation**: Despite training on a large dataset, the model performs poorly on both the training and test sets. It fails to capture the non-linear relationships between input features and student outcomes.

- o **Root cause**: The model has high bias; it is too simplistic to capture the true patterns in the data.

- o **Solution**: The data science team replaces the linear model with a polynomial regression model and later tests a neural network. Both alternatives significantly improve performance, showing better alignment with the actual relationships in the data.

- **Case study 2: High variance in student performance prediction:**

  - o **Problem**: To increase accuracy, the same university tries a deep neural network with many layers to model the same dataset.

  - o **Observation**: The model achieves near-perfect accuracy on the training set but performs poorly on unseen test data.

  - o **Root cause**: This is a classic case of high variance, the model is overfitting the training data and failing to generalize.

  - o **Solution**: The team implements dropout regularization, reduces the number of layers, and uses cross-validation to monitor generalization. This leads to a more balanced model with improved test accuracy.

Understanding and addressing bias and variance is essential for creating ML models that generalize well to unseen data. By using performance metrics, learning curves, and appropriate techniques, you can achieve the right balance and build robust models. Remember, the goal is not perfection in training, but reliability in real-world scenarios. With these tools and strategies, you are well-prepared to identify and handle bias and variance effectively in your ML projects.

Interpreting key evaluation metrics

Evaluation metrics are essential for understanding the performance of ML models, particularly for classification tasks. Choosing the right metric helps ensure that a model meets the requirements of the problem it aims to solve. Common metrics such as **Area Under the Receiver Operating Characteristic Curve (AUC-ROC)**, precision, recall, and F1 score provide insights into different aspects of a model's performance. This section explains these metrics in detail, how to interpret them, and their appropriate use cases.

AUC-ROC

AUC-ROC is a metric that evaluates the ability of a classification model to distinguish between classes. It plots the **true positive rate (TPR)** against the **false positive rate (FPR)** at various threshold settings. The **area under this curve (AUC)** represents the model's overall performance.

An AUC of 1 indicates a perfect classifier, while an AUC of 0.5 suggests a model that performs no better than random guessing, as illustrated in *Figure 11.3*.

Example: Imagine a spam filter. A model with a high AUC-ROC effectively differentiates between spam and legitimate emails.

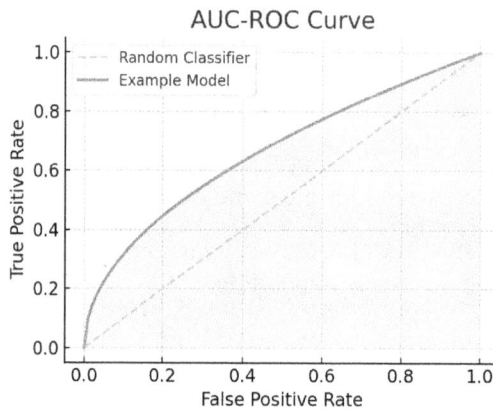

Figure 11.3: AUC-ROC curve

The ROC curve shows the tradeoff between the true positive rate and false positive rate across thresholds. The shaded AUC quantifies classifier performance, the closer the curve hugs the top-left, the better.

Precision

Precision measures the proportion of true positive predictions among all positive predictions. It is particularly useful in scenarios where false positives have significant consequences.

It is calculated as the number of true positives divided by the sum of true and false positives:

Precision = True positives / (True positives + False positives)

Example: In a fraud detection system, high precision ensures that flagged transactions are genuinely fraudulent, reducing unnecessary investigations.

Recall

Recall measures the proportion of actual positive instances that are correctly identified by the model. It is critical in situations where missing a positive instance has serious implications.

It is calculated as the number of true positives divided by the sum of true positives and false negatives:

$$Recall = True\ positives\ /\ (True\ positives + False\ negatives)$$

Example: In a medical diagnosis model, high recall ensures that most patients with a condition are correctly identified.

F1 score

The F1 score is the harmonic mean of precision and recall, providing a balanced metric that accounts for both false positives and false negatives. It is particularly useful when precision and recall are equally important.

It is calculated using the formula:

$$F1\ score = 2 * (Precision * Recall)\ /\ (Precision + Recall)$$

Example: In text classification, where both missing a relevant category and falsely assigning a category can have negative consequences, the F1 score provides a balanced measure.

Here is a quick comparison table for all metrics:

Metric	Best used for	Example use case
AUC-ROC	Imbalanced datasets	Spam classification
Precision	High cost of false positives	Fraud detection
Recall	High cost of false negatives	Medical diagnosis
F1 score	Balanced trade-off	Text classification

Table 11.2: Key evaluation metrics with best-use scenarios and example applications

Offline vs. online model evaluation techniques

Model evaluation is a critical step in ensuring ML models perform as expected. Evaluation methods can be broadly categorized into offline and online techniques. Each approach serves a distinct purpose and is used at different stages of model development and deployment. Understanding the differences and appropriate use cases for each method is crucial for building robust ML solutions. This section explores offline and online model evaluation techniques, their advantages and limitations, and when to use them. We will also provide practical examples and illustrations to clarify these concepts.

Offline model evaluation

Offline model evaluation refers to the process of assessing a machine learning model's performance using historical data. This method is performed in a controlled environment without exposing the model to live user interactions. Offline evaluation is often the first step in understanding how well a model generalizes to unseen data. Common offline evaluation methods include:

- **Train-test split**: Dividing the dataset into training and testing subsets to evaluate the model.

- **Cross-validation**: Splitting the data into multiple folds and training/testing the model on different folds.

- **Metrics-based evaluation**: Using metrics like accuracy, precision, recall, and AUC-ROC to assess performance.

Example: A data scientist builds a recommendation system for an e-commerce website. The model is evaluated offline using historical user purchase data to measure how accurately it predicts future purchases.

The following are the advantages of offline evaluation:

- No risk of impacting live users.
- Allows rapid iteration and experimentation.
- Easy to debug and interpret.

The following are the limitations of offline evaluation:

- Does not account for real-world conditions.
- May not reflect user behavior in a live environment.

Online model evaluation

Online model evaluation involves testing a model in a live environment with real user interactions. This method provides insights into how the model performs under actual conditions, making it essential for validating its impact on business metrics. Common online evaluation methods include:

- **A/B testing**: Comparing the performance of two versions of a model or system by exposing them to different user groups.

- **Multi-armed bandit testing**: Dynamically adjusting the proportion of traffic sent to different models based on performance.

- **Shadow testing**: Running a new model in parallel with the existing one to compare predictions without affecting users.

Example: A streaming service tests a new recommendation algorithm by exposing 10% of users to the new model while the remaining 90% continue using the old one. Metrics like click-through rate and watch time are measured to evaluate performance.

Let us look at the advantages of online evaluation:

- Provides insights into real-world performance.
- Measures the model's impact on key business metrics.
- Can uncover unexpected user behaviour.

Next, take a look at the limitations of online evaluation:

- Risk of negatively impacting user experience.
- Slower iteration cycle compared to offline evaluation.
- Requires careful planning to avoid biases in results.

The following is a quick comparison of offline and online techniques:

Criteria	Offline evaluation	Online evaluation
Environment	Controlled (historical data)	Live (real user interactions)
Risk	No user impact	Potential user impact
Speed	Faster iterations	Slower due to live testing
Insights	Limited to historical patterns	Real-world user behavior
Use case	Initial model testing	Validating real-world performance

Table 11.3: Offline vs. online model evaluation, key differences in setup, risk, speed, and insights

Both offline and online model evaluation techniques are essential for building effective machine learning models. While offline evaluation provides a safe and efficient way to test models, online evaluation ensures they perform well in real-world conditions. By understanding the strengths and limitations of each method, data scientists can choose the right approach at different stages of the ML pipeline. Combining these techniques leads to robust and reliable models that deliver value in practical applications.

Model comparison using performance metrics

Model comparison is a critical step in ML, enabling data scientists to choose the best-performing model for a given task. Performance metrics provide quantitative insights into how well models meet their objectives and help identify trade-offs between different approaches. Selecting the appropriate metric ensures that the chosen model aligns with the problem's goals and constraints. This section explores key performance metrics, practical examples of their use, and methods to systematically compare models. We also include visual illustrations and tables for better clarity.

Key performance metrics

Understanding the strengths and limitations of various performance metrics is essential for effective model comparison. Here are some of the most commonly used metrics:

- **Accuracy**: Accuracy measures the proportion of correctly classified instances out of the total instances. It is simple to calculate and useful when the dataset has a balanced distribution of classes.

  Formula: *Accuracy = (True positives + True negatives) / Total instances*

  Example: In a binary classification task for predicting email spam, an accuracy of 95% means the model correctly classified 95% of emails as spam or non-spam.

- **Precision**: Precision measures the proportion of true positive predictions out of all positive predictions. It is crucial in scenarios where false positives are costly.

  Formula: *Precision = True positives / (True positives + False positives)*

  Example: In fraud detection, high precision ensures that flagged transactions are genuinely fraudulent, reducing unnecessary alerts.

- **Recall**: Recall measures the proportion of actual positive instances that are correctly identified by the model. It is critical when missing positive instances have significant consequences.

  Formula: *Recall = True positives / (True positives + False negatives)*

  Example: In medical diagnoses, high recall ensures that most patients with a condition are correctly identified, minimizing missed cases.

- **F1 score**: The F1 score is the harmonic mean of precision and recall, balancing the trade-off between the two. It is particularly useful when precision and recall are equally important.

  Formula: *F1 score = 2 * (Precision * Recall) / (Precision + Recall)*

  Example: In text classification, where both false positives and false negatives can have adverse effects, the F1 score provides a balanced view.

- **AUC-ROC**: AUC-ROC evaluates a model's ability to distinguish between classes. The AUC measures the model's overall performance.

  Example: In a credit scoring system, a high AUC-ROC indicates that the model effectively separates high-risk and low-risk customers.

Comparison of models

To select the best model, it is essential to systematically compare its performance across relevant metrics. This process helps highlight trade-offs and identify the model that best meets the requirements.

Example: Comparing two fraud detection models using precision, recall, and F1 score to determine which is better suited for minimizing false positives and capturing all fraudulent cases.

To make informed decisions in ML, comparing models across key performance metrics is essential. This approach reveals strengths and weaknesses, helping you select the model that best aligns with your objectives.

Refer to the following table:

Metric	Model A	Model B	Best choice
Accuracy	95%	92%	Model A
Precision	90%	85%	Model A
Recall	80%	88%	Model B
F1 Score	84%	86%	Model B

Table 11.4: Comparison of models across evaluation metrics

Model comparison using performance metrics is a structured approach to selecting the best model for a given task. By analyzing metrics such as accuracy, precision, recall, F1 score, and AUC-ROC, data scientists can identify trade-offs and align model selection with business goals. Combining metrics with practical examples and systematic comparisons ensures that the chosen model is not only accurate but also effective in real-world applications.

Utilizing AWS tools for ML model evaluation

Evaluating ML models effectively is crucial for ensuring they perform well in real-world scenarios. AWS offers a suite of tools designed to streamline and enhance the model evaluation process. These tools provide capabilities for monitoring, bias detection, experimentation, and performance tracking, making them essential for any ML pipeline.

This section explores the key AWS tools for ML model evaluation, their features, and how to use them effectively. Practical examples and comparisons illustrate their application in various scenarios.

Amazon SageMaker Model Monitor

Amazon SageMaker Model Monitor is designed to continuously monitor the performance of deployed models. It identifies data quality issues, such as drift in input data or predictions, and alerts users when performance metrics fall below acceptable thresholds.

The following are the key features of Amazon SageMaker:

- Automatic detection of data drifting.

- Continuous monitoring of prediction quality.

- Integration with AWS CloudWatch for alerts and logging.

Example: A model predicting customer churn is deployed in production. Model Monitor tracks changes in input data, such as shifts in customer demographics, and flags any deviations that could impact predictions.

Example configuration for SageMaker Model Monitor:

```
from sagemaker.model_monitor import DefaultModelMonitor

monitor = DefaultModelMonitor( role=sagemaker_execution_role, instance_
count=1, instance_type="ml.m5.large", volume_size_in_gb=20, max_runtime_in_
seconds=3600, )

monitor.create_monitoring_schedule( endpoint_input=endpoint_name, output_s3_
uri="s3://my-bucket/monitoring-output", schedule_cron_expression="cron(0 * ? *
* *)", # Run hourly statistics_config={"enableCloudWatchMetrics": True} )
```

This configuration sets up hourly monitoring for a deployed model and stores reports in an S3 bucket. It also enables CloudWatch integration for tracking key metrics.

Amazon SageMaker Clarify

Amazon SageMaker Clarify helps detect and mitigate bias in datasets and models. It also provides explainability reports, allowing users to understand the factors influencing model predictions.

The following are the key features of Amazon SageMaker Clarify:

- Bias detection in datasets and model predictions.

- Explainability reports using **SHapley Additive exPlanations** (**SHAP**) values play a central role in interpreting the predictions made by ML models. SHAP is a game-theoretic approach that assigns each feature an importance value for a particular prediction, helping data scientists understand not just how accurate a model is, but also why it made a specific decision.

- Integration with SageMaker workflows for seamless use.

Example: A hiring recommendation model is analyzed with Clarify to ensure gender and ethnicity bias are minimized. The tool highlights any imbalances and suggests adjustments to the dataset.

Amazon SageMaker Experiments

Amazon SageMaker Experiments tracks and organizes ML experiments. It helps data scientists compare multiple model versions and training runs by storing metadata and performance metrics.

Key features of Sagemaker Environments are as follows:

- Experiment tracking and visualization.

- Comparison of different training runs.

- Integration with SageMaker Studio for a streamlined workflow.

Example: A data scientist trains three versions of a model with different hyperparameter settings. Experiments track the performance metrics, allowing for easy comparison and selection of the best-performing version.

AWS best practices for Model Evaluation

The following are the AWS best practices for Model Evaluation in production:

- **Enable continuous monitoring** using **Amazon SageMaker Model Monitor** to detect data drift, schema changes, and prediction quality degradation.

- Use **Amazon SageMaker Clarify** during both training and inference to ensure ongoing fairness and explainability.

- Set up **automated alerts via CloudWatch** for real-time notifications when evaluation metrics breach defined thresholds.

- Leverage **Amazon SageMaker Experiments** to track versioned evaluation metrics, enabling reproducibility and auditing.

- Store all evaluation artifacts in **Amazon S3** with proper versioning and permissions for compliance.

- Integrate model evaluation checks as part of **CI/CD pipelines** using **SageMaker Pipelines** to enforce quality gates before deployment.

Comparison of AWS tools

While each AWS Tool serves a specific purpose, understanding their differences and complementary roles is crucial.

The following table summarizes the key features and use cases of these tools:

Tool	Primary purpose	Key features	Use case
Model Monitor	Monitor deployed models	Data drift detection, quality alerts	Production model tracking
Clarify	Bias detection and explainability	Bias reports, SHAP values	Ethical AI, fair predictions
Experiments	Experiment tracking	Metadata storage, run comparison	Hyperparameter optimization

Table 11.5: AWS tools compared by purpose, key features, and common use cases

AWS provides powerful tools to streamline ML model evaluation. From monitoring deployed models with SageMaker Model Monitor, to ensuring fairness with SageMaker Clarify, and tracking experiments with SageMaker Experiments, these tools cover all aspects of evaluation. By understanding their features and applications, data scientists can ensure their models are robust, ethical, and aligned with business goals.

Conclusion

This chapter covered essential strategies for evaluating machine learning models to ensure they are reliable, accurate, and aligned with business goals. A solid understanding of evaluation concepts is crucial for both the AWS Certified Machine Learning – Specialty (MLS-C01) exam and real-world ML deployment. We began by exploring bias and variance, identifying how underfitting and overfitting impact model performance. Techniques like regularization, data augmentation, and feature engineering help strike the right balance for generalization. Next, we examined key evaluation metrics, including AUC-ROC, precision, recall, and F1 score and how to select the right metric based on the problem context. We also compared offline and online evaluation methods, such as A/B testing and shadow deployment. A structured model comparison process was emphasized, as well as the use of AWS tools like SageMaker Model Monitor, Clarify, and Experiments to support real-time tracking, bias detection, and experiment management. Evaluating ML models is an ongoing process critical to production readiness and long-term success.

In the next chapter, you will learn how to monitor, optimize, and scale ML systems using AWS tools like CloudWatch and CloudTrail. You will explore best practices for auto-scaling, load balancing, and multi-region deployment to ensure performance and availability.

Multiple choice questions

1. **What is a common indicator of high bias in a machine learning model?**
   a. High training accuracy but low-test accuracy
   b. High test accuracy but low training accuracy
   c. Both training and test accuracy are low
   d. Model performs well on noisy data

2. **Which metric is most suitable for evaluating models on imbalanced datasets?**
   a. Accuracy
   b. AUC-ROC
   c. Precision
   d. Recall

3. **What does SageMaker Model Monitor primarily detect?**
   a. Bias in datasets
   b. Drift in input data and predictions
   c. Training data errors
   d. Hyperparameter optimization issues

4. **What is the formula for calculating precision?**
   a. True positives / (True positives + False positives)
   b. True positives / (True positives + False negatives)
   c. True negatives / (True negatives + False negatives)
   d. True negatives / (True negatives + False positives)

5. **What is the main advantage of online model evaluation?**
   a. Rapid debugging and iteration
   b. Low risk of user impact
   c. Real-world performance insights
   d. Easy interpretability of metrics

6. **Which AWS Tool is best suited for detecting bias in datasets?**
   a. SageMaker Model Monitor
   b. SageMaker Experiments
   c. SageMaker Clarify
   d. SageMaker Autopilot

7. **What is the purpose of cross-validation in offline model evaluation?**
   a. To optimize hyperparameters
   b. To test model performance on multiple subsets of data
   c. To improve real-world performance
   d. To track model experiments

8. **Which metric balances precision and recall?**
   a. Accuracy
   b. F1 score
   c. AUC-ROC
   d. Mean squared error

9. **What type of evaluation involves comparing a new model to an existing one without affecting users?**
   a. A/B testing
   b. Shadow testing
   c. Multi-armed bandit testing
   d. Offline evaluation

10. **Which AWS Tool helps track and organize ML experiments?**
   a. SageMaker Model Monitor
   b. SageMaker Clarify
   c. SageMaker Experiments
   d. SageMaker Ground Truth

Answer key

1. c.
2. b.
3. b.
4. a.
5. c.
6. c.
7. b.
8. b.
9. b.
10. c.

CHAPTER 12
Building ML Solutions for Performance and Scalability

Introduction

In today's AI-driven landscape, building **machine learning** (**ML**) solutions that perform efficiently, and scale seamlessly is crucial for meeting business demands and ensuring robust system reliability. This chapter focuses on leveraging AWS services to monitor, optimize, and scale ML solutions for high performance and availability. We will discuss monitoring tools like *AWS CloudTrail* and *Amazon CloudWatch*, explore strategies for deploying ML solutions across multiple regions and availability zones, and cover best practices for resource allocation, auto-scaling, and load balancing. By mastering these techniques, you will be equipped to design scalable and performant ML systems that adhere to AWS best practices.

Structure

This chapter covers the following topics:

- Monitoring AWS environments with AWS CloudTrail and Amazon CloudWatch
- Multi-region ML deployment
- Creating and managing AMIs and Docker containers
- Right-sizing resources and load balancing
- Adhering to AWS best practices for ML solutions

Objectives

In this chapter, you will learn key strategies for deploying ML solutions across multiple regions and availability zones to enhance system availability, reduce latency, and improve fault tolerance. You will gain expertise in creating and managing **Amazon Machine Images** (**AMIs**) and Docker containers to ensure consistent, portable, and scalable deployments. The concept of auto-scaling will be covered to help you dynamically adjust resources based on demand, promoting cost-efficiency and uninterrupted performance. Additionally, you will develop skills to right-size resources and implement load balancing to optimize compute, storage, and networking needs while minimizing costs. Finally, you will adopt AWS best practices to design and maintain ML architectures that align with the AWS Well-Architected Framework.

These insights and hands-on techniques will prepare you to confidently tackle the Building ML Solutions for Performance and Scalability section of the AWS Certified Machine Learning - Specialty (MLS-C01) exam, ensuring you are ready to design, build, and scale ML systems effectively.

Monitoring AWS environments with AWS CloudTrail and Amazon CloudWatch

Monitoring is a cornerstone of any robust ML solution in the cloud. AWS provides powerful tools like AWS CloudTrail and Amazon CloudWatch to enable users to monitor, troubleshoot, and optimize their environments effectively. This section explains these tools in detail, using first principles to establish a foundation, practical examples to demonstrate their usage, and illustrations to make the concepts clear.

AWS CloudTrail

AWS CloudTrail provides detailed logs of every API request made within your AWS account. By enabling CloudTrail, you can gain insights into the activities occurring in your account, including actions taken by users, roles, and services.

The following are the key features of AWS CloudTrail:

- **Event logging**: CloudTrail captures information such as who made the request, when it occurred, and what actions were taken.

- **Governance and compliance**: Logs can be stored securely in S3 and analyzed to meet compliance requirements.

- **Integration with other AWS services**: CloudTrail integrates with services like Amazon Athena for log analysis.

Example:

Imagine you have an ML solution deployed using Amazon SageMaker, and you notice an unexpected change in a notebook instance. You can use AWS CloudTrail to trace back and identify who initiated the change and when it occurred. By analyzing the logs, you can ensure unauthorized activities are detected and resolved promptly.

CloudTrail Investigation Workflow for ML workloads:

1. Go to the AWS CloudTrail Console.

2. Filter events using Event Name (e.g., `UpdateNotebookInstance`) and Resource Name (e.g., `ml-notebook-name`).

3. Identify the IAM user or role that initiated the action.

4. Review the time and source IP address for anomaly detection.

5. Export logs to Amazon Athena or CloudWatch Logs for deeper analysis.

6. Respond appropriately (e.g., revoke access, roll back changes, notify security).

Amazon CloudWatch

Amazon CloudWatch is a monitoring and observability service that provides metrics, logs, and alarms for AWS resources. It helps you gain visibility into the performance and health of your ML solutions.

Key features of Amazon CloudWatch are as follows:

- **Metrics collection**: CloudWatch collects metrics such as CPU usage, memory utilization, and application latency.

- **Alarms and notifications**: Create alarms to notify you when specific thresholds are breached.

- **Custom dashboards**: Build dashboards to visualize performance metrics in real time.

Example:

Suppose you are training a large machine learning model in Amazon SageMaker. By using CloudWatch, you can monitor metrics like *CPU* and *GPU utilization* during the training process. If resource utilization exceeds optimal thresholds, CloudWatch can send an alarm, allowing you to adjust the resources or terminate the job to save costs.

Here is a quick comparison between AWS CloudTrail and Amazon CloudWatch:

Feature	AWS CloudTrail	Amazon CloudWatch
Purpose	Tracks API calls and activities	Monitors resource performance.
Data type	Logs of API requests	Metrics and logs of resource utilization.
Use case	Governance and auditing	Performance monitoring and alarms.
Integration	Works with S3, Athena	Works with Lambda, SNS, and dashboards.
Example	Tracking changes to resources	Monitoring CPU usage of ML models.

Table 12.1: AWS CloudTrail vs. CloudWatch

The following are the practical tips for using AWS CloudTrail and Amazon CloudWatch:

- **Enable logging and monitoring early**: Ensure CloudTrail and CloudWatch are configured at the start of your ML project

- **Use tags and filters**: Use resource tags and filters in CloudWatch to organize and manage monitoring data effectively

- **Set up alerts**: Configure CloudWatch alarms to receive notifications when metrics deviate from expected values

- **Review logs regularly**: Periodically review CloudTrail logs for unusual activities or security incidents

- **Integrate with other AWS services**: Leverage tools like Amazon SNS for notifications and AWS Lambda for automated responses

The following is a sample CloudWatch Alarm Configuration (Python SDK - Boto3):

```
import boto3
cloudwatch = boto3.client('cloudwatch')
cloudwatch.put_metric_alarm(
AlarmName='HighCPUUtilization-SageMakerTraining',
MetricName='CPUUtilization',
Namespace='AWS/SageMaker',
Statistic='Average', Period=300,
EvaluationPeriods=1,
Threshold=80.0,
ComparisonOperator='GreaterThanThreshold',
Dimensions=[ {'Name': 'EndpointName', 'Value': 'your-endpoint-name'} ],
AlarmActions=['arn:aws:sns:us-east-1:123456789012:MyAlarmTopic'],
AlarmDescription='Alarm when SageMaker CPU utilization exceeds 80%',
ActionsEnabled=True )
```

This alarm notifies users if CPU utilization exceeds 80% during training or inference, helping optimize compute use and avoid cost overruns.

Note on cost implications:

While detailed logging with CloudTrail and CloudWatch provides robust observability and security, it can incur additional storage and data transfer costs, especially when logging high-volume resources (e.g., frequent SageMaker training jobs or inference endpoints).

To control costs:

- Use log filters and metric retention policies.
- Archive logs in S3 with lifecycle policies.
- Enable sampling or logging only key actions when possible.

Multi-region ML deployment

Deploying ML solutions across multiple regions and availability zones is essential for achieving high availability, fault tolerance, and low-latency access for global users. This topic explores strategies to distribute ML workloads effectively while adhering to AWS's best practices. Using the first principles, we will demystify the concepts of regions and availability zones, illustrate practical examples, and provide a framework for deploying ML solutions with scalability and reliability.

Refer to the following figure:

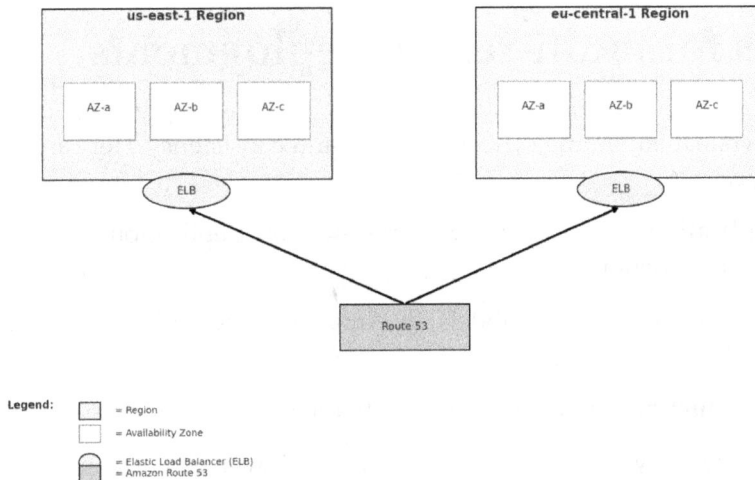

Figure 12.1: *Multi-region and multi-AZ ML deployment on AWS*

Figure 12.1 illustrates a highly available ML architecture with deployments in two AWS regions (**us-east-1** and **eu-central-1**), each spanning multiple AZs. **Elastic Load Balancers (ELBs)** distribute traffic across AZs, while Amazon Route 53 routes user traffic to the closest region based on latency.

Understanding AWS regions and availability zones

AWS divides its global infrastructure into regions and availability zones to ensure high availability and resilience for applications. Regions are geographically distinct locations (e.g., `us-west-1`, `ap-south-1`, and so on), while availability zones are isolated data centers within a region.

Understanding AWS's global architecture is essential for building robust ML solutions. The following are key features that support high availability, low latency, and fault tolerance:

- **Regions**: Used to serve users in specific geographical areas, ensuring low latency.

- **AZs**: Isolated yet interconnected zones within a region to provide fault isolation.

- **Global infrastructure**: Redundancy in regions and AZs ensures resilience against disasters.

Example: Suppose you are deploying a movie recommendation system that needs to serve users in North America, Europe, and Asia. By using AWS Regions, you can deploy the ML models close to users in each geography (e.g., `us-east-1`, `eu-central-1`, or `ap-northeast-To` ensure high availability within each region, you deploy the model across multiple AZs, such as two or three AZs within each region. This setup minimizes latency and ensures that the solution remains operational even if one AZ experiences an outage.

Strategies for multi-region deployments

Deploying ML solutions across multiple regions involves replicating data, models, and configurations while maintaining synchronization and consistency. Here are some of the most effective strategies:

- **Data replication**: Use Amazon S3 Cross-Region Replication to ensure datasets are available in all regions.

- **Model replication**: Store models in Amazon ECR and use automated scripts to replicate them across regions.

- **Latency reduction**: Route user requests to the nearest region using Amazon Route 53.

- **Disaster recovery**: Implement backups and failover mechanisms using AWS Elastic Disaster Recovery.

With multi-region strategies in place, the next step is to focus on optimizing availability and fault tolerance within a single region by leveraging multiple AZs.

Strategies for multi-AZ deployments

Deploying across multiple AZs ensures high availability within a region. Key considerations for this approach include:

- **Load balancing**: Use Elastic Load Balancing to distribute traffic evenly across AZs.

- **Elasticity**: Leverage auto-scaling groups to add or remove resources dynamically based on demand.

- **Shared storage**: Use Amazon EFS or FSx for shared file systems accessible by instances in multiple AZs.

- **Health checks**: Configure health checks to detect and reroute traffic away from unhealthy AZs.

To achieve high availability and resilience within a single region, deploying ML solutions across multiple AZs is a key strategy.

The following table outlines the differences between multi-region and multi-AZ deployments to help determine the best approach based on your application's needs:

Aspect	Multi-region deployment	Multi-AZ deployment
Scope	Global	Regional
Use case	Serve global users, disaster recovery	High availability within a region
Latency	Reduces latency for global users	Low latency for regional users
Cost	Higher due to multiple regions	Lower compared to multi-region
Complexity	Requires replication and synchronization	Simpler configuration within a region

Table 12.2: Comparison of multi-region and multi-AZ deployments

Practical tips for multi-region and multi-AZ deployments

To effectively manage and scale your ML deployments across multiple regions and availability zones, it is important to follow practical strategies that enhance reliability, performance, and cost-efficiency.

The following are some key tips to guide successful implementation:

- **Start small**: Begin with a single region and expand to multiple regions as demand grows.

- **Automate**: Use AWS CloudFormation or Terraform to automate deployments across regions and AZs.

- **Test failover**: Regularly test failover scenarios to ensure disaster recovery readiness. Simulate region or AZ outages using controlled chaos engineering practices (e.g., failover drills) to ensure your system responds as expected. Monitor **Recovery Time Objective (RTO)** and **Recovery Point Objective (RPO)** against your SLAs. Use Route 53 with health checks and weighted routing: Configure DNS failover with Amazon Route 53 to automatically reroute traffic to a healthy region if a primary region becomes unavailable.

- **Monitor performance**: Use Amazon CloudWatch to monitor latency, request volumes, and resource health.

- **Cost management**: Cost management is a critical consideration when deploying ML solutions across regions and AZs. For predictable workloads, it is recommended to use Savings Plans or Reserved Instances, which can significantly reduce compute costs across services like *EC2*, *Amazon SageMaker*, and *ECS*. When storing machine learning artifacts such as models, datasets, or logs, Amazon S3 Intelligent-Tiering provides a cost-effective solution by automatically moving data between storage tiers based on access patterns. To further control expenses, teams should avoid unnecessary cross-region replication, which can incur high data transfer charges unless such replication is mandated for compliance or disaster recovery purposes. Finally, for training jobs that are not latency-sensitive, Spot Instances offer a low-cost alternative in non-critical regions. Meanwhile, on-demand or reserved instances are more appropriate for inference endpoints in production, where reliability and availability are paramount.

Creating and managing AMIs and Docker containers

Creating and managing **Amazon machine images** (**AMIs**) and Docker containers are key skills for deploying and maintaining scalable and portable ML solutions in the AWS Cloud. This topic explores the principles of AMIs and Docker containers, describes how to create and manage them effectively, and provides practical examples to clarify their roles in ML solution deployments.

Amazon machine images

An AMI is a template that contains the software configuration (OS, application server, and applications) required to launch an EC2 instance. AMIs provide the foundation for replicable and consistent ML environments.

Key features of AMIs are as follows:

- **Preconfigured environment**: AMIs include operating systems, application configurations, and required software.

- **Versioning**: Maintain different versions of AMIs to track updates and changes.

- **Customization**: Create custom AMIs tailored to specific ML workflows.

- **Regional availability**: AMIs are region-specific but can be copied across regions.

Example:

Imagine you frequently train models using TensorFlow on EC2 instances. Instead of setting up the environment each time, you create a custom AMI with TensorFlow, necessary libraries, and preconfigured settings. By using this AMI, you can launch instances with a consistent environment, saving setup time and reducing errors.

Docker containers

Docker containers package applications and their dependencies into a portable and lightweight format, ensuring that ML models run consistently across different environments. Containers are especially useful for microservices and distributed ML workflows.

Key features of Docker containers are as follows:

- **Portability**: Containers run consistently across development, testing, and production environments.

- **Isolation**: Applications run in isolated environments, avoiding conflicts with other processes.

- **Lightweight**: Containers share the host OS kernel, making them more efficient than virtual machines.

- **Flexibility**: Easily scale ML solutions by running multiple container instances.

Example:

Suppose you deploy a PyTorch model for inference. By creating a Docker container with the PyTorch runtime, model files, and inference scripts, you can ensure that the same container runs seamlessly across your local machine, AWS ECS, or Kubernetes.

When choosing between AMIs and Docker containers for deploying ML solutions, it is important to understand their differences in flexibility, resource usage, and deployment style.

The following table provides a side-by-side comparison to help guide this decision:

Aspect	AMIs	Docker containers
Definition	Template for launching EC2 instances	Portable unit with app and dependencies
Use case	Static configurations, full VMs	Dynamic and lightweight deployments

Resource usage	Higher (entire OS)	Lower (shares OS kernel)
Flexibility	Region-specific	Runs on any Docker-enabled host
Examples	Preconfigured EC2 environment	Containerized ML model deployment

Table 12.3: Comparison of AMIs and Docker containers across key aspects

Practical tips for using AMIs and Docker containers

To effectively manage and deploy ML environments using AMIs and Docker containers, it is important to follow best practices that enhance performance, flexibility, and maintainability. Below are practical tips to help you get the most out of these deployment options:

- **Optimize AMIs**: Minimize unnecessary software in AMIs to reduce size and improve launch times.

- **Use Docker for flexibility**: Choose Docker containers for rapid deployment and microservices.

- **Version control**: Maintain version control for both AMIs and Docker images to track changes.

- **Automate**: Use CI/CD pipelines to automate building, testing, and deploying containers.

- **Monitor usage**: Regularly monitor AMI and container usage to optimize costs and resources.

With AMIs and Docker containers forming the foundation for consistent and portable ML deployments, the next step is to ensure these environments can scale efficiently based on workload demands. Now, we will discuss about how to auto-scale ML solutions on AWS Auto Scaling for ML solutions.

Auto-scaling is a critical capability for building robust, cost-effective, and scalable ML solutions on AWS. By dynamically adjusting the number of compute resources based on demand, auto-scaling ensures high availability and optimized resource utilization. This section covers the fundamentals of auto-scaling, its importance for ML workloads, and practical strategies for its implementation.

Overview of auto-scaling

Auto-scaling refers to the automatic adjustment of the number of compute resources in response to changes in workload demand. AWS provides the auto-scaling service to manage this process, ensuring that applications run efficiently without manual intervention.

Let us see why auto-scaling is crucial for ML solutions:

- **Dynamic workloads**: ML solutions often experience fluctuating workloads during training, inference, or batch processing.

- **Cost efficiency**: Automatically scaling down during low usage periods reduces operational costs.

- **High availability**: Ensures that resources are available to meet unexpected spikes in demand.

- **Performance optimization**: Matches resource capacity with current workload, preventing under-or over-provisioning.

Auto-scaling plays a vital role in maintaining the efficiency and scalability of ML workloads without constant manual oversight. Before diving into practical examples, it is important to understand why auto-scaling is especially crucial for ML solutions.

Example:

Consider a real-time fraud detection system that processes transaction data. During peak hours, such as *Black Friday*, the volume of transactions may surge. Auto-scaling can dynamically add instances to handle the increased workload. During off-peak hours, it scales down to minimize costs while maintaining operational efficiency.

Here are the key components of auto-scaling:

- **Launch configuration**: Defines the instance type, AMI, and other settings for launching new instances

- **Scaling policies**: Specify when and how the system scales in or out

- **CloudWatch alarms**: Monitor metrics like CPU utilization and trigger scaling actions

- **Target tracking scaling:** Automatically adjusts capacity to maintain a specified metric value

The following are some of the use cases of auto-scaling in ML solutions:

- **Model training**: Scale up instances to train large models and scale down when training completes

- **Batch inference**: Handle high volumes of data by adding instances temporarily

- **Real-time inference**: Match the number of serving instances with the current query load

- **Pipeline orchestration**: Scale compute resources dynamically in data pipelines

To choose the right scaling strategy for your ML infrastructure, it is helpful to understand the trade-offs between manual scaling and auto-scaling.

The following table highlights the key differences across critical aspects:

Aspect	Manual scaling	Auto-scaling
Scalability	Requires manual intervention	Automatic and dynamic adjustment
Response time	Slow to adapt to workload changes	Real-time adjustments
Cost efficiency	Higher due to over-provisioning	Optimized with minimal resource usage
Complexity	Simpler but less efficient	More complex to set up, but highly efficient
Best use case	Static workloads	Dynamic workloads with unpredictable patterns

Table 12.4: Comparison of manual scaling and auto-scaling

The following are the practical tips for implementing auto-scaling:

- **Set accurate metrics**: Use relevant CloudWatch metrics like CPU usage, memory utilization, or custom application metrics.

- **Use predictive scaling**: Leverage AWS Auto Scaling predictive scaling to anticipate workload trends.

- **Test scaling policies**: Simulate high-demand scenarios to validate scaling policies

- **Combine with spot instances**: Use a mix of spot and on-demand instances for cost efficiency.

- **Monitor regularly**: Continuously monitor scaling actions to ensure they align with business goals.

Right-sizing resources and load balancing

Right-sizing resources and implementing load balancing are foundational principles for designing efficient and cost-effective ML solutions in the AWS Cloud. Right-sizing ensures that compute, storage, and networking resources are neither over-provisioned nor under-provisioned, while load balancing distributes incoming traffic across resources to optimize performance and ensure high availability. This section explores these concepts in detail, with practical examples and illustrations to enhance understanding.

Right-sizing resources

Right-sizing refers to optimizing the allocation of AWS resources to match the workload's requirements. It involves selecting the appropriate instance types, storage options, and configurations to minimize costs while maintaining performance.

The following are the key principles of right-sizing:

- **Understand workload requirements**: Analyze compute, memory, storage, and networking needs.

- **Choose the right instance type**: Use tools like AWS Instance Selector to identify optimal EC2 instances.

- **Monitor resource utilization**: Leverage Amazon CloudWatch to track usage and identify inefficiencies.

- **Iterate regularly**: Continuously evaluate and adjust resource allocations as workloads evolve.

Example: Suppose you are training a machine learning model on Amazon SageMaker. Initially, you use a high-end instance type but monitoring reveals that CPU utilization is consistently below 50%. By switching to a smaller instance, you reduce costs without compromising performance.

Load balancing

Load balancing involves distributing incoming traffic across multiple resources to ensure even utilization, minimize latency, and improve fault tolerance. AWS provides **Elastic Load Balancing (ELB)** to handle these tasks.

Key features of ELB are as follows:

- **Traffic distribution**: Routes traffic to healthy instances across multiple availability zones.

- **Health checks**: Continuously monitor the health of resources and avoid routing traffic to failed instances.

- **Scalability**: Works seamlessly with auto-scaling groups to handle dynamic workloads

- **Integration**: Compatible with EC2, ECS, Fargate, and other AWS services.

After ensuring that your ML infrastructure can scale efficiently with changing demand through auto-scaling, the next step is to maintain performance and availability under heavy or unpredictable traffic. This is where load balancing becomes essential.

Example: Consider a real-time image recognition application deployed on multiple EC2 instances. An application load balancer distributes incoming requests evenly across instances, ensuring low latency and preventing any single instance from becoming overwhelmed.

To optimize both cost and performance in ML deployments, it is important to understand the distinction between right-sizing and load balancing.

The following table compares these two strategies across key aspects to help guide their appropriate use:

Aspect	Right-sizing	Load balancing
Definition	Optimizing resource allocation.	Distributing traffic across resources.
Focus area	Individual resource efficiency.	System-wide traffic management.
Objective	Minimize costs and waste.	Ensure high availability and fault tolerance.
Tools	AWS Instance Selector, CloudWatch.	Elastic load balancer, Route 53.
Best use case	Static or predictable workloads.	Dynamic or high-traffic applications.

Table 12.5: Comparison of right-sizing and load balancing in AWS

The following are the practical tips for right-sizing and load balancing:

- **Leverage AWS tools**: Use tools like AWS Compute Optimizer for right-sizing recommendations.

- **Test and monitor**: Continuously test the impact of changes and monitor metrics to ensure desired outcomes.

- **Combine strategies**: Implement right-sizing and load balancing together for optimal efficiency.

- **Automate adjustments**: Use auto-scaling policies to dynamically adjust resources based on load.

- **Plan for growth**: Design for scalability, anticipating the increase in future workload.

Adhering to AWS best practices for ML solutions

Adhering to AWS best practices is crucial for building ML solutions that are secure, scalable, and cost-efficient. AWS provides a comprehensive set of guidelines and tools based on the AWS Well-Architected Framework. This section explores these best practices in detail, providing practical examples and illustrations to help implement them effectively.

AWS Well-Architected Framework

The AWS Well-Architected Framework provides a structured approach for evaluating and improving architectures. It focuses on six key pillars to ensure best practices for cloud solutions, including ML workflows.

The following are the key pillars of the Well-Architected Framework:

- **Operational excellence**: Focuses on operations automation and continuous improvement

- **Security**: Protects data and systems through best practices like encryption and access control
- **Reliability**: Ensures workloads can recover from failures and meet customer demands
- **Performance efficiency**: Optimizes resources for workload performance
- **Cost optimization**: Minimizes costs while maintaining performance and functionality
- **Sustainability**: Encourages efficient use of resources to minimize environmental impact

Example: When deploying ML models, especially in sensitive domains like finance, it is essential to follow AWS security best practices to protect data and infrastructure.

Here is a practical example of how to implement these practices using Amazon SageMaker:

- Use Amazon VPC to isolate your ML environment.
- Enable encryption for data in transit and at rest using AWS KMS.
- Apply least privilege principles for IAM roles to restrict access to resources.

Performance optimization in ML solutions

Optimizing performance involves selecting appropriate compute resources, improving data processing workflows, and leveraging AWS services like **Amazon SageMaker** and *AWS Batch*.

Key strategies for performance optimization include:

- **Use spot instances**: Reduce costs for batch ML workloads by using spot instances.
- **Optimize data storage**: Use Amazon S3 for scalable and cost-effective storage.
- **Leverage SageMaker Pipelines**: Automate end-to-end ML workflows for faster iterations.
- **Monitor performance**: Use CloudWatch metrics to identify bottlenecks.

Implementing AWS's Well-Architected Framework ensures that ML solutions are secure, efficient, and scalable.

The following table outlines key best practices across each pillar, along with practical examples tailored to ML deployments:

Pillar	Best practices	Example
Operational excellence	Automate model deployments	Use SageMaker for CI/CD pipelines
Security	Encrypt data and restrict access	Enable KMS and IAM policies
Reliability	Design for fault tolerance	Deploy across multiple AZs

Performance efficiency	Optimize resource selection	Use GPU instances for training
Cost optimization	Minimize unused resources	Apply auto-scaling for inference
Sustainability	Reduce energy consumption	Optimize batch processing schedules

Table 12.6: Best practices across AWS Well

The following are the practical tips for adopting best practices:

- **Use AWS Well-Architected Tool**: Review workloads using the AWS Well-Architected Tool for detailed recommendations.

- **Regularly update security policies**: Ensure policies evolve with new AWS features and threats.

- **Monitor and optimize costs**: Use AWS Cost Explorer and Trusted Advisor to track expenses.

- **Leverage managed services**: Use services like SageMaker to reduce operational complexity.

- **Document and iterate**: Maintain clear documentation of architectures and update them as requirements change

Conclusion

This chapter covered essential strategies and AWS tools for designing scalable, efficient, and resilient ML solutions. You learned how to monitor ML environments using AWS CloudTrail and Amazon CloudWatch, gaining insights into performance and operational health. We explored deploying ML workloads across multiple regions and availability zones to ensure fault tolerance and low latency, supported by data replication, load balancing, and health checks.

Tools like AMIs and Docker containers were introduced to enable consistent and portable deployments, while auto-scaling and right-sizing were highlighted as key techniques for optimizing cost and performance under dynamic workloads. Together with load balancing, these methods help maintain high availability and responsiveness. Finally, we tied these strategies into the AWS Well-Architected Framework, which ensures your ML systems align with best practices across security, reliability, cost, and sustainability.

With this foundation in place, you are now prepared to move to the next chapter. You will learn how to select the right AWS ML services based on data needs, use cases, and business objectives, helping you design solutions that are not only technically sound but also aligned with strategic goals.

Multiple choice questions

1. **What is the primary purpose of AWS CloudTrail in monitoring AWS environments?**

    a. To monitor resource performance and set alarms

    b. To track API calls and actions in your AWS account

    c. To automatically scale resources based on demand

    d. To optimize cost and performance of ML solutions

2. **Which AWS service is best suited for collecting and visualizing performance metrics of ML workloads?**

    a. Amazon SageMaker

    b. AWS CloudTrail

    c. Amazon CloudWatch

    d. AWS Elastic Load Balancer

3. **You are deploying a ML model across multiple AWS regions to serve users in North America and Asia. Which of the following is the most appropriate reason for this setup?**

    a. To simplify monitoring and logging

    b. To reduce compute costs

    c. To ensure low latency and high availability for global users

    d. To avoid the use of DNS routing tools

4. **Which of the following is not a feature of Docker containers?**

    a. Portability across environments

    b. Full operating system emulation

    c. Lightweight resource usage

    d. Isolation from other applications

5. **Our team is deciding between manual and auto-scaling for an ML inference endpoint that experiences unpredictable traffic spikes. What is the main tradeoff when choosing auto-scaling?**

    a. Auto-scaling provides greater control but slower adaptation

    b. Auto-scaling improves availability but may require careful threshold tuning

    c. Manual scaling is more reliable during traffic surges

    d. Auto-scaling eliminates the need for monitoring tools

6. **Which AWS service helps distribute incoming traffic across multiple resources?**

    a. Amazon EC2 Auto-scaling

    b. AWS Elastic Load Balancer

    c. Amazon CloudTrail

    d. AWS Batch

7. **You are using AWS CloudTrail and Amazon CloudWatch for monitoring your ML infrastructure. What is one tradeoff of enabling detailed CloudWatch logging for all endpoints and resources?**

    a. To maximize latency for global users

    b. To optimize resource allocation and reduce costs

    c. To distribute workloads evenly across instances

    d. To simplify ML deployment pipelines

8. **Which of the following is a key pillar of the AWS Well-Architected Framework?**

    a. Operational flexibility

    b. Infrastructure optimization

    c. Sustainability

    d. Application debugging

9. **Which AWS service can be used to replicate data across regions for global ML solutions?**

    a. Amazon Route 53

    b. Amazon S3 Cross-Region Replication

    c. AWS Elastic Disaster Recovery

    d. AWS Glue

10. **What is a benefit of using AMIs for ML deployments?**

    a. Automatic distribution of traffic across resources

    b. Ensures consistent environment setup for EC2 instances

    c. Enables lightweight and portable ML models

    d. Reduces the need for encryption in data processing

Answer key

1. b.

2. c.

3. c.

4. b.

5. b.

6. b.

7. c.

8. c.

9. b.

10. b.

Join our Discord space

Join our Discord workspace for latest updates, offers, tech happenings around the world, new releases, and sessions with the authors:

https://discord.bpbonline.com

CHAPTER 13

Recommending and Implementing Appropriate ML Services

Introduction

In this chapter, we will focus on understanding and utilizing the appropriate ML services within the AWS ecosystem to address diverse business challenges. The AWS Certified Machine Learning - Specialty (MLS-C01) exam expects candidates to have in-depth knowledge of the key ML services offered by AWS and the decision-making process for implementing these services effectively.

This chapter helps you confidently recommend and implement the most appropriate ML solutions.

You will learn how to leverage pre-built ML services such as *Amazon Polly, Lex*, and *Transcribe*. You will also explore how to evaluate trade-offs between building custom models and using SageMaker's built-in algorithms.

Additionally, we explore how to manage AWS service quotas, optimize costs, and utilize infrastructure resources such as Spot Instances for deep learning tasks.

Structure

The chapter covers the following topics:

- Overview of AWS ML application services

- Understanding and managing AWS service quotas
- Leveraging Bedrock, SageMaker JumpStart, and AutoML for fast-track ML development
- Custom models vs. Amazon SageMaker built-in algorithms
- Cost considerations and infrastructure planning on AWS
- Utilizing Spot instances for deep learning with AWS Batch

Objectives

By the end of this chapter, you will gain a solid understanding of AWS Machine Learning application services and their practical use cases. You will explore tools like Amazon Polly, Lex, and Transcribe to address natural language processing and speech-related challenges in ML solutions. In addition, you will learn how to monitor and manage AWS service quotas to ensure optimal resource usage and performance. This chapter will also help you make informed decisions about when to use custom models versus SageMaker's built-in algorithms, based on business needs, development time, and complexity. You will develop the skills to plan and manage AWS infrastructure for ML projects, focusing on cost optimization, scalability, and selecting the right instance types. Finally, you will learn how to use Spot Instances for deep learning tasks by configuring and deploying workloads on AWS Batch, enabling cost-effective and efficient processing at scale.

By mastering these topics, you will be equipped to confidently tackle questions on recommending and implementing AWS ML services in the certification exam and apply these skills effectively in real-world scenarios.

Overview of AWS ML application services

ML application services on AWS simplify the integration of AI capabilities into various applications without requiring in-depth knowledge of complex ML algorithms or infrastructure. This section focuses on three key AWS services: Amazon Polly, Amazon Lex, and Amazon Transcribe. Each service serves specific business needs, ranging from text-to-speech conversion and chatbot development to speech-to-text transcription.

Amazon Polly

Amazon Polly is a text-to-speech service that uses advanced deep learning technologies to convert text into natural-sounding speech. It supports multiple languages and voices, making it ideal for building applications that require voice interaction.

The following are the key features of Amazon Polly:

- **Wide language and voice support**: Offers over 60 voices across 30+ languages.

- **Real-time processing**: Converts text to speech in real-time for live applications.

- **Custom lexicons**: Allows customization of speech output with phonetic lexicons.

- **Neural text-to-speech (NTTS)**: Delivers enhanced, human-like speech quality.

Example

Consider a customer service application for a global e-commerce platform. Using Amazon Polly, the application can dynamically generate spoken responses in the customer's preferred language, enhancing accessibility and user experience.

Amazon Lex

Amazon Lex is an ML service designed to build conversational interfaces such as chatbots and virtual assistants. It provides **automatic speech recognition (ASR)** and **natural language understanding (NLU)** to process spoken and text inputs effectively.

These are the key features of Amazon Lex:

- **Multi-turn conversations**: Supports dynamic, context-aware interactions.

- **Integration with AWS Lambda**: Allows executing business logic seamlessly.

- **Omnichannel support**: Integrates with platforms like *Facebook Messenger* and *Slack*.

- **Built-in speech recognition**: Processes spoken inputs for voice-based bots.

Example:

Imagine an airline implementing a chatbot to handle customer inquiries. Amazon Lex enables the chatbot to understand and respond to queries like flight status, booking, or cancellation, enhancing efficiency and customer satisfaction.

Amazon Transcribe

Amazon Transcribe is a service that automatically converts spoken language into written text, making it a powerful tool for applications requiring transcription.

Key features of Amazon Transcribe are as follows:

- **Automatic punctuation**: Generates transcripts with appropriate punctuation.

- **Custom vocabulary**: Improves transcription accuracy for domain-specific terms.

- **Speaker identification**: Differentiates between speakers in multi-speaker audio.

- **Real-time and batch processing**: Handles both live and pre-recorded audio files.

Example

A healthcare provider can use Amazon Transcribe to generate accurate transcripts of doctor-patient conversations, which can then be stored for record-keeping or further analysis.

Here is a quick comparison of Amazon Polly, Lex, and Transcribe:

Feature	Amazon Polly	Amazon Lex	Amazon Transcribe
Purpose	Text-to-speech	Conversational AI	Speech-to-text
Key strength	Natural-sounding voices	Multi-turn conversations	Speaker identification
Primary use case	Accessibility, voice apps	Chatbots, virtual assistants	Transcription for analysis

Table 13.1: Comparison of Amazon Polly, Lex, and Transcribe

Understanding and managing AWS service quotas

AWS service quotas are limits that AWS imposes on the resources you can use within your account to ensure fair usage and efficient management of infrastructure. These quotas can be either soft limits, which are adjustable, or hard limits, which are fixed. Understanding and effectively managing service quotas is essential for optimizing resource usage, avoiding bottlenecks, and ensuring smooth operation of your ML workflows on AWS.

Key concepts of AWS Service Quotas

AWS Service Quotas govern the maximum number of resources or operations you can utilize in a specific region or globally. For example, the number of EC2 instances, API requests, or the size of storage resources might be restricted by quotas.

Next, we will take a look at the types of quotas:

- **Soft quotas**: Adjustable limits that you can request to increase based on your managing service quotas are essential when scaling ML workloads on AWS. Below are two common scenarios that illustrate how service quotas can impact your workflow and what actions you may need to take:

- **Example 1**: EC2 Instance Quotas

  Imagine you are launching multiple EC2 instances for training deep learning models. By default, each AWS region has a quota, such as 20 on-demand instances. If your workload requires 50 instances, you must proactively request a quota increase through the AWS Service Quotas console to avoid deployment delays.

- **Example 2**: SageMaker Endpoint Limits

  When deploying models with Amazon SageMaker, there is a limit to the number of active endpoints per account. If you are testing multiple models simultaneously, you may hit this limit. To proceed, you should monitor your current usage and request a quota increase if needed, ensuring uninterrupted testing and deployment.

These examples highlight the importance of regularly reviewing and managing service quotas to prevent unexpected bottlenecks and ensure smooth ML operations.

Managing AWS Service Quotas

To effectively manage service quotas, AWS provides tools and best practices that allow you to monitor, request changes, and optimize your resource usage.

Let us take a look at the steps to manage service quotas:

- **Identify quotas**: Use the AWS Management Console or service quotas dashboard to view applicable limits.

- **Monitor usage**: Enable CloudWatch metrics to track resource usage and receive alerts when approaching limits.

- **Request increases**: Submit requests for soft quota increases through the service quotas console.

- **Optimize resources**: Consolidate workflows or use resource-saving strategies like Spot Instances to stay within limits.

Tools for managing service quotas

Efficient quota management is essential for maintaining the scalability and reliability of your ML workloads on AWS. Fortunately, AWS offers several tools to help you track usage and request quota increases before they impact your operations.

AWS provides various tools to help you manage and monitor service quotas effectively:

- **Service quotas dashboard**: A centralized view to monitor and request quota increases.

- **AWS CLI**: Automate quota management with commands to retrieve limits or submit increase requests.

- **CloudWatch metrics**: Monitor resource usage and set alerts for quota thresholds.

Understanding the different types of AWS service quotas is important for effectively managing resources and planning for scalability.

The following table outlines the key quota types, whether they can be adjusted, and common examples:

Quota type	Adjustable	Common examples
Soft quota	Yes	EC2 instances, API Gateway requests
Hard quota	No	IAM roles per account
Default quota	Yes (within limits)	New account limits like S3 buckets

Table 13.2: Overview of AWS quota types, indicating their adjustability and typical use cases across

The following are the best practices for quota management:

- **Plan resource usage**: Forecast resource needs based on project requirements.

- **Set alerts**: Use CloudWatch alarms to monitor usage.

- **Automate requests**: Leverage AWS CLI or SDKs to submit quota increase requests programmatically.

- **Regular reviews**: Periodically review and optimize resource utilization.

Leveraging Bedrock, SageMaker JumpStart, and AutoML for FastTrackML Development

Amazon Bedrock allows you to build and scale generative AI applications using foundation models from providers like Anthropic, AI21, and Cohere via a simple API without managing any infrastructure. It is ideal for rapid prototyping, personalization, and deploying conversational agents.

The following are the key features:

- No need to manage ML infrastructure.

- Easy integration into existing applications via API.

- Supports popular foundation models (Claude, Jurassic, etc.).

Use case example:

A customer support platform can integrate Amazon Bedrock with Anthropic's Claude model to create multilingual, contextual chatbots without needing deep ML expertise.

SageMaker JumpStart

SageMaker JumpStart provides access to pre-built models, solution templates, and training resources that accelerate ML adoption.

The following are the key features:

- 1-click deployment of popular models (e.g., XGBoost, BERT)

- Solution templates for tasks like fraud detection, image classification
- Integration with SageMaker Studio

Use case example:

A healthcare startup uses SageMaker JumpStart's pre-trained model for classifying radiology images, reducing model development time from weeks to hours.

SageMaker AutoML

SageMaker Autopilot automatically preprocesses data, selects the best algorithms, tunes hyperparameters, and provides explainability reports, while still giving you access to the underlying notebooks.

The following are the key features:

- Full visibility and control over generated models.
- Generates candidate models with performance metrics.
- Explainability tools (feature importance, model diagnostics).

Use case example:

A retail company uploads its customer churn dataset and uses Autopilot to quickly build a predictive model with minimal manual tuning, saving valuable data science resources.

Custom models vs. Amazon SageMaker built-in algorithms

Choosing between developing custom ML models and utilizing Amazon SageMaker's built-in algorithms is a key decision in any ML project. This decision impacts resource allocation, project timelines, and the overall success of the solution. In this section, we will break down the fundamental differences, advantages, challenges, and use cases for both approaches, providing a clear decision-making framework for practitioners.

Custom models

Custom models are designed from the ground up, tailored to meet the specific requirements of a business problem. These models often involve extensive experimentation and optimization to deliver the desired results.

Here we will see a few important advantages of custom models:

- **Flexibility**: Allows complete control over the model architecture, training process, and hyperparameter tuning.

- **Specialized solutions**: Can address unique and complex problems that pre-built algorithms might not solve.

- **Advanced capabilities**: Suitable for cutting-edge research and domain-specific challenges.

While there are many advantages, there are a few challenges that you might face while working with custom models:

- **Resource demands**: Requires expertise in ML and significant computational resources.

- **Longer development cycles**: Development and testing can be time-consuming.

- **Higher costs**: Typically involves more investment in terms of both time and money.

Example:

Consider a fintech company aiming to detect fraudulent transactions. A custom model allows for the integration of domain-specific features and complex relationships unique to the financial sector, enhancing detection accuracy.

Amazon SageMaker built-in algorithms

Amazon SageMaker offers a collection of pre-built algorithms optimized for various ML tasks such as classification, regression, clustering, and anomaly detection. These algorithms are scalable and require minimal setup, making them ideal for common use cases.

The following are the advantages of SageMaker built-in algorithms:

- **Ease of use**: Pre-configured and ready to deploy with minimal effort.

- **Cost-effectiveness**: Reduces development costs by leveraging pre-built solutions.

- **Scalability**: Optimized for large-scale datasets and distributed environments.

The following are the challenges of SageMaker built-in algorithms:

- **Limited customization**: May not fully meet specific business requirements.

- **Dependency on AWS ecosystem**: Heavily tied to AWS infrastructure.

- **General-purpose nature**: May not perform optimally for niche or complex problems.

Example:

An e-commerce company building a recommendation system for products can use SageMaker's factorization machine algorithm. This approach ensures rapid deployment and reliable performance without requiring extensive customization.

You can see a comparison of custom models vs. SageMaker built-in algorithms in the following table:

Criteria	Custom models	SageMaker built-in algorithms
Flexibility	Highly flexible and customizable	Limited customization
Ease of use	Requires expertise in ML	Pre-configured, beginner-friendly
Cost	Higher development and operational costs	Cost-effective for common tasks
Best use case	Complex, domain-specific problems	General-purpose ML applications
Time to market	Longer development time	Faster deployment
Inference latency	Varies by implementation	Optimized (<100 ms typical)

Table 13.3: Comparison of custom models and SageMaker

Decision-making framework

To decide whether to use custom models or SageMaker's built-in algorithms, consider the following:

- **Business requirements**: Clearly define the problem and evaluate whether it requires a customized solution.

- **Resource availability**: Assess the availability of data scientists, time, and computational resources.

- **Time constraints**: Use built-in algorithms for faster prototyping and deployment.

- **Cost considerations**: If budget is a concern, opt for built-in algorithms to minimize costs.

- **Scalability needs**: For large-scale applications, SageMaker's built-in algorithms are often better suited.

Cost considerations and infrastructure planning on AWS

Cost considerations and infrastructure planning are integral components of building effective and efficient ML solutions on AWS. By understanding how to balance performance with cost, organizations can achieve their business objectives without overspending. AWS provides a variety of tools and services to optimize infrastructure usage and manage costs efficiently.

Key principles of cost optimization

AWS enables cost optimization by providing scalable, pay-as-you-go infrastructure and tools for monitoring and managing expenses. Its key principles include:

- **Right-sizing resources**: Select instance types and sizes that align with workload requirements.

- **Auto-scaling**: Dynamically adjust resources based on demand.

- **Use reserved instances and savings plans**: Commit to long-term usage for lower costs.

- **Spot instances**: Leverage unused capacity for cost savings.

Cost components in AWS

Understanding the key cost components is crucial for planning and managing budgets effectively. These components include:

- **Computer costs**: Charges for using EC2 instances, Lambda functions, and other computer services.

- **Storage costs**: Costs associated with storing data in services like *S3, EBS,* or *Glacier.*

- **Data transfer costs**: Charges for data moving in and out of AWS services.

- **ML service costs**: Usage of SageMaker, Polly, Lex, and Transcribe services.

- **Networking costs**: VPC, load balancers, and other networking-related expenses.

Infrastructure planning best practices

Effective infrastructure planning involves designing systems that meet performance and scalability needs while minimizing costs. The best practices for infrastructure planning include:

- **Leverage serverless architectures**: Reduce infrastructure management overhead by using services like *AWS Lambda.*

- **Monitor and optimize usage**: Regularly review usage with tools like *AWS Cost Explorer* and *Trusted Advisor.*

- **Architect for scalability**: Use elastic load balancing and auto-scaling groups to handle fluctuating workloads.

- **Enable consolidated billing**: Combine accounts for better cost management and volume discounts.

Practical examples

To illustrate how AWS services can be applied in real-world scenarios, consider the following examples that highlight cost optimization strategies using EC2 instances:

- **Example 1**: Right-sizing EC2 Instances

  A startup running a recommendation engine initially uses large EC2 instances, leading to high costs. By switching to smaller, right-sized instances, they reduce computer expenses without affecting performance.

- **Example 2**: Using Spot Instances for training

  A media company leverages Spot Instances to train a deep learning model for image recognition. Spot Instances provide up to 90% savings compared to on-demand instances, significantly lowering training costs.

The following table is a comparison of AWS cost-optimization options:

Cost-optimization method	Advantages	Considerations
Right-sizing resources	Optimizes usage for cost savings	Requires monitoring and fine-tuning
Spot instances	Up to 90% savings	May experience interruptions
Auto-scaling	Handles demand fluctuations	Requires configuration
Reserved instances	Lower long-term costs	Requires commitment
Serverless architectures	No infrastructure management	Not suitable for all workloads

Table 13.4: Comparison of AWS cost-optimization methods

Tools for cost management

Effectively managing costs is essential when building and scaling ML solutions on AWS. Without visibility into usage and spending, projects can quickly exceed budget, undermining both efficiency and business value. To help with this, AWS offers several tools that enable proactive cost monitoring, optimization, and planning:

- **AWS Cost Explorer**: Visualize and analyze cost trends over time.

- **AWS Trusted Advisor**: Receive recommendations for cost savings.

- **AWS Budgets**: Set custom budgets and receive alerts.

- **Amazon CloudWatch**: Monitor resource usage and performance.

Cost considerations and infrastructure planning are pivotal for maximizing the ROI of AWS ML solutions. By applying best practices and leveraging AWS tools, businesses can build scalable, cost-efficient infrastructures while staying within budget. A thoughtful approach to cost optimization not only reduces expenses but also ensures sustainable growth.

Utilizing Spot Instances for deep learning with AWS Batch

Deep learning workloads require significant computational resources, often leading to high costs. AWS Spot Instances, coupled with AWS Batch, provide an efficient and cost-effective solution for handling these workloads. By leveraging unused EC2 capacity, Spot Instances offer significant cost savings, while AWS Batch automates job scheduling and management, making it easier to process large-scale deep learning tasks.

Understanding AWS Spot Instances

AWS Spot Instances allow you to use spare EC2 capacity at a discounted price, offering savings of up to 90% compared to on-demand instances. These instances are ideal for fault-tolerance and flexible workloads, such as deep learning model training, where interruptions can be managed.

The following are some of the key features of Spot Instances:

- **Significant cost savings**: Pay substantially less compared to on-demand prices.

- **Availability**: Access spare capacity in multiple regions and instance types.

- **Interruptions**: Instances may be terminated if AWS needs the capacity, but mechanisms like Checkpoints and Spot Fleet mitigate this risk.

Example:

A company training a **convolutional neural network (CNN)** for image classification can use Spot Instances to handle the computational demands at a fraction of the cost, ensuring budget efficiency without compromising performance.

Overview of AWS Batch

AWS Batch is a fully managed service that enables developers and data scientists to run batch computing workloads efficiently. By integrating with Spot Instances, AWS Batch ensures seamless scheduling and resource allocation for deep learning tasks.

The following are the key features of AWS Batch:

- **Automated job scheduling**: Automatically schedules jobs based on priority and resource requirements.

- **Seamless integration**: Supports Spot Instances and other EC2 instance types.

- **Scalability**: Dynamically scales resources to match workload demands.

- **Cost optimization**: Minimizes costs by intelligently using Spot Instances for suitable workloads.

Practical workflow example

Now that we have explored various AWS cost-optimization strategies, let us see how they come together in a real-world ML scenario. The following example demonstrates how to train a deep learning model using AWS Batch with Spot Instances, highlighting an efficient and cost-effective workflow:

- **Define the job**: Create a job definition specifying the Docker container, input data, and compute requirements.

- **Submit the job**: Submit the job to an AWS Batch job queue configured to use Spot Instances.

- **Monitor and manage**: Use the AWS Management Console or CLI to monitor job progress and handle interruptions.

- **Retrieve results**: Once the job is complete, retrieve the trained model or processed outputs from the designated storage.

Example use case:

A media company processing video frames for object detection uses AWS Batch with Spot Instances. The system dynamically scales resources to process millions of frames cost-effectively, maintaining high throughput.

The following table shows a comparison of Spot Instances and on-demand instances for deep learning:

Criteria	Spot instances	On-demand instances
Cost	Up to 90% savings	Full price
Availability	Dependent on spare capacity	Always available
Interruption	Possible, requires fault-tolerance	No interruption risk
Best use case	Flexible, fault-tolerant workloads	Critical workloads
Scalability	Highly scalable, cost-effective	Scalable but more expensive

Table 13.5: Comparison of Spot Instances and on-demand instances

Utilizing Spot Instances with AWS Batch provides a robust and cost-efficient solution for handling deep learning workloads. By combining significant cost savings with intelligent job scheduling, organizations can optimize their resources and reduce expenses without compromising performance. Adopting best practices ensures reliability and maximizes the benefits of this approach.

Conclusion

This chapter provided a practical guide to selecting and implementing the right AWS ML services for various use cases. It covered how tools like Amazon Polly, Lex, and Transcribe enhance workflows in NLP and conversational AI, and emphasized the importance of managing AWS service quotas using tools like CloudWatch and the Service Quotas Dashboard. Readers also learned to evaluate trade-offs between custom models and SageMaker's built-in algorithms, and explored cost optimization strategies such as right-sizing, Spot Instances, auto-scaling, and serverless deployments. These insights help in building scalable, cost-effective ML solutions aligned with business needs and prepare readers for the AWS Certified Machine Learning – Specialty exam.

In the next chapter, you will learn how to secure ML workloads using AWS best practices like encryption, access controls, and network isolation.

Multiple choice questions

1. **What is the primary purpose of Amazon Polly?**

    a. To build conversational chatbots

    b. To convert text into natural-sounding speech

    c. To transcribe spoken language into text

    d. To identify anomalies in datasets

2. **Which of the following is a key feature of Amazon Lex?**

    a. Speaker identification

    b. Multi-turn conversations

    c. Neural text-to-speech

    d. Automatic punctuation

3. **What type of AWS service quota can be adjusted by submitting a request?**

    a. Hard quota

    b. Default quota

    c. Soft quota

    d. Regional quota

4. **When should you choose custom models over SageMaker's built-in algorithms?**

    a. For faster deployment

    b. For general-purpose ML tasks

    c. For niche, domain-specific problems

    d. To reduce operational costs

5. **Which AWS Tool can be used to monitor resource usage and set alerts for approaching limits?**

    a. AWS Trusted Advisor

    b. Amazon CloudWatch

    c. AWS Batch

    d. AWS Lambda

6. **What is one of the main advantages of using Spot Instances for deep learning tasks?**

    a. Guaranteed uninterrupted availability

    b. Up to 90% cost savings

    c. No need for checkpointing

    d. Access to spare EC2 capacity at a lower price

7. **Which AWS ML service is best suited for creating virtual assistants?**

    a. Amazon Polly

    b. Amazon Transcribe

    c. Amazon Lex

    d. AWS Batch

8. **What is the purpose of AWS Batch in a deep learning workflow?**

    a. To convert speech into text

    b. To automate batch job scheduling and resource allocation

    c. To build conversational chatbots

    d. To manage service quotas

9. **Which of the following is not a best practice for using Spot Instances with AWS Batch?**

    a. Implementing checkpoints to save progress

    b. Combining multiple instance types in Spot Fleets

    c. Relying solely on one instance type in a single availability zone

    d. Monitoring Spot Instance pricing trends

10. **What is a common cost component in AWS that directly relates to data storage?**

    a. Compute costs

    b. Data transfer costs

    c. ML service costs

    d. Storage costs

Answer key

1. b.

2. b.

3. c.

4. c.

5. b.

6. b.

7. c.

8. b.

9. c.

10. d.

Join our Discord space

Join our Discord workspace for latest updates, offers, tech happenings around the world, new releases, and sessions with the authors:

https://discord.bpbonline.com

CHAPTER 14

Applying AWS Security Practices to ML Solutions

Introduction

In the rapidly evolving world of **artificial intelligence/machine learning (AI/ML)**, ensuring the security of your solutions is paramount. As you design, build, and deploy ML applications on AWS, safeguarding sensitive data, ensuring compliance with industry standards, and protecting your resources from threats are essential components of success. AWS provides a robust set of security tools and best practices tailored to the unique challenges of ML workloads.

This chapter explores the application of AWS security practices to ML solutions, emphasizing key concepts such as identity management, encryption, and secure deployment within the AWS Cloud. By mastering these principles, you will be well-prepared to implement secure and reliable ML solutions while meeting the requirements of the AWS Certified Machine Learning - Specialty (MLS-C01) exam.

Structure

The chapter covers the following topics:

- AWS identity and access management for ML solutions
- Managing S3 bucket policies and security groups
- Utilizing VPCs for secure ML deployments

- Encryption and anonymization techniques in ML

- Case study: Securing a customer churn prediction model on AWS

Objectives

By the end of this chapter, you will gain a deep understanding of AWS **Identity and Access Management (IAM)**, including how to create policies that provide secure and efficient access to ML resources. You will learn how to configure and manage S3 bucket policies and security groups to protect data assets and prevent unauthorized access. The chapter also covers the role of **virtual private clouds (VPCs)** in establishing isolated, secure environments for model training, inference, and deployment. In addition, you will explore advanced encryption and anonymization techniques that safeguard sensitive data throughout its lifecycle in ML workflows. Finally, you will become familiar with AWS-recommended best practices for securing ML solutions, equipping you with the skills to mitigate security risks and maintain compliance. By mastering these topics, you will be well-prepared to answer certification exam questions related to ML security and apply these practices confidently in real-world applications.

AWS identity and access management for ML solutions

AWS IAM is the cornerstone of secure ML solutions in the AWS Cloud. IAM enables you to control access to your AWS resources by defining who (identity) is authenticated and authorized to use those resources. For ML applications, this control is critical as it protects sensitive data, ML models, and associated resources from unauthorized access.

IAM policies

IAM policies are JSON documents that define permissions for an identity (user, group, or role) or resource. In the context of ML solutions, IAM policies ensure that only authorized entities can access specific resources, such as S3 buckets containing training datasets or SageMaker notebooks for model development.

For example, let us look at the following IAM policy for read-only access to an S3 Bucket:

```
{
    "Version": "2012-10-17",
    "Statement": [
      {
        "Effect": "Allow",
        "Action": "s3:GetObject",
        "Resource": "arn:aws:s3:::my-ml-data-bucket/*"
```

```
        }
    ]
}
```

IAM roles

IAM roles are another essential component of access management for ML solutions. Unlike users, roles do not have long-term credentials. Instead, roles provide temporary access to AWS resources based on policies. For example, a SageMaker notebook instance can assume a role to access training data in S3 without embedding credentials in the application.

To assign a role to a SageMaker notebook instance, you need to:

1. Create an IAM role with the required permissions (e.g., S3 read access).

2. Attach the role to the SageMaker notebook instance during its setup.

3. Ensure the policy grants it the least privilege.

Fine-grained access control

Fine-grained access control enables you to specify detailed permissions for users, roles, or resources. For example, you can limit access to a specific folder in an S3 bucket containing test datasets while granting full access to the training dataset folder.

Users vs. roles

The following table summarizes the differences between IAM users and IAM roles:

IAM users	IAM roles
Assigned to a person or an application with long-term credentials	Used by applications or AWS services with temporary credentials
Requires manual credential management	Credentials are automatically rotated

Table 14.1: Comparison of IAM users and IAM roles

Best practices for IAM in ML

Implementing IAM best practices is essential for securing ML environments and minimizing risk. The following practices help ensure that access to ML resources is properly managed and aligned with security standards.

The following are the principles of least privilege by granting only the permissions necessary for a task:

- Use IAM roles instead of embedding credentials in your application code.

- Regularly audit IAM policies and access logs to ensure compliance and detect unauthorized access.

- Leverage AWS Organizations to centrally manage permissions across multiple accounts.

Managing S3 bucket policies and security groups

Amazon S3 and security groups are critical components in AWS for controlling access and ensuring the security of your resources. Managing S3 bucket policies involves defining permissions to allow or deny access to objects stored in an S3 bucket, while security groups act as virtual firewalls to control inbound and outbound traffic for your AWS resources. These tools, when used effectively, can help protect sensitive data, such as training datasets and ML model outputs, from unauthorized access.

S3 bucket policies

S3 bucket policies are JSON-based access control policies that apply to an entire bucket. These policies allow you to define granular permissions based on actions, principles, and resources. For ML workflows, S3 bucket policies can secure training datasets, ensure compliance with data regulations, and enable controlled sharing.

For example, here is an S3 bucket policy for public read access:

```
{
    "Version": "2012-10-17",
    "Statement": [
      {
        "Effect": "Allow",
        "Principal": "*",
        "Action": "s3:GetObject",
        "Resource": "arn:aws:s3:::my-public-bucket/*"
      }
    ]
}
```

This policy allows any user to read objects from the bucket **my-public-bucket**. While public read access might be useful for sharing non-sensitive data, it is critical to use such policies judiciously.

Security groups

Security groups act as virtual firewalls for your Amazon EC2 instances and other resources. They control inbound and outbound traffic at the instance level. For ML solutions, security groups are essential for ensuring that only authorized users and systems can access your ML models, APIs, or data sources.

For example, let us see how to set up a security group for a SageMaker endpoint. To configure a security group, follow these steps:

1. Allow inbound traffic from specific IP addresses or security groups for inference requests.

2. Deny all other inbound traffic by default.

3. Allow outbound traffic to necessary services, such as S3 for storing model outputs.

Combining bucket policies and security groups

In many scenarios, you will use both bucket policies and security groups to enforce security. For example, bucket policies can secure the data at the S3 level, while security groups can restrict access to resources that process this data.

S3 bucket policies vs. security groups

The following table highlights the differences between S3 bucket policies and security groups:

S3 bucket policies	Security groups
Applies to S3 buckets and objects	Applies to AWS resources like EC2 instances and SageMaker endpoints.
Defines access permissions for data stored in S3	Controls network traffic to and from resources.
Written in JSON format	Configured through AWS Management Console or CLI.

Table 14.2: Comparison of S3 bucket policies and security groups

Best practices

To maintain a secure and well-managed AWS environment, it is important to follow established best practices when configuring S3 bucket policies and security groups. The following recommendations help ensure data protection, access control, and continuous monitoring:

- Implement the principle of least privilege by granting only necessary permissions in S3 bucket policies.

- Use IP address whitelisting and port restrictions in security groups.

- Regularly review and update bucket policies and security group rules to adapt to changing requirements.

- Enable logging and monitoring with services like Amazon CloudTrail and AWS Config to track access and changes.

Utilizing VPCs for secure ML deployments

Amazon VPC enables you to launch AWS resources in a logically isolated network. For ML deployments, VPCs provide a secure environment where sensitive data, models, and APIs can operate without exposure to the public internet. This isolation ensures compliance with data security standards and protects ML workloads from external threats.

Basics of VPC

VPC is a customizable network that allows you to define subnets, routing tables, and gateways. Each VPC is isolated from others, offering a secure environment for your ML workloads. For example, you can create private subnets for storing training datasets and public subnets for hosting APIs that serve model predictions.

The following example illustrates a simple VPC architecture designed for a secure and scalable ML deployment. It outlines how different components can be isolated and connected to balance accessibility and security:

- A public subnet with a SageMaker endpoint to provide inference services

- A private subnet with an EC2 instance for preprocessing training data

- A NAT gateway for allowing the private subnet to download dependencies without exposing it to the internet

Security groups and network ACLs

VPCs leverage security groups and network **access control lists** (**ACLs**) to manage traffic. Security groups act as firewalls for resources within the VPC, while ACLs provide an additional layer of network-level security.

To configure security groups for a SageMaker notebook instance, follow these steps:

1. Allow inbound traffic only from specific IP ranges or security groups.

2. Deny all inbound traffic by default.

3. Allow outbound traffic to essential AWS services, such as S3.

Using PrivateLink for ML endpoints

AWS PrivateLink allows you to securely access AWS services without using the public internet. This is particularly useful for ML endpoints that need to serve predictions while maintaining strict data security. By integrating PrivateLink, you ensure that all traffic remains within the AWS network, reducing exposure to external threats.

VPC vs. public deployments

The following table compares VPC-based deployments with public deployments for ML solutions:

VPC deployment	Public deployment
Resources are isolated within a private network	Resources are exposed to the public internet
Enhanced security and compliance	Increased risk of unauthorized access
Requires additional setup and configuration	Easier to set up but less secure

Table 14.3: Comparison of VPC-based and public deployments for ML solutions

Best practices for VPCs in ML

To ensure secure and efficient networking for ML workloads, it is important to follow best practices when configuring VPCs. The following recommendations help enhance data protection, visibility, and connectivity within your ML infrastructure:

- Use private subnets for storing sensitive data and training models.
- Enable flow logs to monitor network traffic and detect unauthorized access.
- Leverage AWS services like PrivateLink and Transit Gateway to enhance connectivity and security.
- Regularly review and update VPC configurations to address evolving security needs.

By following these VPC best practices, you can build a secure and well-structured network foundation for your ML workloads. With networking safeguards in place, the next critical focus is protecting data itself, both at rest and in transit, using encryption and anonymization techniques.

Encryption and anonymization techniques in ML

Data security and privacy are critical in ML workflows, particularly when handling sensitive or personal information. Encryption and anonymization techniques help protect data throughout its lifecycle, ensuring compliance with data protection regulations and safeguarding against unauthorized access. This section explores key concepts, techniques, and best practices for securing ML data using encryption and anonymization.

Encryption basics

Encryption is the process of converting plaintext data into ciphertext using cryptographic algorithms. Only authorized parties with the correct decryption key can access the original data. In ML, encryption is used to secure data during storage, transmission, and processing.

Amazon S3 offers **server-side encryption (SSE)** with options such as:

- **SSE-S3**: Encryption keys are managed by AWS.
- **SSE-KMS**: Encryption keys are managed using AWS **Key Management Service (KMS)**.
- **SSE-C**: Customer provides and manages their own encryption keys.

Anonymization techniques

Anonymization removes or masks personal identifiers in data, making it impossible to trace back to individuals. This ensures that datasets can be used for ML training while preserving privacy. Common anonymization techniques include:

- **Generalization**: Replacing specific details with broader categories.
- **Suppression**: Removing sensitive attributes.
- **Tokenization**: Replacing sensitive data with tokens.

Tokenization can be used to anonymize sensitive customer information in datasets. For example, replacing names with unique tokens (e.g., `User123`) ensures privacy while retaining the dataset's utility for ML.

Combining encryption and anonymization

For comprehensive security, encryption and anonymization are often combined. Encryption protects data at rest and in transit, while anonymization ensures privacy even if data is accessed. For example, encrypting anonymized data provides an additional layer of security.

Encryption vs. anonymization

The following table highlights the differences between encryption and anonymization:

Encryption	Anonymization
Protects data by converting it to ciphertext	Removes or masks personal identifiers
Requires decryption keys for access	Does not require keys; data remains usable but anonymized
Focuses on data security	Focuses on data privacy

Table 14.4: Comparison of encryption and anonymization

Best practices

To effectively protect sensitive data in ML workflows, it is essential to implement strong encryption and anonymization practices. The following best practices help ensure data security, privacy, and compliance throughout the ML lifecycle:

- Use AWS KMS for managing encryption keys securely and efficiently.

- Anonymize sensitive attributes in datasets before sharing or using them for ML.

- Regularly audit encryption and anonymization processes to ensure compliance with evolving regulations.

- Employ multi-layered security by combining encryption, anonymization, and access controls.

AWS services for security

AWS offers a range of services to help implement encryption and anonymization techniques:

- **AWS KMS**: Manage encryption keys.

- **AWS CloudTrail**: Track API calls and detect unauthorized access.

- **Amazon Macie**: Automate the identification of sensitive data.

- **AWS Glue DataBrew**: Clean and anonymize datasets with minimal coding.

With these AWS services, you can implement encryption and anonymization effectively within your ML workflows. Now that you've seen the tools available, it is important to understand how to apply them within a broader security framework.

AWS best practices for ML solution security

Security is a critical component of building and maintaining ML solutions on AWS. Adhering to AWS best practices ensures that your ML solutions remain secure, compliant, and resilient against potential threats. This section explores the essential AWS security best practices for ML solutions, focusing on concepts such as identity management, encryption, monitoring, and incident response.

Least privilege access

The principle of least privilege involves granting users, applications, or services only the permissions that they need to perform their tasks. This minimizes the risk of accidental or intentional misuse of resources.

The following example shows how to configure an IAM policy that grants read-only access to objects in an S3 bucket used for ML training data:

```
{
    "Version": "2012-10-17",
    "Statement": [
      {
        "Effect": "Allow",
        "Action": "s3:GetObject",
        "Resource": "arn:aws:s3:::ml-training-data/*"
      }
    ]
}
```

In this example, the policy allows read-only access to a specific S3 bucket used for ML training data.

Data encryption

Encrypting data at rest and in transit is essential for protecting sensitive information. AWS services like Amazon S3, AWS KMS, and Amazon SageMaker provide built-in encryption options.

The following steps demonstrate how to enable encryption in Amazon S3 to protect your data at rest and ensure compliance with security best practices:

1. Navigate to your S3 bucket in the AWS Management Console.

2. Select **Properties** and enable server-side encryption.

3. Choose between SSE-S3, SSE-KMS, or SSE-C based on your security requirements.

Network security

Protecting your ML solutions at the network level involves using VPCs, security groups, and network ACLs. These tools help isolate and secure resources from unauthorized access.

Here are the steps you need to take to configure a security group for an ML endpoint:

1. Create a security group in the AWS Management Console.

2. Allow inbound traffic only from specific IP ranges.

3. Deny all other traffic by default.

Monitoring and logging

Monitoring and logging are vital for detecting and responding to security incidents. AWS offers services like Amazon CloudWatch, AWS CloudTrail, and Amazon GuardDuty to track activities, identify vulnerabilities, and detect anomalies.

The following example outlines how to use AWS CloudTrail to enable audit logging, helping you track user activity and detect potential security issues in your ML environment:

1. Enable AWS CloudTrail in your account.

2. Configure log delivery to an S3 bucket.

3. Review logs regularly for unauthorized activities.

Incident response

An effective incident response plan includes preparing for, detecting, and mitigating security incidents. AWS offers tools like AWS Config and AWS Security Hub to support incident response efforts.

The following example illustrates how to automate security responses using AWS Config by defining rules, setting remediation actions, and monitoring compliance through the dashboard:

1. Define compliance rules in AWS Config.

2. Set up remediation actions to automatically resolve non-compliant configurations.

3. Monitor compliance status using the AWS Config Dashboard.

Preventive vs. detective security measures

The following table compares preventive and detective security measures:

Preventive measures	Detective measures
Implement least privilege access policies	Monitor activities using AWS CloudTrail
Encrypt data at rest and in transit	Detect anomalies with Amazon GuardDuty
Use VPCs and security groups to isolate resources	Analyze logs for unauthorized activities

Table 14.5: Comparison of preventive and detective security measures

AWS security best practices

To maintain a strong security posture for ML solutions on AWS, it is essential to follow key security best practices. The following recommendations help ensure consistent protection, compliance, and awareness across your team and infrastructure:

- Regularly update IAM policies and permissions.

- Enable MFA for all users.

- Use AWS Trusted Advisor to identify security gaps.

- Continuously educate team members about security practices.

Case study: Securing a customer churn prediction model on AWS

A telecom company wants to build a customer churn prediction model using Amazon SageMaker. The dataset contains sensitive customer information (e.g., age, contract type, usage patterns). The company must meet strict data security requirements, including encryption, controlled access, and compliance with privacy regulations.

Low security architecture low involves the following steps:

1. **Data ingestion and storage**:
   a. Raw data is uploaded to a private S3 bucket.
   b. SSE-KMS encryption is enabled.
   c. The bucket policy only allows access via an IAM role with s3:GetObject permission.

2. **Model development**:
   a. SageMaker notebook is launched in a private subnet inside a VPC.
   b. IAM role attached to notebook grants least privilege (only S3 read, no write).
   c. Security group restricts notebook access to specific Ips.

3. **Data anonymization**:
   a. Data is anonymized using AWS Glue DataBrew before training.
   b. PII is removed or tokenized.

4. **Model training**:
   a. Training is executed on SageMaker within the same VPC.
   b. Temporary IAM role is used for access to anonymized data.
   c. All activity is logged using AWS CloudTrail.

5. **Model deployment**:
   a. Trained model is deployed using SageMaker endpoint.
   b. Endpoint sits in a public subnet with a security group allowing access only from the company's internal IP range.
   c. AWS PrivateLink is used to access the model securely from BI dashboards.

6. **Monitoring and compliance**:
   a. CloudTrail logs API calls.
   b. GuardDuty detects anomalies.
   c. AWS Config ensures encryption and network configurations are compliant.

Summary insights: This case study demonstrates how AWS security practices are applied across the ML lifecycle, from ingestion to deployment and monitoring. It ties together IAM, encryption, VPC isolation, and security best practices in a practical and exam-relevant way.

Conclusion

This chapter focused on the key security principles needed to protect ML solutions in the AWS Cloud, emphasizing confidentiality, integrity, and availability. It began with IAM, highlighting the principle of least privilege and the use of IAM policies, roles, and groups to control access and reduce risk. Data protection was addressed through encryption at rest and in transit, as well as anonymization to safeguard sensitive datasets during training and inference. The chapter also explored network security using VPCs, along with security groups, network ACLs, and AWS PrivateLink to isolate ML environments and block unauthorized access. Continuous monitoring and auditing were emphasized using AWS tools like CloudWatch, CloudTrail, and Config to detect vulnerabilities and respond to incidents proactively. Together, these layers form a comprehensive security strategy that aligns with AWS best practices and regulatory requirements. By mastering these tools and techniques, you can build secure, resilient ML systems and be better prepared for the AWS Certified Machine Learning – Specialty exam.

In the next chapter, we will cover how to deploy and operationalize ML solutions, including strategies for productionizing models, managing workflows at scale, setting up CI/CD pipelines, and monitoring performance in real-world environments.

Multiple choice questions

1. **Which AWS service is primarily used to manage access permissions for ML solutions?**

    a. AWS CloudTrail

    b. AWS Identity and Access Management

    c. Amazon CloudWatch

    d. AWS Key Management Service

2. **What is the principle of least privilege in the context of AWS security?**

    a. Granting access to all AWS services by default

    b. Granting only the permissions necessary to perform a specific task

    c. Removing all permissions for inactive users

    d. Using encryption for all resources

3. **Which of the following options is not a valid server-side encryption method in Amazon S3?**

    a. SSE-S3

    b. SSE-KMS

    c. SSE-RSA

    d. SSE-C

4. **What does a security group control in an AWS VPC?**

    a. Access to individual S3 buckets

    b. Traffic to and from EC2 instances

    c. The encryption of data in transit

    d. Monitoring and logging of user activities

5. **What is the main purpose of AWS PrivateLink?**

    a. To manage encryption keys securely

    b. To securely access AWS services without using the public internet

    c. To create isolated networks within a VPC

    d. To automate ML workflows

6. **Which of the following best describes data anonymization?**

    a. Encrypting data to protect it from unauthorized access

    b. Removing or masking personal identifiers to protect privacy

    c.   Converting plaintext data into ciphertext

    d.   Using ML to detect sensitive data automatically

7. **Which AWS service helps monitor and detect unauthorized activities in ML solutions?**

    a.   Amazon SageMaker

    b.   AWS GuardDuty

    c.   AWS Config

    d.   AWS Glue

8. **What is the key difference between S3 bucket policies and security groups?**

    a.   S3 bucket policies control access at the network level, while security groups control data access

    b.   S3 bucket policies are used for controlling access to objects, while security groups manage network traffic

    c.   Security groups are written in JSON format, while S3 bucket policies are configured in the console

    d.   Both are used to encrypt sensitive data

9. **Which AWS service can automate responses to non-compliant configurations in ML environments?**

    a.   Amazon CloudWatch

    b.   AWS Config

    c.   Amazon GuardDuty

    d.   AWS PrivateLink

10. **What is the recommended way to secure sensitive ML datasets stored in S3?**

    a.   Use public access for easy sharing

    b.   Enable server-side encryption and restrict access with IAM policies

    c.   Store datasets in a public subnet

    d.   Only anonymize the datasets without additional encryption

Answer key

1. b.

2. b.

3. c.

4. b.

5. b.

6. b.

7. b.

8. b.

9. b.

10. b.

Join our Discord space

Join our Discord workspace for latest updates, offers, tech happenings around the world, new releases, and sessions with the authors:

https://discord.bpbonline.com

CHAPTER 15

Deploying and Operationalizing ML Solutions

Introduction

Deploying **machine learning** (**ML**) models is a crucial step in transforming a trained model into a functional solution that delivers real-world value. The process goes beyond just making predictions; it involves exposing the model for consumption, ensuring its reliability, updating it when necessary, and monitoring its ongoing performance. Successful deployment requires a well-architected infrastructure that allows models to integrate seamlessly with applications, scale as needed, and maintain efficiency over time.

In this chapter, we will explore how to effectively deploy and operationalize ML solutions using AWS services. We will cover how to expose ML models through endpoints, interact with them efficiently, and manage access control. Additionally, we will delve into understanding model behavior in production, implementing A/B testing to compare models, and designing retraining pipelines to keep models up to date. Debugging and troubleshooting techniques are also essential for maintaining reliability, so we will examine common failure points, logging practices, and tools to diagnose and resolve model issues. Lastly, we will discuss performance monitoring and mitigation strategies to ensure long-term model accuracy and efficiency.

By the end of this chapter, you will have the knowledge and skills necessary to confidently deploy ML models in production, maintain them effectively, and troubleshoot issues as they arise. These concepts align with the AWS Certified Machine Learning – Specialty (MLS-C01) exam, preparing you to answer related questions with confidence.

Structure

This chapter covers the following topics:

- Exposing and interacting with ML model endpoints
- In-depth understanding of ML models and their behaviours
- Implementing A/B testing for ML models
- Retraining and updating ML models
- Debugging and troubleshooting techniques for ML models
- Performance monitoring and mitigation strategies

Objectives

This chapter prepares you to deploy and manage machine learning models in the AWS ecosystem. You will learn to expose models via endpoints, configure inference settings, and secure deployments using services like *Amazon SageMaker* and *AWS Lambda*. These skills enable you to build scalable, API-driven ML solutions. You will explore how to monitor model performance, detect drift, and improve interpretability to maintain reliability over time. A/B testing will be covered to help you compare model versions, analyze results, and make informed deployment decisions with minimal risk.

You will also learn to automate retraining and updates using SageMaker Pipelines, scheduling jobs, managing versions, deploying without downtime, and rolling back if needed. Debugging skills will help you identify inference issues, use logs effectively, and resolve problems with AWS tools. Finally, you will gain experience setting up automated monitoring with services like SageMaker Model Monitor and CloudWatch to detect performance drops, trigger alerts, and optimize resources.

By the end of this chapter, you will be ready for AWS certification exams and, more importantly, equipped with the real-world skills needed to deploy, manage, and maintain production-ready ML systems.

Exposing and interacting with ML model endpoints

Once ML model is trained, it must be made accessible to users, applications, or other systems for inference. This process involves exposing the model through an endpoint, that is, a URL or an interface where the model can receive input and return predictions. AWS provides several methods to deploy ML models as endpoints, including Amazon SageMaker endpoints, AWS Lambda for serverless inference, and Amazon EC2 for custom deployments.

Understanding how to deploy and interact with these endpoints is crucial for ensuring models are scalable, secure, and cost-effective. In this section, we will break down the concept of ML model endpoints, explore various deployment options, and provide practical examples of how to expose and interact with ML models in production environments.

An ML model endpoint is a deployed service that allows external applications or users to send input data and receive model predictions. It functions like an API, providing a standardized way to interact with the trained model. Endpoints can be configured to handle different workloads, including real-time inference, batch processing, and asynchronous inference. Endpoints are essential for productionizing ML models, as they provide a bridge between the model and the end user. They ensure that ML models are available for real-world applications, whether it is fraud detection in banking, product recommendations in e-commerce, or medical diagnosis in healthcare.

Types of ML model endpoints

AWS offers multiple ways to expose ML models as endpoints, each suited to different use cases. The three most common types of endpoints are:

- **Real-time inference endpoints**: Designed for applications that require immediate responses from the model.

- **Batch processing endpoints**: Used for processing large datasets where predictions can be computed in bulk.

- **Asynchronous inference endpoints**: Suitable for scenarios where requests can be queued and processed later, reducing costs.

The following table provides a comparison of common ML model endpoint types, outlining their typical use cases and example applications to help you choose the appropriate deployment strategy based on performance and latency requirements:

Endpoint type	Use case	Example
Real-time inference	Low-latency applications requiring immediate responses.	Chatbots, fraud detection, real-time recommendation systems.
Batch processing	Large-scale predictions that do not require immediate responses.	Customer segmentation, risk modeling, document classification.
Asynchronous inference	Tasks that can tolerate delayed responses to save cost.	Processing medical images, summarizing large texts, video analysis.

Table 15.1: Comparison of ML model endpoint types and their use cases

Setting up Amazon SageMaker endpoint

Amazon SageMaker provides a managed service for deploying ML models as endpoints. It allows developers to easily deploy models, manage scalability, and handle security configurations without needing to manage infrastructure manually.

The following are the steps to deploy a model as an Endpoint in SageMaker:

1. Train and save the model in Amazon S3.

2. Create a model object in SageMaker pointing to the model artifacts.

3. Configure an inference endpoint with the appropriate instance type and scaling options.

4. Deploy the model and test the endpoint using API requests.

The following Python script demonstrates how to deploy an ML model as an endpoint in Amazon SageMaker using the Boto3 SDK:

```python
import boto3 sagemaker = boto3.client('sagemaker')
# Define model configuration
model_name = 'my-ml-model'
 primary_container = {
   'Image': 'container-image-URL',
    'ModelDataUrl': 's3://my-bucket/my-own-model.tar.gz'

}
# Create the model in SageMaker
 sagemaker.create_model(
    ModelName=model_name,
    PrimaryContainer=primary_container,
    ExecutionRoleArn='SageMakerRole'
```

In-depth understanding of ML models and their behaviors

Understanding how ML model behaves in production is crucial for ensuring its reliability, accuracy, and fairness. ML models do not operate in isolation; they are influenced by data distribution, model architecture, and external factors such as real-world variability. This section explores how models behave under different conditions, the concept of model drift, and how to interpret model outputs effectively.

By developing a deep understanding of ML model behaviors, practitioners can proactively detect performance degradation, handle biases, and improve decision-making processes. This section provides insights into model interpretability, data distribution shifts, and best practices for monitoring and evaluating ML models over time.

Understanding model predictions

At its core, ML model maps input data to an output prediction. This can be a classification (e.g., predicting whether an email is spam or not) or a regression task (e.g., predicting house prices). The behavior of the model depends on the type of learning algorithm used and the data it was trained on. For example, a logistic regression model outputs probabilities, while a deep learning model might produce embeddings that represent complex relationships in data. Understanding the nature of model outputs is essential for debugging, improving performance, and ensuring fairness.

Consider a model that predicts whether an image contains a cat or a dog. The output will be as follows:

Image ID	Prediction (Cat)	Prediction (Dog)
image_001.jpg	0.85	0.15
image_002.jpg	0.30	0.70

Table 15.2: Classification model output probabilities

In this case, the model assigns a probability to each category. A threshold (e.g., 0.5) is often used to determine the final classification. However, misclassifications can occur, especially if the model has not seen certain variations of cats or dogs during training.

Model drift and performance degradation

Over time, ML models can experience performance degradation due to changes in the data distribution, known as model drift. There are two primary types of drift:

- **Concept drift**: When the relationship between input features and target labels changes over time.
- **Data drift**: When the distribution of input features shifts due to external factors.

Consider a credit scoring model trained on data from five years ago. If the economic landscape changes, factors such as income and credit usage may shift, making previous patterns less relevant. This results in data drift, which can lead to incorrect predictions and increased loan default rates.

The following table shows the comparison of concept drift vs. data drift:

Type of drift	Description	Example
Concept drift	The relationship between input features and labels changes over time.	A fraud detection model trained on past fraudulent transactions may fail to detect new fraud techniques.
Data drift	The distribution of input features changes due to external factors.	A demand forecasting model for retail experiences shifts due to new customer demographics.

Table 15.3: Comparison of concept drift vs. data drift

Model interpretability and explainability

Understanding why a model makes certain predictions is crucial for debugging and compliance. Model interpretability refers to the ability to explain how a model arrives at its conclusions. Techniques such as **Shapley Additive Explanations** (**SHAP**) and **Local Interpretable Model-agnostic Explanations** (**LIME**) help provide insights into model decisions.

The following table highlights the relative importance of key features used in a loan approval model, helping to understand which inputs most influence the model's decisions:

Feature	Importance score
Credit score	0.40
Annual income	0.35
Loan amount	0.25

Table 15.4: Importance scores in a loan approval model

These insights help stakeholders understand why a loan was approved or denied, making the model more transparent.

The following are the best practices for ensuring model reliability:

- Continuously monitor model performance using tools like Amazon SageMaker Model Monitor.

- Implement drift detection techniques and retrain models when necessary.

- Use interpretable models or apply explainability techniques to improve trust.

- Validate model outputs using test datasets and real-world evaluation metrics.

By following these best practices, ML models can remain accurate, fair, and useful over time.

Understanding ML models and their behaviors is essential for ensuring their effectiveness in real-world applications. By recognizing the causes of performance degradation, improving model interpretability, and monitoring drift, organizations can build reliable AI-driven solutions. As ML models continue to evolve, maintaining transparency and adaptability will be critical for long-term success.

Implementing A/B testing for ML models

A/B testing is a fundamental technique used in ML deployment to compare two or more model versions before selecting the best-performing one for production. By systematically testing variations of a model, organizations can make data-driven decisions to improve accuracy, efficiency, and user experience. A/B testing ensures that changes to an ML model lead to positive outcomes rather than unintended consequences.

This section will explore the principles of A/B testing, its importance in ML workflows, implementation strategies, and best practices. Practical examples and comparisons will be provided to help clarify the key concepts involved in deploying A/B tests for ML models in real-world scenarios.

A/B testing, also known as split testing, is a controlled experiment where two versions of a model (A and B) are deployed simultaneously, and their performance is measured using predefined metrics. The goal is to determine which model provides better results based on objective evaluation criteria such as accuracy, latency, or user engagement.

In the context of ML models, A/B testing helps to:

- Validate performance improvements before full deployment.
- Reduce risks associated with deploying an underperforming model.
- Continuously optimize models based on real-world data.

For example, an e-commerce company may test two recommendation models: Model A uses collaborative filtering, while Model B incorporates deep learning. By running an A/B test, the company can determine which approach leads to higher customer engagement and conversion rates.

A successful A/B test consists of several key components, as follows:

- **Control group (Model A)**: The existing model currently in production.
- **Treatment group (Model B)**: The new model variation being tested.
- **Randomized assignment**: Users or requests are randomly assigned to either Model A or Model B.
- **Evaluation metrics**: Performance is measured using relevant KPIs (e.g., accuracy, response time, engagement rates).
- **Statistical analysis**: Statistical methods such as confidence intervals and p-values help determine if the observed differences are significant.

By carefully designing these components, A/B testing ensures reliable and actionable results.

The following table shows a comparison of Model A vs. Model B:

Aspect	Model A (Control)	Model B (Treatment)
Accuracy	85%	89%
Latency	200 ms	180 ms
User Engagement	7% increase in clicks	12% increase in clicks

Table 15.5: Comparison of Model A vs. Model B in A/B testing

In this example, Model B outperforms Model A in accuracy, latency, and user engagement, making it the better candidate for deployment.

To effectively conduct A/B testing for ML models, follow these structured steps:

1. **Define objectives**: Clearly outline the purpose of the test, such as improving accuracy or reducing inference latency.

2. **Select models for comparison**: Choose the control and treatment models to be evaluated.

3. **Determine metrics**: Identify **key performance indicators (KPIs)** such as precision, recall, or business-specific metrics.

4. **Deploy models in parallel**: Use cloud-based ML deployment strategies like *Amazon SageMaker Multi-Model Endpoints* to serve both models simultaneously.

5. **Distribute traffic randomly**: Assign requests or users randomly to ensure unbiased results.

6. **Collect data**: Gather prediction outputs, user interactions, and feedback.

7. **Perform statistical analysis**: Use hypothesis testing methods to determine significance.

8. **Decide on model deployment**: Deploy the best-performing model and retire the underperforming one.

Following this process ensures an objective evaluation and minimizes risks in production deployment.

A practical example of A/B testing a sentiment analysis model is to enhance customer feedback analysis, a company compares two sentiment analysis models. The current model (Model A) uses traditional NLP methods, while the new one (Model B) is powered by deep learning. To evaluate their performance, the company runs an A/B test, randomly routing customer feedback to one of the two models.

The following table shows the comparison between sentiment analysis model performance:

Metric	Model A (NLP-based)	Model B (Deep learning)
Accuracy	78%	85%
Precision	74%	82%
Recall	76%	84%

Table 15.6: Sentiment analysis model performance comparison

Based on the test results, Model B performs significantly better in accuracy, precision, and recall, justifying its deployment in production.

To ensure accurate and meaningful results from A/B testing, consider the following best practices:

- Ensure a sufficiently large sample size to achieve statistical significance.

- Randomly assign traffic to eliminate bias.

- Monitor test duration to avoid seasonal or external influences.

- Validate assumptions before drawing conclusions from the results.

- Automate model rollout and rollback procedures for seamless transitions.

By following these best practices, organizations can confidently make decisions about ML model improvements and deployments.

A/B testing is a powerful technique for evaluating and optimizing ML models before full-scale deployment. By comparing multiple models under real-world conditions, organizations can ensure data-driven decision-making, reduce risk, and improve model performance. Implementing structured A/B tests allows teams to iterate efficiently and continuously enhance their ML solutions.

Retraining and updating ML models

ML models are not static; they need to evolve over time as data patterns change. A model that was highly accurate at deployment may become less effective due to shifts in real-world conditions, also known as model drift. To maintain optimal performance, ML models must be regularly retrained and updated with fresh data.

This section explores the fundamentals of retraining and updating ML models, why it is essential, the different approaches to implementing retraining workflows, and best practices for maintaining high-performing ML solutions in production environments. Real-world examples and comparisons will be provided to illustrate key concepts.

Retraining ML models is essential to prevent performance degradation over time. Several factors necessitate retraining, including:

- **Data drift**: When the statistical properties of incoming data change, causing the model to make less accurate predictions.

- **Concept drift**: When the relationship between input features and target labels shifts, making past training data outdated.

- **Model performance decline**: Over time, external factors such as new user behaviours or market conditions can reduce model accuracy.

- **Regulatory and business requirements**: Organizations may need to update models to comply with evolving industry standards or policies.

Consider a fraud detection model used by a bank. Initially, the model is trained on transaction data to identify fraudulent patterns. However, as fraudsters adapt and develop new tactics, the original model may fail to detect newer types of fraud. By retraining the model with the latest transaction data, it can learn new fraud patterns and maintain high accuracy.

There are several approaches to retraining ML models, depending on business needs and resource availability:

- **Periodic retraining**: Models are retrained at fixed intervals (e.g., weekly, monthly) to incorporate fresh data.

- **Trigger-based retraining**: Retraining is initiated when model performance drops below a threshold.

- **Continuous learning**: The model continuously updates itself with new data, often using streaming techniques.

The following table shows the comparison of retraining approaches:

Retraining approach	Description	Use case
Periodic retraining	Model is retrained at scheduled intervals.	Retail demand forecasting, sentiment analysis.
Trigger-based retraining	Retraining is initiated when performance drops below a threshold.	Fraud detection, predictive maintenance.
Continuous learning	Model updates itself dynamically with new data.	Recommendation systems, real-time anomaly detection.

Table 15.7: Comparison of retraining approaches

Implementing automated retraining pipeline

Automating the retraining process reduces manual effort and ensures models stay up-to-date. AWS provides various tools to build automated retraining pipelines, such as *Amazon SageMaker Pipelines, AWS Step Functions,* and *AWS Lambda*.

The following are the steps to build an automated retraining pipeline:

- **Monitor model performance**: Use Amazon SageMaker Model Monitor to track performance metrics.

- **Trigger retraining**: Set up triggers based on performance thresholds or time schedules.

- **Ingest new data**: Load fresh training data from Amazon S3 or streaming sources.

- **Train the model**: Use SageMaker training jobs to fine-tune the model.

- **Evaluate the new model**: Compare performance with the previous model before deployment.

- **Deploy the updated model**: Replace the old model with the new one using SageMaker endpoints.

Let us discuss an example of automating retraining for a customer churn prediction model.

A telecom company wants to improve its customer retention by predicting churn rates. The initial ML model is trained on historical customer data, but customer behavior changes over time. To keep the model effective, an automated retraining pipeline is implemented using Amazon SageMaker. Whenever the model's prediction accuracy falls below 80%, a retraining job is triggered, and a new model is deployed if it outperforms the previous version.

To ensure successful retraining and updating of ML models, follow these best practices:

- Monitor model performance continuously to detect degradation early.

- Use version control** for models to track changes and rollback if necessary.

- Validate new models** thoroughly before deploying them in production.

- Automate data preprocessing** to streamline retraining workflows.

- Consider cost implications** when retraining models frequently.

By adhering to these best practices, organizations can maintain reliable and high-performing ML models.

Retraining and updating ML models is a crucial process to ensure their continued effectiveness in dynamic environments. By understanding the reasons for retraining, choosing the appropriate retraining approach, and implementing automated workflows, organizations can keep their ML solutions relevant and high-performing. As data evolves, maintaining an efficient retraining strategy becomes a key factor in sustaining long-term success in machine learning applications.

Debugging and troubleshooting techniques for ML models

ML models, like any software system, can encounter issues that impact their performance, accuracy, or deployment. Debugging and troubleshooting ML models is essential to ensure they function correctly and continue to deliver reliable results over time. Unlike traditional software debugging, ML debugging involves analyzing data, training processes, model behavior, and deployment pipelines to identify and resolve issues.

This section explores the key techniques for debugging ML models, common challenges encountered, and strategies to troubleshoot issues effectively. Practical examples and comparative tables are included to illustrate these concepts clearly.

Debugging ML models requires understanding the types of errors that can occur. These errors generally fall into three main categories, as follows:

- **Data issues**: Poor-quality data, missing values, or biased datasets leading to inaccurate predictions.

- **Model issues**: Incorrect model selection, overfitting, underfitting, or improper hyperparameter tuning.

- **Deployment issues**: Errors in integrating the model into production, latency problems, or scalability concerns.

Each of these errors requires a different approach to debugging and troubleshooting, which we will explore in detail in the following sections.

The following table shows the comparison of ML errors and their causes:

Error type	Cause	Example
Data issues	Missing values, biased dataset, incorrect feature scaling.	A face recognition model trained only on light-skinned individuals fails on dark-skinned faces.
Model issues	Overfitting, underfitting, incorrect model architecture.	A complex neural network overfits on small datasets and fails on new inputs.
Deployment issues	Inference latency, versioning issues, API integration errors.	A fraud detection model takes too long to process transactions, delaying approvals.

Table 15.8: Comparison of ML errors and their causes

Debugging data issues

Since ML models rely heavily on data, debugging starts with analyzing the dataset. Some common techniques for debugging data-related issues include:

- **Checking for missing values**: Use data imputation techniques or remove incomplete records.

- **Detecting data biases**: Analyze feature distributions to ensure diversity and fairness.

- **Feature scaling verification**: Ensure numerical features are correctly normalized or standardized.

For example, a housing price prediction model trained on a dataset missing key location-based features may make poor predictions for properties in different areas. Debugging in this case involves re-examining the data pipeline and ensuring all relevant features are included.

Debugging model issues

ML model performance depends on selecting the right architecture and tuning hyperparameters. Common debugging strategies for model-related issues include:

- **Checking for overfitting and underfitting**: Compare training and validation performance to identify excessive bias or variance.

- **Hyperparameter tuning**: Experiment with different learning rates, batch sizes, and architectures.

- **Examining loss curves**: Analyze training loss vs. validation loss to detect model convergence problems.

For instance, if an image classification model achieves 98% accuracy on training data but only 60% on test data, it is likely overfitting. To fix this, techniques such as dropout regularization or increasing dataset diversity can be applied.

Debugging deployment issues

Deploying an ML model introduces additional complexities such as API integration, latency optimization, and model version control. Some best practices for troubleshooting deployment issues include:

- **Monitoring inference latency**: Use AWS CloudWatch to track response times and scale resources accordingly.

- **Validating model outputs in production**: Compare real-world predictions with expected outputs to detect drift.

- **Ensuring compatibility with the deployment environment**: Check dependency versions and API formats to prevent integration failures.

For example, a chatbot powered by an NLP model may return incorrect responses after a model update. This could be due to a change in tokenization or embedding methods, requiring developers to carefully track model updates and their effects.

Tools for debugging ML models

Several tools can assist in debugging ML models, helping to analyze data, monitor performance, and detect errors:

- **Amazon SageMaker Debugger:** Provides insights into model training by detecting anomalies in gradients and loss functions.

- **TensorBoard**: Helps visualize training progress and track model performance.

- **AWS CloudWatch Logs**: Monitors model predictions and system performance in production.

- **SHAP and LIME**: Explainability tools that help interpret model decisions.

Using these tools allows ML engineers to identify and resolve issues faster, ensuring smooth model deployment and operation.

Debugging and troubleshooting ML models is an essential skill for ensuring accuracy, efficiency, and reliability. By understanding different types of errors, using the proper debugging techniques, and leveraging tools like AWS SageMaker Debugger and CloudWatch, ML practitioners can diagnose and fix issues effectively. A structured approach to debugging ensures that ML models continue to deliver high-quality predictions in production environments.

Performance monitoring and mitigation strategies

Ensuring that the ML model continues to perform optimally in production is as important as its initial development. Performance monitoring helps detect issues such as model drift, prediction latency, and degradation in accuracy. Mitigation strategies are then applied to resolve identified issues before they impact business operations.

This section discusses key performance monitoring techniques, tools available in the AWS ecosystem, and mitigation strategies for maintaining high-performing ML models. Real-world examples and comparisons will help illustrate these concepts.

ML models operate in dynamic environments where data distributions, user behaviours, and system requirements change over time. Without proper monitoring, models can become ineffective, leading to incorrect predictions and business losses. Performance monitoring helps to:

- Detect model drift before accuracy drops significantly.

- Ensure low-latency predictions for real-time applications.

- Identify security vulnerabilities in ML inference.

- Optimize computational resources to balance cost and performance.

For example, a demand forecasting model for retail stores might work well initially, but if consumer preferences change seasonally, the model may start underperforming. Monitoring KPIs helps detect these issues early.

Key metrics for ML model monitoring

To effectively monitor ML model performance, organizations must track specific metrics that reflect the model's reliability, accuracy, and efficiency. These include:

- **Prediction accuracy**: Measures how often the model's predictions match actual outcomes.

- **Inference latency**: Tracks the time taken for the model to return a prediction.

- **Model drift**: Identifies changes in data distribution that may impact model performance.

- **Resource utilization**: Monitors CPU, GPU, and memory usage to optimize infrastructure costs.

By continuously tracking these metrics, ML teams can detect performance issues before they impact end users.

The following table shows the comparison of ML performance metrics:

Metric	Description	Example
Prediction accuracy	Measures how often the model's predictions are correct.	A medical diagnosis model has 92% accuracy in detecting diseases.
Inference latency	Time taken for the model to return predictions after receiving input.	A chatbot response time increases from 100ms to 500ms, affecting user experience.
Model drift	Measures how much the data distribution changes over time.	A credit scoring model trained on past trends fails when economic conditions shift.
Resource utilization	Tracks CPU, GPU, and memory consumption to optimize costs.	A deep learning model consumes excessive GPU power, leading to higher cloud costs.

Table 15.9: Comparison of ML performance metrics

Tools for performance monitoring in AWS

AWS provides various tools to monitor ML models in production and identify performance issues in real time:

- **Amazon SageMaker Model Monitor**: Detects model drift and data quality issues.

- **AWS CloudWatch**: Tracks system-level metrics such as latency, resource usage, and request throughput.

- **AWS X-Ray**: Helps analyze latency issues by tracing end-to-end requests.

- **Amazon SageMaker Clarify**: Monitors bias and fairness in ML models.

Using these tools, organizations can establish robust monitoring pipelines to detect and address performance degradation.

Mitigation strategies for performance issues

When performance issues are detected, different mitigation strategies can be applied to restore model efficiency:

- **Retraining the model**: If model drift is detected, retraining with fresh data helps maintain accuracy.

- **Optimizing infrastructure:** Adjusting instance types and scaling settings can reduce latency.

- **Implementing A/B testing:** Deploying new model versions alongside old ones ensures smooth transitions.

- **Caching frequent predictions**: Reduces redundant computations for repetitive queries.

For example, ML-based stock price prediction model that suddenly starts producing inconsistent results may benefit from a retraining pipeline that updates the model with the latest market trends.

Example: Handling model drift in an e-commerce recommendation system

An e-commerce platform uses a ML model to recommend products based on past customer behavior. Initially, the model performs well, but over time, customer preferences evolve, leading to a decline in recommendation accuracy. To address this, the platform monitors model drift and updates the recommendation model on a weekly basis, ensuring that customers continue to receive relevant and personalized suggestions.

To maintain high-performing ML models, follow these best practices:

- Establish automated monitoring pipelines to continuously track key performance metrics.

- Set up alerts to detect performance degradation and trigger timely interventions.

- Use version control to track model changes and compare performance across iterations.

- Conduct periodic A/B testing before deploying new models to production environments.

These practices help keep ML models accurate, efficient, and cost-effective over time.

Performance monitoring is a critical aspect of ML deployment. By leveraging AWS monitoring tools, tracking key metrics, and applying mitigation strategies, organizations can ensure that their machine learning solutions remain reliable and aligned with business objectives. A robust monitoring framework enables proactive issue detection and resolution—ultimately ensuring long-term success for AI-driven applications.

Conclusion

In this chapter, we learnt to successfully deploy and operationalize ML solutions, which is essential for ensuring that models deliver consistent, accurate, and scalable predictions in real-world applications. This chapter has explored the key aspects of deploying ML models, managing endpoints, implementing A/B testing, retraining models, debugging issues, and monitoring performance to maintain optimal efficiency. We began by discussing exposing and interacting with ML model endpoints, highlighting how different deployment strategies, such as real-time, batch, and asynchronous inference, impact model accessibility and performance. We then explored understanding ML models and their behaviors, emphasizing the importance of detecting model drift, improving explainability, and ensuring fairness in decision-making processes.

A/B testing for ML models was covered as a critical technique for validating new model versions before full deployment, allowing teams to compare performance metrics and make data-driven decisions. To keep models relevant, we examined retraining and updating ML models, outlining strategies for maintaining accuracy through periodic, trigger-based, and continuous retraining approaches. We also addressed debugging and troubleshooting techniques, demonstrating how to identify and resolve issues related to data quality, model performance, and deployment integration. Finally, we discussed performance monitoring and mitigation strategies, stressing the need for continuous monitoring using tools like AWS CloudWatch and Amazon SageMaker Model Monitor to detect and mitigate performance degradation proactively.

By mastering these deployment and operationalization principles, ML practitioners can ensure their models remain reliable, scalable, and adaptable in changing environments. Whether deploying AI-driven customer recommendations, fraud detection systems, or real-time analytics solutions, a well-defined deployment strategy combined with ongoing monitoring and improvement is key to long-term ML success.

In the next chapter, you will find a comprehensive assessment designed to help you evaluate your readiness for the AWS Machine Learning certification exam, ensuring you are fully prepared to apply these concepts in both exam and real-world settings.

Multiple choice questions

1. **What is the primary purpose of exposing ML model endpoints?**
   a. To allow external applications to send data and receive predictions
   b. To store trained models in a database for offline access
   c. To generate new training data automatically
   d. To improve the security of ml models by restricting access

2. **Which of the following is not a common type of ML model endpoint deployment?**
   a. Real-time inference
   b. Batch processing
   c. Asynchronous inference
   d. Hard-coded inference

3. **What is the main benefit of using A/B testing for ml models?**
   a. It helps compare different models and determine which one performs better
   b. It reduces computational costs by eliminating redundant training data
   c. It ensures that all models perform the same way in production
   d. It permanently replaces an old model without evaluating the new one

4. **Which of the following is an example of model drift?**
   a. ML model consistently returns low-latency responses
   b. A recommendation system stops showing relevant products due to changing user preferences
   c. A deep learning model uses too much gpu memory during training
   d. ML model fails due to incorrect hyperparameter tuning

5. **What is a key reason to retrain an ML model?**
   a. To reduce the cost of running ML workloads
   b. To ensure the model continues to perform well as data distributions change
   c. To make the model compatible with different programming languages
   d. To replace feature engineering with automated feature selection

6. **Which AWS Tool is specifically designed to monitor model drift and data quality?**

   a.   AWS Lambda

   b.   Amazon SageMaker Model Monitor

   c.   AWS CloudFormation

   d.   AWS IAM

7. **What is the primary advantage of using continuous learning as a retraining approach?**

   a.   It updates the model in real-time as new data arrives

   b.   It eliminates the need for training data altogether

   c.   It prevents any model performance degradation

   d.   It requires no computational resources

8. **Which of the following is not a common debugging strategy for ML models?**

   a.   Checking for missing or biased data

   b.   Using feature importance techniques like shap or lime

   c.   Increasing model complexity without validation

   d.   Monitoring loss curves during training

9. **Which metric is crucial for evaluating ML model inference efficiency?**

   a.   Training accuracy

   b.   Inference latency

   c.   Number of training epochs

   d.   Number of layers in the model

10. **What is a common mitigation strategy when an ML model shows degraded performance?**

   a.   Ignore the issue and allow the model to adjust itself

   b.   Use random guessing as a fallback method

   c.   Retrain the model with updated data

   d.   Reduce dataset size to simplify computations

Answer key

1. a.
2. d.
3. a.
4. b.
5. b.
6. b.
7. a.
8. c.
9. b.
10. c.

Join our Discord space

Join our Discord workspace for latest updates, offers, tech happenings around the world, new releases, and sessions with the authors:

https://discord.bpbonline.com

Appendix

Multiple choice questions

1. **A data scientist needs to store training data for ML model that will be accessed frequently during training but archived after model deployment. The data is approximately 500 GB. Which storage solution provides the most cost-effective approach?**

   a. Amazon EBS with General Purpose SSD (GP3)

   b. Amazon S3 Standard with lifecycle policy to transition to S3 Glacier

   c. Amazon EFS with Infrequent Access storage class

   d. Amazon S3 Intelligent-Tiering

2. **A company wants to implement real-time fraud detection for credit card transactions. The system must process thousands of transactions per second. Which AWS service combination is most appropriate?**

   a. Amazon Kinesis Data Streams + AWS Lambda + Amazon SageMaker endpoint

   b. Amazon S3 + AWS Batch + Amazon SageMaker batch transform

   c. Amazon RDS + Amazon EC2 + Amazon SageMaker notebook

   d. AWS Glue + Amazon EMR + Amazon SageMaker training job

3. **ML engineer is preparing a dataset for training and notices that 15% of the feature values are missing. The dataset has both numerical and categorical features. What is the best approach to handle missing values?**

   a. Remove all rows with missing values

   b. Replace missing numerical values with the mean and categorical values with the mode

   c. Use supervised learning to predict missing values based on other features

   d. Replace all missing values with zero

4. **When performing feature engineering on text data for sentiment analysis, which technique would be most effective for handling words that appear very frequently but carry little semantic meaning?**

   a. TF-IDF normalization

   b. Stop word removal

   c. Stemming

   d. N-gram generation

5. **A data scientist wants to identify outliers in a dataset before training a model. Which visualization technique is most appropriate for detecting outliers in numerical features?**

   a. Histogram

   b. Scatter plot matrix

   c. Box plot

   d. Correlation heatmap

6. **A retail company wants to build a recommendation system for its e-commerce platform. They have user purchase history and product metadata. Which ML approach is most suitable?**

   a. Supervised learning with logistic regression

   b. Unsupervised learning with K-means clustering

   c. Collaborative filtering

   d. Time series forecasting

7. **A company needs to classify images into 50 different categories. They have 1,000 labeled images per category. Which approach would be most effective?**

   a. Train a convolutional neural network from scratch

   b. Use transfer learning with a pre-trained CNN

   c. Apply K-means clustering

    d.   Use a random forest classifier with pixel values as features

8. **For a binary classification model predicting customer churn, which metric would be most important if the cost of losing a customer is much higher than the cost of retention efforts?**

    a.   Accuracy

    b.   Precision

    c.   Recall

    d.   F1-score

9. **A model is showing high training accuracy (95%) but poor validation accuracy (70%). What is the most likely issue and solution?**

    a.   Underfitting; increase model complexity

    b.   Overfitting; add regularization

    c.   Poor data quality; clean the dataset

    d.   Insufficient training time; train longer

10. **When optimizing hyperparameters for a deep learning model, which technique is most efficient for exploring a large hyperparameter space?**

    a.   Grid search

    b.   Random search

    c.   Bayesian optimization

    d.   Manual tuning

11. **A company wants to deploy a ML model that needs to handle traffic spikes during flash sales. Which deployment option provides the best scalability?**

    a.   Amazon SageMaker real-time endpoint with auto-scaling

    b.   Amazon EC2 instance with custom application

    c.   AWS Lambda function

    d.   Amazon SageMaker batch transform

12. **For monitoring a deployed ML model, which metric is most important to track for detecting model drift?**

    a.   Latency

    b.   Throughput

    c.   Prediction distribution

    d.   Memory usage

13. **ML pipeline needs to process data from multiple sources including databases, APIs, and file systems. Which AWS service is best suited for orchestrating this workflow?**

    a. AWS Step Functions

    b. Amazon SageMaker Pipelines

    c. AWS Data Pipeline

    d. Amazon Simple Workflow Service

14. **When implementing A/B testing for ML model, what is the most important consideration?**

    a. Statistical significance of results

    b. Model training time

    c. Infrastructure costs

    d. Data storage requirements

15. **A company needs to ensure that their ML models comply with data privacy regulations. Which technique should they implement?**

    a. Data anonymization

    b. Model compression

    c. Feature selection

    d. Hyperparameter tuning

16. **For natural language processing tasks, which Amazon SageMaker built-in algorithm is most appropriate for extracting topics from a large collection of documents?**

    a. BlazingText in Word2Vec mode

    b. Latent Dirichlet Allocation

    c. Object2Vec

    d. Sequence-to-Sequence

17. **A data scientist needs to handle a severely imbalanced dataset where the minority class represents only 2% of the data. Which technique would be most effective?**

    a. Oversampling using SMOTE

    b. Undersampling the majority class

    c. Adjusting class weights

    d. Ensemble methods with balanced subsets

18. **When training a deep learning model on Amazon SageMaker, which instance type would be most cost-effective for experimentation and prototyping?**

    a. ml.p3.2xlarge (GPU instance)

    b. ml.m5.xlarge (CPU instance)

    c. ml.c5.4xlarge (Compute optimized)

    d. Spot Instances with automatic checkpoint saving

19. **A time series forecasting model needs to predict daily sales for the next 30 days. The data shows strong seasonality and trend. Which algorithm would be most appropriate?**

    a. Linear regression

    b. Random forest

    c. LSTM neural network

    d. K-means clustering

20. **For a computer vision model that needs to detect objects in real-time video streams, which AWS service combination provides the best performance?**

    a. Amazon Rekognition Video

    b. Amazon SageMaker with a custom CNN model on GPU instances

    c. AWS Lambda with pre-trained models

    d. Amazon Kinesis Video Streams with AWS Batch

21. **A company wants to implement automated model retraining when model performance degrades. Which AWS services should be used?**

    a. Amazon CloudWatch + AWS Lambda + Amazon SageMaker

    b. Amazon S3 + AWS Glue + Amazon EMR

    c. Amazon Kinesis + AWS Step Functions + Amazon EC2

    d. Amazon DynamoDB + AWS Batch + Amazon ECS

22. **When working with tabular data for a regression problem, which feature engineering technique is most effective for handling categorical variables with high cardinality?**

    a. One-hot encoding

    b. Label encoding

    c. Target encoding

    d. Binary encoding

23. **A ML model needs to process sensitive healthcare data. Which AWS service provides the necessary compliance features?**

    a. Amazon SageMaker with VPC configuration

    b. Amazon EC2 in private subnet

    c. AWS Lambda with encryption

    d. Amazon S3 with server-side encryption

24. **For training large language models, which Amazon SageMaker feature helps reduce training costs?**

    a. Managed Spot Training

    b. Pipe mode

    c. Distributed training

    d. Model compression

25. **A recommendation system needs to handle cold start problems for new users. Which approach is most effective?**

    a. Content-based filtering

    b. Collaborative filtering

    c. Hybrid approach combining content and collaborative filtering

    d. Popular item recommendations

26. **When evaluating a multi-class classification model, which metric provides the best overall assessment of model performance?**

    a. Macro-averaged F1 score

    b. Micro-averaged F1 score

    c. Weighted F1 score

    d. Accuracy

27. **A company needs to process streaming data for real-time anomaly detection. Which architecture pattern is most suitable?**

    a. Batch processing with daily updates

    b. Stream processing with sliding window analysis

    c. On-demand processing with manual triggers

    d. Scheduled processing with fixed intervals

28. **For optimizing inference latency in production, which technique is most effective?**

    a. Model quantization

    b. Feature selection

    c. Ensemble methods

    d. Cross-validation

29. **ML pipeline needs to handle schema evolution in the input data. Which approach provides the best flexibility?**

    a. Fixed schema validation

    b. Schema inference and validation

    c. Manual schema updates

    d. Schema-less processing

30. **When implementing explainable AI for a healthcare prediction model, which technique provides the most interpretable results?**

    a. SHapley Additive exPlanations

    b. Feature importance from tree-based models

    c. Partial dependence plots

    d. Local Interpretable Model-agnostic Explanations

31. **A company wants to reduce the cost of storing training data that is accessed infrequently. Which S3 storage class transition strategy is most cost-effective?**

    a. Standard | Standard-IA | Glacier | Deep Archive

    b. Standard | Glacier | Deep Archive

    c. Standard | Standard-IA | Deep Archive

    d. Standard | Intelligent-Tiering

32. **For processing large-scale ETL workloads with complex transformations, which AWS service provides the best performance and cost optimization?**

    a. AWS Glue with auto-scaling

    b. Amazon EMR with Spot Instances

    c. AWS Lambda with parallel execution

    d. Amazon EC2 with custom scripts

33. **A neural network model is experiencing vanishing gradients during training. Which technique would be most effective to address this issue?**

    a. Increase learning rate

    b. Use batch normalization

    c. Reduce model depth

    d. Apply dropout regularization

34. **For a fraud detection system that requires sub-second response times, which deployment architecture is most appropriate?**

    a. Synchronous API with load balancing

    b. Asynchronous batch processing

    c. Event-driven serverless architecture

    d. Microservices with caching layer

35. **When working with time series data that has missing values at irregular intervals, which imputation method is most appropriate?**

    a. Forward fill

    b. Linear interpolation

    c. Mean imputation

    d. Seasonal decomposition with imputation

36. **ML model needs to be deployed across multiple AWS Regions for disaster recovery. Which approach ensures consistency?**

    a. Cross-region model replication with versioning

    b. Independent model training in each region

    c. Centralized training with regional inference endpoints

    d. Multi-region training with data federation

37. **ML model needs to be deployed across multiple AWS Regions for disaster recovery. Which approach ensures consistency?**

    a. Distributed data parallel training

    b. Model parallel training

    c. Mixed precision training

    d. Gradient compression

38. **A company needs to implement data lineage tracking for their ML pipeline. Which combination of AWS services provides the best solution?**

    a. AWS Glue Data Catalog + Amazon SageMaker Lineage Tracking

    b. Amazon S3 + AWS CloudTrail

    c. AWS Lake Formation + Amazon QuickSight

    d. Amazon DynamoDB + AWS X-Ray

39. **For a recommendation system handling millions of users and items, which approach provides the best scalability?**

    a. Matrix factorization with dimensionality reduction

    b. Deep learning embeddings with approximate nearest neighbors

    c. Content-based filtering with parallel processing

    d. Graph-based collaborative filtering

40. **When implementing feature stores for ML, which characteristics are most important?**

    a. Low-latency access and versioning

    b. High storage capacity and compression

    c. Complex query capabilities and analytics

    d. Real-time streaming and event processing

41. **A computer vision model for autonomous vehicles needs to handle varying lighting conditions. Which data augmentation technique is most effective?**

    a. Geometric transformations

    b. Color space adjustments

    c. Noise injection

    d. Synthetic data generation

42. **For monitoring model performance in production, which approach provides the earliest detection of model degradation?**

    a. Periodic batch evaluation on test sets

    b. Real-time monitoring of prediction distributions

    c. A/B testing with control groups

    d. Manual review of prediction samples

43. **A company wants to implement federated learning across multiple data sources. Which consideration is most critical?**

    a. Data privacy and security

    b. Model convergence speed

    c. Communication bandwidth

    d. Computational resources

44. **For optimizing hyperparameters of ensemble models, which strategy is most efficient?**

    a. Individual optimization followed by ensemble tuning

    b. Joint optimization of all model hyperparameters

    c.　Sequential optimization with early stopping

    d.　Random search across the full parameter space

45. **When deploying ML models in edge environments, which optimization technique is most important?**

    a.　Model pruning and quantization

    b.　Feature engineering and selection

    c.　Distributed inference

    d.　Dynamic batching

46. **A natural language processing model needs to handle multiple languages. Which approach provides the best performance?**

    a.　Separate models for each language

    b.　Multilingual transformer models

    c.　Language detection with routing

    d.　Translation to common language

47. **For ML system processing financial transactions, which security measure is most critical?**

    a.　End-to-end encryption

    b.　Network segmentation

    c.　Access logging and monitoring

    d.　Multi-factor authentication

48. **When implementing continuous integration for ML models, which validation step is most important?**

    a.　Model performance validation

    b.　Data quality validation

    c.　Infrastructure compatibility testing

    d.　Security vulnerability scanning

49. **A company needs to optimize costs for training multiple ML models with different resource requirements. Which approach is most cost-effective?**

    a.　Dedicated instances for each model

    b.　Shared clusters with resource scheduling

    c.　Spot instances with fault tolerance

    d.　Serverless training with automatic scaling

50. **For a recommendation system that needs to provide explanations for recommendations, which approach is most suitable?**

    a. Association rule mining

    b. Attention-based neural networks

    c. Decision trees with feature importance

    d. Linear models with coefficient interpretation

51. **A time series anomaly detection system needs to adapt to changing patterns over time. Which approach is most effective?**

    a. Sliding window retraining

    b. Online learning algorithms

    c. Ensemble of seasonal models

    d. Rule-based pattern matching

52. **When implementing data versioning for ML experiments, which strategy provides the best traceability?**

    a. Git-based versioning with data snapshots

    b. Database versioning with timestamps

    c. Immutable data lakes with metadata tracking

    d. Blockchain-based audit trails

53. **For ML model serving high-frequency trading applications, which performance optimization is most critical?**

    a. Memory optimization

    b. CPU optimization

    c. Network latency reduction

    d. Storage I/O optimization

54. **A company wants to implement automated feature engineering for their ML pipeline. Which approach provides the best balance of automation and control?**

    a. AutoML platforms with manual review

    b. Rule-based feature generation

    c. Deep feature synthesis

    d. Genetic algorithm-based optimization

55. **When deploying ML models in a multi-cloud environment, which consideration is most important?**

    a. Model format standardization

    b. Data synchronization strategies

    c. Network connectivity optimization

    d. Vendor lock-in prevention

56. **For ML system handling video content analysis, which approach provides the best efficiency?**

    a. Frame-by-frame analysis with temporal smoothing

    b. Keyframe extraction with full analysis

    c. Real-time streaming analysis

    d. Batch processing with parallel workers

57. **A company needs to implement model governance for regulatory compliance. Which practice is most important?**

    a. Model documentation and audit trails

    b. Performance monitoring and alerting

    c. Access control and authorization

    d. Data quality validation and testing

58. **For optimizing the training of large transformer models, which technique provides the best memory efficiency?**

    a. Gradient checkpointing

    b. Layer freezing

    c. Knowledge distillation

    d. Progressive training

59. **When implementing A/B testing for recommendation systems, which metric is most important to track?**

    a. Click-through rate

    b. Revenue per user

    c. Model accuracy

    d. System latency

60. **ML pipeline needs to handle data from IoT sensors with intermittent connectivity. Which architecture pattern is most robust?**

    a. Edge computing with local storage and batch synchronization

    b. Real-time streaming with automatic retry mechanisms

    c. Centralized processing with message queuing

    d. Hybrid approach with local inference and cloud training

61. **For ML model predicting customer lifetime value, which feature engineering approach is most valuable?**

    a. Recency, frequency, monetary analysis

    b. Demographic segmentation

    c. Behavioral pattern analysis

    d. Time-based aggregations

62. **When implementing model ensembles for production deployment, which strategy provides the best balance of performance and complexity?**

    a. Voting ensemble with equal weights

    b. Stacking with meta-learner

    c. Boosting with adaptive weights

    d. Bagging with random sampling

63. **A company needs to implement real-time personalization for their mobile application. Which approach provides the best user experience?**

    a. Pre-computed recommendations with periodic updates

    b. Real-time inference with cached features

    c. Hybrid approach with online and offline components

    d. Edge deployment with on-device models

64. **For monitoring data quality in streaming ML pipelines, which approach is most effective?**

    a. Statistical process control with control charts

    b. Rule-based validation with threshold monitoring

    c. ML-based anomaly detection

    d. Sampling-based quality assessment

65. **When implementing transfer learning for domain adaptation, which strategy is most effective?**

    a. Fine-tuning all layers with reduced learning rate

    b. Freezing early layers and training final layers

    c. Progressive unfreezing during training

    d. Layer-wise adaptive learning rates

66. **ML system needs to handle concept drift in real-time. Which approach provides the best adaptability?**

    a. Online learning with forgetting factors

    b. Ensemble methods with model rotation

    c. Drift detection with model retraining

    d. Active learning with human feedback

67. **For optimizing inference costs in production, which approach provides the best cost-performance trade-off?**

    a. Model compression with minimal accuracy loss

    b. Batch processing with higher latency

    c. Auto-scaling with predictive capacity planning

    d. Spot instances with fault tolerance

68. **When implementing explainable AI for loan approval decisions, which technique provides the most regulatory-compliant explanations?**

    a. Global feature importance rankings

    b. Local explanations for individual predictions

    c. Counterfactual explanations

    d. Simplified proxy models

69. **A company needs to implement privacy-preserving ML across multiple organizations. Which approach is most suitable?**

    a. Differential privacy with noise injection

    b. Secure multi-party computation

    c. Homomorphic encryption

    d. Federated learning with secure aggregation

70. **For ML model deployed in a safety-critical environment, which validation approach is most comprehensive?**

   a. Cross-validation with stratified sampling

   b. Adversarial testing with edge cases

   c. Formal verification with mathematical proofs

   d. Simulation-based testing with synthetic data

Answer key

1. b. Amazon S3 Standard with a lifecycle policy to transition to S3 Glacier provides cost-effective storage for training data that will be archived after use.

2. a. Amazon Kinesis Data Streams + AWS Lambda + Amazon SageMaker endpoint provides the real-time processing capability needed for fraud detection.

3. c. Using supervised learning to predict missing values based on other features provides the most accurate imputation method.

4. b. Stop word removal effectively handles frequently occurring words that carry little semantic meaning.

5. c. Box plots are most appropriate for detecting outliers in numerical features as they clearly show quartiles and outliers.

6. c. Collaborative filtering is the most suitable approach for recommendation systems using user purchase history.

7. b. Transfer learning with a pre-trained CNN is most effective when you have limited labeled data per category.

8. c. Recall is most important when the cost of missing positive cases (false negatives) is high.

9. b. High training accuracy with poor validation accuracy indicates overfitting; adding regularization is the solution.

10. c. Bayesian optimization is most efficient for exploring large hyperparameter spaces.

11. a. Amazon SageMaker real-time endpoint with auto-scaling provides the best scalability for traffic spikes.

12. c. Prediction distribution is most important for detecting model drift as it shows changes in model behavior.

13. b. Amazon SageMaker Pipelines is best suited for orchestrating ML workflows from multiple data sources.

14. a. Statistical significance of results is the most important consideration for valid A/B testing.

15. a. Data anonymization is essential for compliance with data privacy regulations.

16. b. Latent Dirichlet Allocation is most appropriate for topic extraction from document collections.

17. a. Oversampling using SMOTE is most effective for severely imbalanced datasets.

18. d. Spot instances with automatic checkpoint saving provide the most cost-effective solution for experimentation.

19. c. LSTM neural networks are most appropriate for time series with seasonality and trend.

20. b. Amazon SageMaker with custom CNN model on GPU instances provides the best performance for real-time object detection.

21. a. Amazon CloudWatch + AWS Lambda + Amazon SageMaker enables automated model retraining based on performance monitoring.

22. c. Target encoding is most effective for categorical variables with high cardinality.

23. a. Amazon SageMaker with VPC configuration provides necessary compliance features for healthcare data.

24. a. Managed Spot Training helps reduce training costs for large language models.

25. c. Hybrid approach combining content and collaborative filtering is most effective for cold start problems.

26. c. Weighted F1 score provides the best overall assessment for multi-class classification.

27. b. Stream processing with sliding window analysis is most suitable for real-time anomaly detection.

28. a. Model quantization is most effective for optimizing inference latency.

29. b. Schema inference and validation provides the best flexibility for handling schema evolution.

30. a. SHAP provides the most interpretable results for explainable AI in healthcare.

31. a. Standard ▢ Standard-IA ▢ Glacier ▢ Deep Archive provides the most cost-effective transition strategy.

32. b. Amazon EMR with Spot Instances provides the best performance and cost optimization for large-scale ETL.

33. b. Batch normalization is most effective for addressing vanishing gradients.

34. a. Synchronous API with load balancing is most appropriate for sub-second response requirements.

35. b. Linear interpolation is most appropriate for time series with irregular missing values.

36. c. Centralized training with regional inference endpoints ensures consistency across regions.

37. a. Distributed data parallel training should be prioritized for optimizing deep learning performance.

38. a. AWS Glue Data Catalog + Amazon SageMaker Lineage Tracking provides the best data lineage solution.

39. b. Deep learning embeddings with approximate nearest neighbors provides the best scalability.

40. a. Low-latency access and versioning are most important characteristics for feature stores.

41. b. Color space adjustments are most effective for handling varying lighting conditions.

42. b. Real-time monitoring of prediction distributions provides the earliest detection of model degradation.

43. a. Data privacy and security are the most critical considerations for federated learning.

44. b. Joint optimization of all model hyperparameters is most efficient for ensemble models.

45. a. Model pruning and quantization are most important for edge deployment optimization.

46. b. Multilingual transformer models provide the best performance for multiple languages.

47. a. End-to-end encryption is most critical for financial transaction processing systems.

48. b. Data quality validation is the most important step in ML continuous integration.

49. c. Spot Instances with fault tolerance provide the most cost-effective approach for multiple models.

50. b. Attention-based neural networks are most suitable for explainable recommendations.

51. b. Online learning algorithms are most effective for adapting to changing patterns.

52. c. Immutable data lakes with metadata tracking provide the best traceability.

53. c. Network latency reduction is most critical for high-frequency trading applications.

54. a. AutoML platforms with manual review provide the best balance of automation and control.

55. a. Model format standardization is most important for multi-cloud deployments.

56. b. Keyframe extraction with full analysis provides the best efficiency for video content analysis.

57. a. Model documentation and audit trails are most important for regulatory compliance.

58. a. Gradient checkpointing provides the best memory efficiency for large transformer models.

59. b. Revenue per user is the most important metric to track in recommendation system A/B testing.

60. a. Edge computing with local storage and batch synchronization is most robust for intermittent connectivity.

61. a. Recency, frequency, monetary analysis is most valuable for customer lifetime value prediction.

62. a. Voting ensemble is best for production balance.

63. c. Hybrid approach with online and offline components provides the best user experience.

64. c. ML-based anomaly detection.

65. c. Progressive unfreezing during training is most effective for domain adaptation.

66. a. Online learning with forgetting factors provides the best adaptability for concept drift.

67. a. Model compression with minimal accuracy loss provides the best cost-performance trade-off.

68. b. Local explanations for individual predictions provide the most regulatory-compliant explanations.

69. d. Federated learning with secure aggregation is most suitable for privacy-preserving ML across organizations.

70. c. Formal verification with mathematical proofs

Index

www.ingramcontent.com/pod-product-compliance
Lightning Source LLC
Chambersburg PA
CBHW061745210326
41599CB00034B/6794